In a society filled with so much anti-Christian rhetoric, there is no better book to equip Christians to think clearly, soundly, and inoffensively in the face of the devices employed today in opposition to the Christian faith.

—*Norm Geisler*
Author of *Encyclopedia of Christian Apologetics* and *When Skeptics Ask*

Greg Koukl is a master tactician. I know of no one who is more conscientious in his efforts to communicate effectively and winsomely his Christian faith. In this book Greg shares with us his tried and true methods, skills honed through continual practice and revision. Mastering his tactics will make you a more effective ambassador for Christ.

—*William Lane Craig*
Author of *Reasonable Faith—Christian Truth and Apologetics*

Just as a course on tactics is a requirement at all military academies, so too Greg Koukl's *Tactics: A Game Plan for Discussing Your Christian Convictions* should be required training for all Christians and churches. Koukl has made a worthwhile contribution to the literature on apologetics by teaching us how to say what we say. Witty and winsome, this resource is as fun to read as it is to put into practice.

—*Hank Hanegraaff*
Host of the "Bible Answer Man," author of *Christianity in Crisis: The 21st Century* and *The Complete Bible Answer Book, Collector's Edition*

C. S. Lewis once said, "Any fool can write learned language. The vernacular is the real test." In this book Greg Koukl passes Lewis's test with flying colors. There are many great arguments in favor of the Christian faith, but many of them are accessible only to professional apologists and philosophers. Koukl has developed a memorable and practical way to translate these arguments so that all Christians can become winsome and persuasive apologists in everyday conversations, no matter what their day jobs. This book should be required reading for every thoughtful Christian.

—*Jay Wesley Richards*

W9-AZB-680

If you enjoy apologetics, Greg's book *Tactics* is not only a required read, but simply a delightfully entertaining resource. In fact, just try and put it down! Especially for those who struggle with relevant ways to relate to non-Christians while presenting Christian truth, this volume provides many proven methods of natural, non-confrontational dialogue where the purpose is often to simply give an unbeliever something to think about, what Greg calls placing a stone in someone's shoe. Featuring remarkably simple techniques that are easily and fruitfully applied, this incredibly insightful book is one I highly recommend.

—*Gary R. Habermas*
Distinguished Research Professor, Liberty University
Author of *The Case for the Resurrection of Jesus*

With the advantage of a lifetime of experience, Greg Koukl has written what must be considered THE authoritative treatment of how to employ various strategies in conversations with unbelievers about the Christian faith. *Tactics* is not just another apologetics book. It is a sensitive, well-written, widely illustrated treatment of actual situations that often come up when believers share their faith. Koukl not only reminds us that it is not enough to know why you believe, but it is also crucial to know how to communicate those beliefs by adapting to various situations. And *Tactics* shows precisely how to do that.

—*J. P. Moreland*
Distinguished Professor of Philosophy, Talbot School
of Theology, and author of *Kingdom Triangle*

Greg Koukl has been using the methods offered in this book for many years with our Summit students and to great effect. His suggestions, illustrations, and witnessing approach work. This is a well-written, practical, and timely book.

—*David Noebel*
Founder and President, Summit Ministries

In this wise and compelling book, Greg Koukl—who has thought long and hard about not only what to say but how to say it—provides a game plan for equipping believers through an artful method of careful thinking and winsome conversation. If you struggle with how to talk about your faith and respond to questions and objections in a meaningful and effective way—and most of us do—there is no better book to buy, read, and put into practice. I could not recommend it more highly!

—*Justin Taylor*
"Between Two Worlds" blog; Editor, *Suffering and the Sovereignty of God* and *The Supremacy of Christ in a Postmodern World*

Greg Koukl is a wise, seasoned, front-lines apologist. I am happy to recommend a book so full of practical insights and careful guidance for skillfully, winsomely defending the Christian faith.

—*Paul Copan*
Author of *True for You, but Not for Me* and
Will the Real Jesus Please Stand Up?

Tactics is the book I've been waiting for! I love engaging non-Christians in conversation, but in the back of my mind I often think, "What if I get stuck and don't know what to do?" Greg helped me put that fear to rest and gave me practical tools to artfully maneuver in conversations. I enthusiastically recommend *Tactics*. It will revolutionize your conversations with non-Christians.

—*Sean McDowell*
Author of *Ethix*, coauthor of *Understanding Intelligent Design* and *Evidence for the Resurrection*

When I want someone who can help me train ambassadors for Christ, the first person I call is Greg Koukl. Now his proven ideas are in this book. I wish I had known these tactics twenty years ago. They are some of the best I've ever seen to help Christians be more effective ambassadors for Christ. Trust me—if you read Koukl's advice and learn his methods, your impact for Christ will skyrocket.

—*Frank Turek*
Author of *I Don't Have Enough Faith to Be an Atheist*

Greg Koukl is a master of the ideas that undergird the Gospel and one of the finest Christian communicators on the planet. He has spent many thousands of hours in front of the most difficult skeptics and their toughest questions and has developed very effective techniques to bring the truth to the surface of any conversation with love and grace.

I have learned so much over the years by studying his persuasive yet respectful approach to giving reasons for faith. This book presents his methods in a way that is engaging and accessible to every believer. I hope Christians in churches all over the country gather together to study this important book and learn to stand firm for the Gospel in these dark times.

—Craig J. Hazen, PhD
Founder and Director, Graduate Program in
Christian Apologetics, Biola University

TACTICS

10TH
ANNIVERSARY
EDITION

TACTICS

A GAME PLAN
FOR DISCUSSING YOUR
CHRISTIAN
CONVICTIONS

UPDATED AND EXPANDED

GREGORY KOUKL

ZONDERVAN
REFLECTIVE

ZONDERVAN REFLECTIVE

Tactics: 10th Anniversary Edition
Copyright © 2009, 2019 by Gregory Koukl

ISBN 978-0-310-10146-8 (softcover)

ISBN 978-0-310-10148-2 (audio)

ISBN 978-0-310-10147-5 (ebook)

Requests for information should be addressed to:
Zondervan, *3900 Sparks Dr. SE, Grand Rapids, Michigan 49546*

Published in association with the literary agency of Mark Sweeney & Associates, Chicago, Illinois 60611.

Cover photo: iStock

Printed in the United States of America

23 24 25 26 27 LBC 29 28 27 26 25

To Annabeth Noelle,
a light to my heart
and, by God's grace,
a light to her generation

CONTENTS

FOREWORD

When I hosted a national television program called *Faith under Fire*, which featured short debates on spiritual topics, I decided to invite bestselling New Age author Deepak Chopra to be a guest. The topic would be the future of faith. To offer a different perspective, I asked my friend Greg Koukl to represent Christianity. The idea was to tape them as they interacted for about fifteen minutes via satellite, the typical format for a segment of the show.

That plan quickly went out the window.

Greg was simply so engaging and so effective in poking holes in Chopra's worldview that I had to keep the cameras running. Time after time, Greg was able to expose the faulty thinking underlying Chopra's amorphous theology and correct his inaccurate claims about Jesus and the Bible. Before I knew it, we had consumed the entire hour of the show. Chopra—who was accustomed to spouting his opinions unchallenged on television and radio—was left thoroughly defeated and deflated.

As soon as the taping was over, I turned to my producer. "That," I said, "was a textbook example of how to defend Christianity." For the only time in our show's tenure, we decided to devote an entire program to airing one debate.

Why was Greg so incredibly successful in that encounter? He wasn't belligerent or obnoxious. He didn't raise his voice or launch into a sermon. Instead he used the kind of tactics that he describes in this book: winsomely using key questions and other techniques to guide the conversation and unveil the flawed assumptions and hidden contradictions in another person's positions.

That is what makes this book unique. There are plenty of resources that help Christians understand what they believe and why they believe it, and certainly those are vital. But it's equally crucial to know how to engage in a meaningful dialogue with a skeptic or a person from another religious viewpoint. This is the territory that this book covers with wit and wisdom, using examples from Greg's own life and insights gleaned from his years of fruitful ministry.

I had the privilege of having many of the country's top Christian apologists, or defenders of the faith, on my program, and Greg was consistently among the very best. When we needed someone to deal with some of the most difficult challenges facing Christianity for the film based on my book *The Case for Faith*, we again called on Greg, and once more he embodied what it means to be a prepared ambassador for Christ.

Greg is so good that Christians might say, "Well, he is really smart, uniquely gifted, and has a master's degree in this sort of thing. I could never do what he does." But they can—with a little help. One of Greg's driving passions has been to train ordinary Christians in how they can use easy-to-understand tactics to dissect another person's worldview and to advance the case for Christianity. He has been conducting seminars on this topic for quite a while, and I'm so thankful that he has now distilled his best material into this helpful and valuable volume.

We live in a day when militant atheism is on the march. Christianity is coming under attack, not just from bestselling books, skeptical college professors, and television documentaries but increasingly from neighbors and coworkers. It has become a faux pas to claim that only one faith leads to God, that the New Testament is reliable, or that any tenet of neo-Darwinism might be open to question.

Each day, the chances are increasing that you will find yourself in a conversation with someone who dismisses Christianity as a mythology-ridden anachronism. What will you do when they paint you into a rhetorical corner and belittle your beliefs? How will you persuasively present "the reason for the hope that you have" (1 Peter 3:15 NIV)? How will you seize opportunities to get into potentially life-changing spiritual discussions with people you meet?

You've opened the right book. Let Greg be your mentor as you master new approaches to talking with others about Jesus. As Greg likes to say, "You don't need to hit home runs. You don't even need to get on base. Just getting up to bat—engaging others in friendly conversation—will do."

That means everyone can embark on this adventure. Take advantage of Greg's lifetime of study and experience by getting equipped now, so that God can use you "in season and out of season" (2 Tim. 4:2) to be his ambassador in a spiritually confused world.

—Lee Strobel, author of *The Case for the Real Jesus*

PREFACE TO THE SECOND EDITION

I want to start with a prediction. Then I want to make a promise. First, I'm going to describe something significant that will happen in your life if you take some simple steps in a specific direction. Then I'm going to pledge to give you what you need to make sure that happens.

Here's the prediction. If you read this book carefully and begin to practice the game plan I will teach you—even if you ease in slowly at a pace that's comfortable for you—you're going to begin to see remarkable changes in your ability to effectively maneuver in a relaxed and confident way in your conversations with others about Christ, even when they disagree strongly with you.

I feel confident in this somewhat bold conjecture only because of the countless number of people who have told me that is exactly what happened when they began to put the principles in this book into play.

In the decade that has passed since *Tactics* first came out, I have heard the same response over and over again. I've heard it wherever I go, from all sorts of people—from high schoolers to seasoned followers of Christ, from shy Christians to bold believers—who have applied the practical concepts they've discovered in *Tactics*.

Here is what they've told me: "This book changed my life."

Those words both flatter me and humble me, but they do not surprise me. The commonsense concepts found in *Tactics* changed my life too, and I think they will change yours. That's my prediction.

And now the promise. I am going to give you a game plan that will allow you to converse with confidence in any situation, no matter how little you know or how knowledgeable or aggressive or even obnoxious the other person might be.

I have been keeping that promise for more than a decade now with tens of thousands of people who have used this material. I know I've kept the promise because they tell me all the time. Success for you, though, will require making an adjustment in your thinking.

I would like you to consider the significance of an obvious truism: before there can be any harvest, there always has to be a season of gardening. This is clearly the case with agriculture, of course, but it's also true with evangelism. Jesus himself talked about seasons of sowing that precede seasons of reaping (John 4:35–38).[1]

Before someone ever comes to Christ, there is always a period of time—a season, if you will—when they are thinking about the gospel, mulling it over, wondering whether it might be true. They may be putting out little probes by asking questions. They might even be fighting back a bit. But still, they're wondering—maybe praying secretly, *God, are you real?* That's what I did as a college student at UCLA.

When this happens in someone's life, it's an opportunity for you and me to do some spadework, what Francis Schaeffer called "pre-evangelism." As I looked back on decades of serving the Lord—through writing, speaking, doing radio, making TV appearances—I realized that my work consisted principally of gardening, not harvesting.

When I realized that good gardening is the key to a good harvest, my approach began to shift. *If I could be a better gardener,* I thought, *and also teach others to garden better, then eventually the harvest will be better too.* Pretty simple.

To do that, though, I needed something I didn't have, something that was missing from the books I'd studied, the classes I'd taken, and the conferences I'd attended. I needed a way to connect with others. I needed a bridge from the content to the conversation, a link from the scholarship to the relationship.

That is what I'm going to give you in this book. I am going to give you gardening tools. My plan follows Paul's pattern found in Colossians 4:5–6. Here's what he says: "Conduct yourselves with wisdom toward outsiders, making the most of the opportunity. Let your speech always be with grace, as though seasoned with salt, so that you will know how you should respond to each person."

Notice three elements in Paul's injunction. First, he says, *"Be smart."* Make the most of the moment, but watch your steps. Come in slowly, under the radar. Be shrewd, not blunt. Next, he says, *"Be nice."* Show warmth. Probe gently. Be calm and patient. Remember, if anyone gets mad, you'll lose. Finally, he says, *"Be tactical."* Adjust to the individual. Tailor your comments to his special situation. Each circumstance is different. Each person is unique. Treat them that way.

But how do we do that? How do we initiate conversations in a way that doesn't seem weird, that protects us from getting trapped or getting in over our heads? How do we keep from feeling foolish or making the gospel look foolish?

I'll tell you how. You need a method, a tactical game plan, one that is simple to follow yet is tailor-made for each individual—"as though seasoned with salt." The principles I will teach you in this book will allow you to do what Paul advises: be smart, be nice, and be tactical.

When I talk with people about spiritual matters, I'm not looking to close the deal with them. I'm just looking to do a little gardening in their lives. That's all. I want to get them thinking. If I can do that, then I'm satisfied, since I know they are ultimately in God's hands.

If you'll pardon my mixed metaphors, I don't think you need to swing for the fences. I don't think you even need to worry about getting on base. I just want to get you into the batter's box, and our tactical game plan will put you there.

Then watch what God will do.

ACKNOWLEDGMENTS

I am thankful for the many people who have helped shape both the ideas in this book and the way I explain them to others. My wonderful team at Stand to Reason has challenged me, counseled me, and corrected me over the years and has had a major influence on the ideas in this book. My radio callers over nearly three decades have also helped sharpen my tactical skills.

Although the content of the manuscript is mine, I had a great deal of help with the wordsmithing. I am grateful for Nancy Ulrich and her wonderful ear for writing; for Amy Hall's thoughtful insights on structure, flow, and intellectual clarity; and for Susan Osborn of Christian Communicator, who gave the manuscript professional polish.

My agent, Mark Sweeney, smoothed out what is often a bumpy road to publication. He has also been a great sounding board and cheerleader whenever those talents were required.

I am especially grateful for STR's cofounder, the multitalented, multitasking Melinda Penner, who does everything well. She has made my entire professional life possible and stabilized a good deal of my personal life as well.

Finally and foremost, my gratitude to my most patient and durable wife, Steese Annie. Her cheerful heart does me good like a medicine, and her patience and gift of mercy are daily sources of grace to me.

Many of the ideas in this book first appeared in issues of *Solid Ground*, Stand to Reason's bimonthly newsletter, available at *www .str.org*.

PART ONE
THE GAME PLAN

PART ONE

Chapter 1

DIPLOMACY OR D-DAY?

Apologetics—giving reasons or evidence to support Christianity —has a questionable reputation for many believers. By definition, apologists defend the faith. They defeat false ideas. They destroy speculations raised up against the knowledge of God.

Those sound like fightin' words to many people. Circle the wagons. Hoist the drawbridge. Fix bayonets. Load weapons. Ready, aim, fire. It's not surprising, then, that believers and unbelievers alike associate apologetics with conflict. Defenders don't dialogue. They fight.

In addition to the image problem, Christians who want to give an answer to challengers face another barrier. It's too easy for skeptics to ignore our facts, deny our claims, or simply yawn and walk away from the line we've drawn in the sand.

But sometimes they don't walk away. Instead they stand and fight. We wade into battle, only to face a barrage of objections we can't handle. We have ignored one of the first rules of engagement: never make a frontal assault on a superior force. Caught off balance, we tuck our tails between our legs and retreat, maybe for good. Sound familiar?

I'd like to suggest a "more excellent way." Jesus said that when you find yourself as a sheep amid wolves, be innocent but shrewd (Matt. 10:16). Even though there is real warfare going on,[1] I think our engagements should look more like diplomacy than D-Day.

In this book, I would like to teach you how to be diplomatic, able to navigate smoothly and graciously through hazardous encounters. I want to suggest a method I call the Ambassador Model. This approach trades more on friendly curiosity—a kind of relaxed diplomacy—than on confrontation.

I know that people have different emotional reactions to the idea of engaging others in controversial conversations. Some relish the encounter. Others are willing but a bit nervous and uncertain. Still others try to avoid them entirely. What about you?

Wherever you find yourself on this spectrum, I want to help. If you're like a lot of people who pick up a book like this, you would like to make a difference for the kingdom, but you're not sure how to begin. I want to give you a game plan, a strategy that enables you to get involved in a way you never thought you could yet gives you a tremendous margin of safety.

I am going to teach you how to navigate in conversations so that you stay in control—in a good way—even though your knowledge is limited. You may know nothing about answering challenges people raise against what you believe. You may even be a brand-new Christian. It doesn't matter. I am going to introduce you to a handful of effective maneuvers—I call them tactics—that will help keep you in the driver's seat.

Let me give you an example of what I mean.

THE WITCH IN WISCONSIN

Several years ago, while on vacation at our family retreat in northern Wisconsin, my wife and I stopped at a store in town to get some photos digitized. I noticed that the woman helping us had a large pentagram—a five-pointed star often associated with the occult—dangling from her neck.

"Does that star have religious significance," I asked, pointing to the pendant, "or is it just jewelry?"

"Yes, it has religious significance," she answered. "The five points stand for earth, wind, fire, water, and spirit." Then she added, "I'm a pagan."

My wife, caught off guard by the woman's candor, couldn't suppress a laugh, then quickly apologized. "I'm sorry. I didn't mean to be rude. It's just that I've never heard anyone actually admit right out that they are pagan," she explained. She knew the term only as a negative one used by her friends yelling at their kids: "Get in here, you bunch of pagans!"

"So you're Wiccan?" I continued.

She nodded. Yes, she was a witch. "It's an earth religion," the woman explained, "like the Native Americans. We respect all life."

"If you respect all life," I ventured, "then I suppose you're pro-life on the abortion issue."

She shook her head. "No, actually I'm not. I'm pro-choice."

I was surprised. "Isn't that an unusual position for someone in Wicca to take—I mean, since you're committed to respecting all life?"

"You're right. It is odd," she admitted. Then she qualified herself. "I know *I* could never do that," she said, referring to abortion. "I could never kill a baby. I wouldn't do anything to hurt someone else, because it might come back on me."

Now, this was a remarkable turn in the conversation, for two reasons.

First, notice the words she used to describe abortion. By her own admission, abortion was baby killing. The phrase wasn't a rhetorical flourish of mine; this was her own description.[2] I did not have to persuade her that abortion takes the life of an innocent human being. She already knew it.

What she didn't realize, though, was that her candid admission had given me a leg up in the discussion, and I was not going to waste that opportunity. For the rest of the conversation, I abandoned the word abortion. It would be *baby killing* instead.

> Beware when rhetoric becomes a substitute for substance. You always know that a person has a weak position when he tries to accomplish with the clever use of words what argument alone cannot do.

Second, I thought it surprising that her first reason for not hurting a defenseless child was self-interest—something bad might befall *her. Is that the best she can do?* I thought. This comment was worth pursuing, but I ignored it and took a different tack.

"Well, maybe *you* wouldn't do anything to hurt a baby, but other people would," I countered calmly. "Shouldn't we do something to stop them from killing babies?"

"I think women should have a choice," she responded quickly, without thinking.

Now, generally statements like, "Women should have a choice" are meaningless as they stand. Like the statement, "I have a right to take . . ." the claim requires an object. Choose what? Take what? No one has an open-ended right to choose. People only have the right to choose particular things. Whether anyone has a right to choose depends on what choice they have in mind.

In this case, though, there was no ambiguity. The woman had already identified what the choice amounted to: baby killing, to use her words. Even though she personally respected all life, including human life, this was not a belief she was comfortable forcing on others. Women still should have the choice to kill their own babies.

That was her view. She did not state her conviction in those words, of course, but that was clearly what she believed.

When bizarre ideas like these are implied, do not let them lurk in the shadows. Drag them into the light with a request for clarification. Make the implicit idea explicitly obvious. That is what I did next.

"Do you mean women should have the choice to kill their own babies?"

"Well . . ." She thought for a moment. "I think all things should be taken into consideration on this question."

"Okay, tell me: what kind of considerations would make it alright to kill a baby?"

"Incest," she answered.

I was not surprised by her response, since the line is part of the pro-choice playbook, but I don't want you to miss something significant here.

This dear young woman was advancing her view by trotting out standard slogans in favor of abortion: women have a right to choose, all things should be taken into consideration, incest justifies abortions. Yet in this case, her slogans did not defend abortion in the abstract but explicitly promoted baby killing.

The fact hadn't registered with her, though, because her slogans were getting in the way. She was simply reciting her lines without thinking. However, you can see that from where I stood, the conversation was starting to sound a little weird.

This happens all the time, of course, on both sides of the aisle. We trot out our pet slogans—whether secular ones or Christian ones—letting our catchphrases do the work that careful, thoughtful conversation should be doing instead. The habit often obscures the full significance (or ramifications, in this case) of our words.

I decided to take the conversation one step farther, hoping to break the slogan spell.

"Hmm. Let me see if I understand your view," I said. "Let's just say I had a two-year-old child standing next to me who had been conceived as a result of incest. On your view, it seems, I should have the liberty to kill her. Is that right?"

This last question stopped her in her tracks. Though the notion was clearly absurd, it was also clear that she was deeply committed to her pro-choice convictions. She had no snappy slogan to respond with and had to pause for a moment to think about the corner she had backed herself into. Finally, she said, "I'd have mixed feelings about that." It was the best she could do.

Of course, she meant this as a concession, but it was a desperately weak response. ("Killing a two-year-old? Gee, you got me on that one. I'll have to think about it.")

"I hope so," was all I had the heart to say.

At this point, I noticed a line of customers forming behind me.

I realized our conversation was interfering with her work, and my brief opportunity had come to a close.

True, I hadn't gotten to the gospel, but that was not the direction this conversation was going. This wasn't a gospel moment but a gardening moment that involved a vital moral issue. It was time to abandon the pursuit, entrust her to the Lord, and move on. My wife and I finished our transaction, wished her well, and departed.

LESSONS LEARNED

I want you to notice a few things about this short encounter. First, there was no tension, no anxiety, and no awkwardness in the exchange. There were no lines drawn in the sand and no one vigorously protecting their turf. There was no confrontation, no defensiveness, and no discomfort.

The discussion flowed easily and naturally. I was relaxed and so was she. And that's the way I like it. I don't want to get in a fight, for good reason. If anyone gets mad, I lose. People are not inclined to change their minds when they're angry.

Second, even with the relaxed atmosphere, I was in the driver's seat of the conversation the entire time. I was able to stay there, calmly and thoughtfully, by using three important tactics—maneuvers I will explain in greater detail later in the book—to probe the young woman's ideas and challenge her faulty thinking.

To start with, I asked seven specific questions. I used these questions to begin the conversation ("Does that star have religious significance, or is it just jewelry?") and to gain information from her ("So you're Wiccan?"). I then used questions to expose what I thought were weaknesses in how she responded ("Do you mean women should have the choice to kill their own babies?").

I also gently challenged the inconsistent and contradictory nature of her views. On one hand, she was a witch who respected all life. On the other hand, she was pro-choice on abortion, a procedure she candidly characterized as baby killing.

Third, I tried to help her see the logical consequences of her convictions. For her, incest was a legitimate reason to kill a baby. But when asked if it was legitimate to kill a toddler for the same reason, she balked, even though—strictly speaking—this was fully consistent with her view.

The last thing I want you to notice about our conversation is critical: The witch in Wisconsin was doing most of the work. The only effort on my part was to pay attention to her responses and steer the exchange in the direction I wanted it to go, which was not hard at all using my tactics.

Plus, because I was comfortable with being a gardener—doing a little spadework instead of pushing for a harvest before its season[3]—I felt no pressure to squeeze the gospel into the conversation in a way that was artificial, unnatural, and therefore unhelpful. I made the best of the opportunity, knowing that for the moment she was my task, but ultimately she was God's responsibility. I left her to the Lord and moved on.

This is the power of the tactical approach: staying in the driver's seat in conversations so you can direct the discussion, exposing faulty thinking and suggesting more fruitful alternatives along the way.

Regardless of your capabilities, you can maneuver almost effortlessly in conversations just like I did if you learn the material in this book. I have taught these concepts to tens of thousands of people just like you and equipped them with the confidence and ability to have meaningful, productive conversations about spiritual things.

You *can* become an effective ambassador for Christ. It requires only that you pay attention to the guidelines in the chapters that follow and apply what you have learned.

TWENTY-FIRST-CENTURY AMBASSADORS

Representing Christ in any era requires three skills. First, Christ's ambassadors need the basic *knowledge* necessary for the task. They must know the central message of God's kingdom and something about how to respond to the obstacles they'll encounter on their mission.

However, it's not enough for followers of Jesus to have an accurately informed mind. Our knowledge must be tempered with the *wisdom* that makes our message clear and persuasive. This requires the tools of a diplomat, not the weapons of a warrior, tactical skill rather than brute force.

Finally, our *character* can make or break our mission. Knowledge and wisdom are packaged in a person. If that person does not embody the virtues of the Sovereign she serves, she will undermine her message and handicap her efforts.

These three skills—knowledge, an accurately informed mind; wisdom, an artful method; and character, an attractive manner—play a part in every effective encounter with a nonbeliever. The second skill, tactical wisdom, is the main focus of this book.

Keep in mind that strategy and tactics are different. Strategy involves the big picture, the large-scale operation, one's positioning prior to engagement.

Here's how this concept applies to our situation as Christian ambassadors. As followers of Jesus, we have a tremendous strategic advantage. We are well positioned on the field, because our worldview holds up well under serious scrutiny, especially considering the alternatives.

Our strategic advantage includes two areas. The first, called offensive apologetics, makes a positive case for Christianity by offering reasons that support our view—giving evidence for the existence of God or for the resurrection of Christ or for the inspiration of the Bible, for example. The second area, often called defensive apologetics, answers specific challenges meant to undermine or disprove Christianity—responding to attacks on the authority and historical reliability of the Bible or tackling the problem of evil or addressing the challenge of Darwinian macroevolution, to name a few.[4]

Notice that in the way I am using the term, the strategic element focuses on content. Virtually every book ever written on defending

Christianity takes this approach. Faithful Christian authors have filled bookshelves with enough information to deal decisively with every imaginable challenge to classical Christianity. Still, many Christians have an inferiority complex. Why? It might be because they have never been exposed to such excellent information. As a result, they are lacking the first skill of a good ambassador: knowledge.

But I think there is another reason. Something is still missing. A sharp lawyer needs more than facts to make his case in court. He needs to know how to use his knowledge well. In the same way, we need a plan to artfully manage the details of our dialogues with others. This is where the tactical game plan comes in.

TACTICS: THE MISSING PIECE OF THE PUZZLE

In World War II, the Allied forces had a strategic plan for gaining a foothold on the European continent. The Normandy invasion, code-named Operation Overlord, involved a simultaneous attack on five beaches—Utah, Omaha, Gold, Juno, and Sword—on June 6, 1944, also known as D-Day.

No strategy, however brilliant, can win a war, though. The devil, as they say, is in the details. Individual soldiers must hit the beach and engage, deploying assets and destroying obstacles to gain an advantage, dodging bullets all the while.

Though we are following a diplomatic model and not a military one, the military metaphor is still helpful to distinguish strategy from tactics. Tactics—literally "the art of arranging"—focus on the immediate situation at hand. They involve the orderly, hands-on choreography of the particulars. Often a clever commander can gain an advantage over the superior strength or numbers of a larger force through deft tactical maneuvering.

I think you can see the parallel for you as a Christian. You may have personal experience with how the gospel can change someone's life, but how do you design specific responses for specific people so you can have an impact in specific situations?

Tactics can help, because they offer techniques of maneuvering in what otherwise might be difficult conversations. They guide you in arranging your resources in an artful way. They suggest approaches that anyone can use to be more persuasive, in part because they help you to be more reasonable and thoughtful, instead of just emotional, about your convictions as a follower of Christ.

The tactical approach requires as much careful listening as thoughtful response. You have to pay attention so you can adapt to new information. This method resembles one-on-one basketball more than a game of chess. There are plans being played out, but there is constant motion and adjustment.

I have all kinds of odd names for these tactics to help you remember what they are and how they work—names like Columbo; Suicide; Taking the Roof Off; Rhodes Scholar; Just the Facts, Ma'am; and Steamroller. Some you initiate; others you use for self-protection.

In the pages that follow, you will encounter real-life examples of dialogues where I use a tactical approach to address common objections, complaints, or assertions raised against the convictions you and I hold as followers of Jesus. But there is a danger I want you to be aware of, so I need to pause to make an important clarification.

Tactics are not manipulative tricks or slick ruses. They are not clever ploys to embarrass other people and force them to submit to your point of view. They are not meant to belittle or humiliate those who disagree so you can gain notches in your spiritual belt.

> It is not the Christian life to wound, embarrass, or play one-upmanship with colleagues, friends, or even opponents, but it's a common vice that anyone can easily fall into.
>
> —*Hugh Hewitt*[5]

I offer this warning for two reasons.

First, these tactics are powerful and can be abused. It's not difficult to make someone look silly when you master these techniques.

A tactical approach can quickly show people how foolish some of their ideas are. Therefore you must be careful not to use your tactics merely to assault others in a vindictive or abusive way.[6]

Second, the illustrations in this book are abbreviated accounts of real conversations I've had with nonbelievers. In the retelling, I may appear more aggressive than I was in real life. I am certainly not opposed to being assertive, direct, or challenging. However, I never intend to be abrasive or abusive or to gain an advantage by demeaning another person. It's not only bad manners; it's unnecessary when you have the truth and such good reasons to believe it.

My goal, rather, is to find clever ways to exploit someone's bad thinking for the purpose of guiding her to truth, remaining gracious and charitable at the same time. My aim is to manage, not manipulate; to convince, not coerce; to finesse, not fight. I want the same for you.

If you are a little nervous about the prospect of talking to people outside the safety of your Christian circle, let me offer you two words of encouragement.

First, I have been engaging challengers and critics in the marketplace of ideas for more than four decades. The people I talk with—atheists, cultists, skeptics, and secularists of every description—all oppose evangelical Christian views, sometimes vigorously and belligerently. Often they are very smart people.

To be candid, this concerned me at first. I wasn't sure how the responses I'd learned in the safety of my study would fare against the smart guys in public with thousands of people watching or listening. What I discovered in the crucible, though, was that the facts and sound reason are on our side. Most people, even the smart ones, don't give much thought to their opposition to Christianity. How do I know? I have listened to their objections.

It is axiomatic that these learned and intelligent people—academics of all sorts and professionals of every stripe—often make foolish and fundamental mistakes in thinking when it comes to spiritual things. This came as a complete surprise to me at first, but I've seen it over and over.

I have learned we don't have to be frightened of the facts or of the adversaries. Take your time, do your homework, think through the issues. If Christianity is the truth, then no matter how convincing the other side sounds at first, there will always be a fly in the ointment somewhere—a mistake in thinking, a wayward "fact," an unjustified conclusion. Keep looking for it. Sooner or later it will show up.[7] Many times, as you'll soon see, the right tactic will help you discover that flaw and show it for the error it is.

Here is the second word of encouragement: You can do this. I will show you how. I will guide you, step by step, through a game plan that will help you maneuver comfortably and graciously in conversations about your Christian convictions and values. Move at your own pace. Engage at your comfort level. You will discover, though, that the tactical approach provides you with a large margin of safety.

Yes, there is an art to this process, and learning any craft takes time and a little focused effort. It takes practice to turn a volatile situation into an opportunity. If you learn the tactics in this book, though, I promise you will get better at presenting the truth clearly and sometimes even cleverly.

If you are an attentive student, in a very short time you will develop the art of staying in the driver's seat and steering the conversation during your discussions with others. You will learn how to navigate through the minefields to gain a footing or an advantage in conversations. You will be learning to be a better diplomat, an ambassador for Jesus Christ.

WHAT WE LEARNED IN THIS CHAPTER

First, we learned the value of using the tactical approach when discussing Christianity. Tactics help you manage the conversation by getting you into the driver's seat and keeping you there. Tactics also help you maneuver effectively in the midst of disagreement so that your engagements seem more like diplomacy than D-Day.

Second, we defined tactics and distinguished them from strategy.

Strategy involves the big picture, which in our case means the content, information, and reasons why someone should believe Christianity is true. Tactics, on the other hand, involve the details of the engagement, the art of navigating through the conversation itself.

Third, we learned about the dangers of using tactics. Tactics are not manipulative tricks, slick ruses, or clever ploys to belittle or humiliate another person. Instead tactics are used to gain a footing, to maneuver, and to expose the person's bad thinking so you can guide him to truth.

Before we get into the details, though, I would like to address a couple of reservations you may have.

Chapter 2

RESERVATIONS

I have just made you a promise. I said that if you learn the tactics in this book, you will be able to comfortably engage in thoughtful conversations with others about your Christian convictions. At this point, though, you may have some reservations.

For one, trying to make your case with another person, even if done carefully, brings you dangerously close to having an argument. You may be thinking that anything that looks like an argument should be avoided.

In one sense, you'd be right. Squabbling, bickering, and quarreling are not very attractive, and they rarely produce anything good. With these types of disputes, I have a general rule: if anyone in the discussion gets mad, you lose.

Here's what I mean. When you get angry, you look belligerent. You raise your voice. You scowl and glare. You may even start cutting the other person off before he's had an opportunity to make his point. Not only is this bad manners, but it begins to look like your ideas are not as good as you thought they were, so you resort to interruption and intimidation to get your way. You begin to replace persuasion with power. This is not a good strategy. It is never really convincing, even if you're successful in bullying the other person into silence.

These are the liabilities when you get mad. What if you keep your cool, though, and the other person gets mad? Well, you lose in that case too. People who are angry get defensive, and defensive people are not in a very good position to think about whether your ideas are compelling ones. They are too interested in defending their own turf to weigh the merits of an opposing view.

> Always make it a goal to keep your conversations cordial. Sometimes that will not be possible. If a principled, charitable expression of your ideas makes someone mad, there's little you can do about it. Jesus' teaching made some people furious. Just make sure it's your ideas that offend and not you, that your beliefs cause the disruption and not your behavior.

Remember, if anyone gets mad, you lose, so it's good to avoid quarrels. The apostle Paul tells us clearly that as the Lord's representatives, we must not be the kind of people who are looking for a fight. Rather we're to be kind, patient, and gentle toward our opposition (2 Tim. 2:24–25).

There is another sense, though, in which arguments should not be avoided. I realize that to some people, even an amiable defense of a religious view or a moral opinion seems in bad taste. After all, if one person is right, that means others who disagree are wrong, and that sounds judgmental. It smacks of narrow-mindedness, condescension, and arrogance.

This is unfortunate. Let me try to explain why this second kind of arguing—contending in a principled way for something that really matters—is actually a good thing.

ARGUING IS A VIRTUE

Imagine living in a world where you couldn't distinguish between truth and error. You would not be able to tell food from poison or friend from foe. You could not tell good from bad, right from wrong, healthy from unhealthy, or safe from unsafe. Such a world would be a dangerous place. You wouldn't survive long.

What protects us from the hazards of such a world? If you're a Christian, you might be tempted to say, "The Word of God protects us." Certainly, that's true, but the person who says that might be missing something else God has given us that is also vital. God's Word would be useless without it.

Something else is necessary before we can accurately know what God is saying through his Word. Yes, the Bible is first in terms of authority, but something else is first in terms of the order of knowing. We cannot grasp the authoritative teaching of God's Word unless we use our minds properly. Therefore the mind, not the Bible, is the very first line of defense God has given us against error.

> If we do not use our minds properly, as God intended, the Bible will be of no use to guard us from falsehood and protect us from evil.

For some of you this may be a controversial statement, so let's think about it for a moment. To understand the Bible accurately, our mental faculties must be intact and we must use them the way God designed them to be used. We demonstrate this fact every time we disagree on an interpretation of a biblical passage and then give reasons why our view is better than another's. We argue for our point of view, and if we argue well, we separate wheat from chaff, truth from error.

Jesus said, "You shall love the Lord your God with all your heart, and with all your soul, and with all your mind, and with all your strength" (Mark 12:30). Loving God with the mind is not a passive process. It is not enough to have sentimental religious thoughts. Rather, loving God "mindfully" involves coming to conclusions about God and his world based on revelation, observation, and careful reflection.

What is the tool we use in our observations of the world that helps us separate fact from fiction? That tool is reason, the ability to use our minds to sort through observations and draw accurate conclusions about the world. Rationality is one of the tools God has given us to acquire knowledge.

Generally, sorting things out is not a solitary enterprise. It's best done in the company of others who dispute our claims in a principled way and offer competing ideas for us to consider. In short, we argue. Sometimes we are silent partners, listening, not talking, but the process is going on in our minds just the same.

> The ability to argue well is vital for clear thinking. That's why arguments are good things. Arguing is a virtue because it helps us hold to what is true and discard what is false.

This is not rationalism, a kind of idolatry of the mind that places man's thinking at the center of the universe. Rather, it's the proper use of one of the faculties God has given us to understand him and the world he has made.

FIGHT PHOBIC

If truth is central to Christianity, and the ability to argue is central to knowing truth, why do some Christians—even mature believers—push back when Christians try to determine truth through disagreement and thoughtful disputation? Two things come to mind that are especially applicable to those in a Christian setting, usually a church environment.

First, some fear division. They say that when people are free to express strong differences of opinion, especially on theological issues, it threatens unity. Consequently, the minute a disagreement surfaces, someone jumps in to shut down dissent in order to keep the peace. This approach causes problems of its own, though.

True enough, Christians sometimes get distracted by useless disputes. Paul warns against wrangling about words and quarreling about foolish speculations (2 Tim. 2:14, 23). But he also commands us to be diligent workmen, handling the word of truth accurately (2 Tim. 2:15). And because some disagreements are vital, Paul solemnly charges us to "reprove, rebuke, exhort" when necessary (2 Tim. 4:1–2).[1] This cannot be done without some confrontation, but such encounters don't have to be hostile, and disagreement doesn't need to threaten genuine unity.

To be of one mind biblically doesn't mean we all have to share the same opinion. It means rather that we enjoy warm fellowship based on our communion with Christ even when we have differences. It does not mean we abandon all attempts at refining our knowledge by enforcing an artificial unanimity. Instead, true maturity means learning how to disagree in an aggressive fashion yet still maintain a peaceful harmony in the church.

There's a second reason why Christians resist arguments. Some believers, unfortunately, take any opposition as hostility, especially if their view is being challenged. In some circles, it's virtually impossible to take exception to a cherished view or a respected teacher without being labeled malicious.

This is a dangerous attitude for the church because the minute one is labeled mean-spirited simply for raising an opposing view, debate is silenced. If we disqualify legitimate discussion, we compromise our ability to know the truth, and error can thrive without restraint.

Christians should not deal with dissent this way. Instead, we ought to learn how to argue in a principled fashion—fairly, reasonably, and graciously. We need to cultivate our ability to disagree with civility and not take opposition personally. We must also have the grace to allow our views to be challenged with evidence, reasoning, and Scripture. Those who refuse to engage in principled dispute—or worse, prevent others from doing so—have a poor chance of growing in their understanding of truth.

There is no reason to threaten our unity by frivolous debate. However, many debates are worthy of our best efforts. Paul told Timothy, "Retain the standard of sound words," and, "Guard . . . the treasure which has been entrusted to you" (2 Tim. 1:13–14). He told

Titus to choose elders who could "exhort in sound doctrine" and "refute those who contradict"—false teachers, he said, who "must be silenced" (Titus 1:9, 11). This protection of truth is not a passive enterprise. It is active and engaging.

Arguments are good, and dispute is healthy. They clarify the truth and protect us from error and religious despotism. When the church discourages principled debates and a free flow of ideas, the result is shallow Christianity and a false sense of unity. No one gets any practice at learning how to field contrary views in a gracious and productive way. The oneness shared is contrived, not genuine. Worse, the ability to separate wheat from chaff is lost. When arguments are few, error abounds.

DO ARGUMENTS WORK?

Now I want to address another question: do arguments work? The simple answer is yes, they do, but this needs explanation.

Some suspect that using reason isn't spiritual. "After all, you can't argue anyone into the kingdom," they say. "Only the Spirit can change a rebel's heart. Jesus was clear on this. No one can come to him unless the Father draws him [John 6:44]. No intellectual argument could ever substitute for the act of sovereign grace necessary for sinners to come to their senses."

Of course, this last statement is entirely true as far as it goes. The problem is, it does not go far enough. There is more to the story. It doesn't follow that if God's Spirit plays a vital role, then reason and persuasion play none. In the apostle Paul's mind, there was no conflict. Note:

> *According to Paul's custom*, he went to them, and for three Sabbaths *reasoned* with them from the Scriptures, explaining and *giving evidence* that the Christ had to suffer and rise again from the dead. . . . And *some of them were persuaded.*
> —*Acts 17:2–4, emphasis added*

He was *reasoning* in the synagogue every Sabbath and trying to *persuade* Jews and Greeks.

—*Acts 18:4, emphasis added*

And there are many more passages like this.[2] You might also think of examples from your own life where taking a thoughtful approach made a big difference—maybe even a decisive difference—in a person's journey to Christ.

The fact is, you *can* argue someone into the kingdom. It happens all the time.[3] But when arguments are effective, they are not working in a vacuum.

When people say you can't argue anyone into the kingdom, they usually have an alternative approach in mind. They might be thinking that a genuine expression of love, kindness, and acceptance coupled with a simple presentation of the gospel is a more biblical approach.

If you are tempted to think this way, let me say something that may shock you: you cannot love someone into the kingdom. It can't be done. Neither is the simple gospel by itself adequate to do that job.

How do I know? Because many people who were treated with sacrificial love and kindness by Christians never surrendered to the Savior. Many who have heard a clear explanation of God's gift in Christ never put their trust in him.

In each case, something was missing that, when present, always results in conversion. What's missing is that special work of the Father that Jesus referred to—drawing a lost soul into his arms. Of this work Jesus also said, "Of all that He has given Me I lose nothing, but raise it up on the last day" (John 6:39).

According to Jesus, then, two things are true. First, there is a particular work of God that is necessary to bring someone into the kingdom. Second, when present, this work cannot fail to accomplish its goal. Without the work of the Spirit, no argument—no matter how persuasive—will be effective. But neither will any act of love nor any simple presentation of the gospel. Add the Spirit, though, and the equation changes dramatically.

Here's the key principle: without God's work, nothing else works; but with God's work, many things work. Under the influence of the Holy Spirit, love persuades. With Jesus' help, arguments convince. By the power of God, the gospel transforms through each of these methods.

Why do you think God is just as pleased to use a good argument as a warm expression of love? Because both love and reason are consistent with God's character. The same God who is the essence of love (1 John 4:8) also gave the invitation, "Come now, and let us reason together" (Isa. 1:18). Therefore both approaches honor him.

Understanding this truth makes our job as ambassadors much easier. We can be confident that every time we engage, we have an ally. Our job is to communicate the gospel as clearly, graciously, and persuasively as possible. God's job is to take it from there. We may plant the seeds or water the saplings, but God causes whatever increase comes from our efforts (1 Cor. 3:6–8).

> We are not in this alone. Yes, each of us has an important role to play, but all the pressure is on the Lord. Sharing the gospel is our task, but salvation is God's responsibility.

I like to call this principle "100 percent God and 100 percent man." I am wholly responsible for my side of the ledger, and God is entirely responsible for his. I focus on being faithful, but I trust God to be effective. Some will respond, and some will not. The results are his concern, not mine. This lifts a tremendous burden from my shoulders.

When I was a young Christian, the wife of my mentor gave me some solid advice from John 10. In this chapter, Jesus uses a "figure of speech" (v. 6) to describe the work of the Holy Spirit drawing someone to Christ. "My sheep hear My voice," Jesus says. "I know them, and they follow Me; and I give eternal life to them, and they will never perish" (John 10:27–28).[4]

This passage has practical application for evangelism because it helps explain something you might have encountered in conversations with others. Have you ever noticed that sometimes your comments seem to fall on deaf ears, yet at other times they seem profitable?

"When I share my faith," Kathy, my mentor's wife, told me, "I pay attention to how the sheep respond. Most will keep on eating grass. But once in a while, you'll notice that some lift their heads. There is a moment of recognition as they hear the Shepherd's voice."[5]

Kathy understood that it was Jesus' job to change the heart. Since she was confident the Holy Spirit was going before her, she was simply looking for the people who were looking for her. She was looking for those already hungry for the gospel, those whose hearts were being softened by the Spirit. Those were the people she spent her time on. She left the rest alone.[6]

A MODEST GOAL

My confidence that God is responsible for the results helps me in another way. Since I know I play only one part in a larger process of bringing anyone to the Lord, I'm comfortable taking smaller steps toward that end.

It may surprise you to hear this, but I never set out to convert anyone. My aim is never to win someone to Christ. I have a more modest goal, one you might consider adopting as your own. *All I want to do is put a stone in someone's shoe.* I want to give that person something worth thinking about, something he can't ignore because it continues to poke at him in a good way.

Think of it this way. When a batter gets up to the plate, his goal isn't to win the ball game. That's an extended process that takes a team effort. He just wants a chance to get a hit. If he connects, he might get on base and into scoring position. Or he may drive another batter home even if he never makes it to first. In the same way, I never try to hit the winning run. I just want to get up to bat. That's all.

In some circles, there's pressure for Christian ambassadors to close the sale. Get right to the meat of the message. Give the simple gospel. If the person doesn't respond, you've still done your part. Shake the dust off your feet and move on.

In my view, though, this is not good advice. You don't have to get to the foot of the cross in every encounter. You don't have to try to close every deal. I think it's often better if you don't try. I have a number of reasons for this recommendation.

First, the simple gospel is no longer simple. Yes, the truth is still the truth. It hasn't changed, but the world has changed dramatically. The basic theological concepts and the language we've used to convey them are largely unintelligible now to many in our culture, especially the emerging generation. Basic four-steps-to-salvation approaches sound clunky, contrived, and overly simplistic. Religious slogans often substitute for thoughtful substance, making believers unattractive, unconvincing, and largely ineffective.

Second, objections abound, now more than ever. Books hostile to classical Christianity raise sophisticated challenges and populate bestseller lists. Most people have not read them, of course, but they know they're out there, and they know their authors are making rounds in the media and in public debates. They're convinced the smart guys have weighed in and found Christianity wanting, so they have little interest in giving us a hearing.[7]

Third, not all Christians are good closers. Yes, some are effective at getting a decision. For those with that gift, harvesting takes little effort. Nothing fancy is required; the simple gospel does the trick. That's because when the fruit is ripe, all it takes is a little bump for it to fall into the basket. But something else is needed before the harvester can harvest: gardeners working for a season until the fruit is ripe.

I want you to think about what Jesus said to his disciples after his conversation with the Samaritan woman outside the city of Sychar (John 4:27–38). He told them that, contrary to their conviction, Sychar was a field ripe for harvest. They would do the reaping, though they hadn't done the sowing. Others did the heavy lifting, but the disciples would get the easy pickings. "One sows and another reaps," Jesus said (v. 37).

In this single sentence, Jesus made three things clear. First, there was one team working as a group in the same field. Second, there were two seasons of labor—a planting season and a gathering season. Third, there were two types of workers—sowers and reapers, gardeners and harvesters. Both were vital in their proper season, working productively and happily together to the same end, "so that he who sows and he who reaps may rejoice together" (v. 36).

Here is the takeaway I do not want you to miss. Since the harvesting is easy when the fruit is ripe, and since the lion's share of the labor is in the gardening, I suspect we need more gardeners than harvesters. That means there is a place for you, even if you do not fancy yourself a good closer.

I am convinced that most Christians—including me—are not harvesters. Instead we are ordinary gardeners, tending the field so others can bring in the crop in due season. Some Christians, aware of their difficulty in harvesting, get discouraged and never go into the field at all. If this describes you, then you need to know it's okay to sow, even if you don't reap. There'd be no harvest at all without sowers like you. Ironically, I think harvesting comes easily for some because many ordinary gardeners went before them—planting, watering, weeding—cultivating healthy growth until the fruit was ready to pick.

Here is the final reason I do not think it wise to make a beeline for the cross in every conversation: in most situations, the fruit is not ripe. The nonbeliever is simply not ready. She may have just begun to consider Christianity. Dropping a message on her that is, from her point of view, meaningless or simply unbelievable doesn't accomplish anything. It may be the worst thing you can do. She rejects a message she doesn't understand, and then she's harder to reach the next time.

Think of your journey to Christ. Chances are, you didn't go from a standstill to total commitment. Instead God dealt with you over time. There was a period of reflection as you sorted out the details.

A few years back, I spoke to a Jewish attorney who didn't understand why he needed to believe in Jesus (you'll find the full story in chapter 7). In his case, I didn't try to build to a point of decision, where I asked, "Do you want to receive Christ?" Instead I put a stone in his shoe. I gave him two questions to consider. He needed to digest vital information before he'd be ready for a genuine commitment. If he ever made a decision to trust Jesus, I wanted it to be informed and thoughtful, a choice that lasted, not an emotional reaction made in the heat of the moment, one he'd later abandon.

One spring, I spoke at the University of California, San Diego, to an audience of four hundred students in the center of campus. Most were not Christians. I'd heard that the general attitude on campus was that Christians are stupid. That sounded like a good opener for my talk.

"I understand many of you think Christians are stupid," I said to the audience. "Well, some of them are," I admitted. "But many non-Christians are stupid too, so I don't know how that helps you. What I want to do this evening is show you that *Christianity* is not stupid."

Then I shared with them my modest goal. "I'm not here to convert you tonight," I said. "Instead I want to put a stone in your shoe." After that, I lectured on the failure of moral relativism. I wasn't there to close the sale. I just wanted to give them something to think about.

As it turned out, while taking questions from the audience afterward, I was able to give more detail about the gospel, but only after I had laid the groundwork by making the message not only sensible to them but reasonable. I took one step at a time.

> I encourage you to consider the strategy I use when God opens a door of opportunity for me. I pray quickly for wisdom, then ask myself, *What one thing can I say in this circumstance, what one question can I ask, what single idea can I offer that will get the other person thinking?* Then I simply try to put a stone in the person's shoe.

WHAT WE LEARNED IN THIS CHAPTER

I opened this chapter by addressing a handful of reservations you might have about developing your tactical skill as an ambassador. There is a difference between an argument and a fight. Unfriendly quarrels are not productive. If anyone in the conversation gets mad, then you lose. Arguments, on the other hand, are good things. Arguing is a virtue because it advances clear thinking. If done well, it helps refine our understanding of the truth.

When Christians avoid principled conflict on things that matter because they fear disunity or division, they cripple the church in three ways. First, Scripture commands that we guard the truth within our ranks. But where arguments are few, error abounds. Second, believers are denied the opportunity to learn how to argue among themselves in a fair, reasonable, and gracious way. Third, the outcome for fight-phobic churches is often not genuine oneness but a contrived unanimity, a shallow and artificial peace.

For those who are tempted to think that presenting arguments and evidence is not spiritual because only God can change a rebellious heart, I made two observations. First, without the work of God, nothing else will work—not arguments, not love, not even the simple gospel. Second, with the help of the Holy Spirit, God is pleased to use many things. Love and reason are especially appealing to him because both are consistent with his nature. With God's help, arguments work all the time. Jesus used them, Peter used them, and Paul used them—all to great effect. We should use them too.

Understanding God's central role in the process removes a tremendous burden. We can focus on our job—being clear, gracious, and persuasive—and leave the results to God (a principle I call "100 percent God and 100 percent man"). We're looking for those who are looking for us—people whose hearts are already being touched by the Spirit. We can be alert for those sheep who hear Jesus' voice and lift their heads, without troubling—or unnecessarily annoying—those who are not yet ready.

Finally, I encouraged you to adopt for your encounters the modest goal that I have found so effective. Instead of trying to get to the cross in every encounter, just aim to put a stone in someone's shoe. Try to give the person something to think about. Be content to plant a thought or an idea that might later flourish under God's sovereign care. Be a good gardener, then trust the Lord to bring in the harvest in his proper time.

Chapter 3

GETTING IN THE DRIVER'S SEAT

The Columbo Tactic

Let's start this chapter by putting you in a tough spot. I want you to imagine yourself in the following situations.

- *Scene 1:* You're at a dinner party with some of your close friends from church. The conversation ranges naturally over a number of interesting spiritual topics. Suddenly, to your surprise and embarrassment, the host's fifteen-year-old son announces with some belligerence that he doesn't believe in God anymore. "It's simply not rational," he says. "There is no proof." No one had any idea he'd been moving in this direction. There's a stunned silence. What will you say?
- *Scene 2:* It's the night of your weekly Bible study group. During the discussion of the Sunday sermon on the Great Commission, a newcomer remarks, "Who are we to say Christianity is better than any other religion? I think the essence of Jesus' teaching is love, the same as all religions. It's not our job to tell other people how to live or believe." The rest of the group fidgets awkwardly but says nothing. How do you respond?

- *Scene 3:* You're riding the university shuttle with a friend who notices a Bible in your backpack. "I've read the Bible before," he says. "It's got some interesting stories, but people take it too seriously. It was only written by men, after all, and men make mistakes." You try to recall the points your pastor made a few weeks earlier about the Bible's inspiration but come up empty-handed. What do you say?

- *Scene 4:* You're sitting at the car dealer, watching TV and waiting with other customers for your car to be serviced. A television news program highlights religious groups trying to influence important moral legislation. The person sitting next to you says, "Haven't these people ever heard of separation of church and state? Those Christians are always trying to force their views on everyone else. You can't legislate morality. Why don't they just leave the rest of us alone?" Other people are listening, and you don't want to create a scene, but you feel you must say something. What's your next move?

TEN-SECOND WINDOW

In each of these cases you have an opportunity, but there are obstacles. First, you must speak up quickly because the opportunity will not last long. You have only about ten seconds before the door closes. Second, you're conflicted. You want to say something, but you're also concerned about being sensitive, keeping the peace, preserving friendships, and not looking extreme.

What if I told you there was an easy escape from the challenge that each situation presents, a way to minimize the awkwardness and engage the other person productively and gracefully? What if you had a simple plan in place that would guide you in your next move? Would that give you the confidence to take a small step toward addressing challenges like these?

I have such a plan. My plan helps me know how to use that critical ten-second window to my best advantage. It acts as a guide to direct my next steps. When I consider each of these scenes, a host of questions comes to mind. In the next chapter, I'll give you the backstory to these questions. For the moment, though, think about how the following responses begin to address the content of the person's remarks yet still draw him into an interactive conversation in a very intentional way.

- *Challenge 1:* "It's not rational to believe in God. There is no proof."

  What do you mean by "God"—that is, what kind of God do you reject? What specifically is irrational about believing in God? Since you're concerned about proof for God's existence, what kind of evidence would you find acceptable? What arguments for God have you considered, and what did you find wrong with them?
- *Challenge 2:* "Christianity is basically the same as all other religions. The main similarity is love. We shouldn't tell others how to live or believe."

  How much have you studied other religions to compare the details and find a common theme? Why would the similarities be more important than the differences? I'm curious—what do you think Jesus' attitude was on this issue? Did he think all religions were basically equal? Isn't telling people to love one another just another example of doing what you're objecting to—telling others how they should live and believe?
- *Challenge 3:* "You can't take the Bible too seriously, because it was only written by men, and men make mistakes."

  Do you have any books in your library? Do you find any truth in those books, also written by humans who are prone to error? Is there a reason you think the Bible is less truthful or reliable than other books you own? Do people *always* make mistakes in what they write? If not, then why would you dismiss the Bible simply on that basis? Do you think that, if God did exist, he would be able to use humans to write down exactly what he wanted? If not, why not?

■ *Challenge 4:* "It's wrong to force your views on other people. You can't legislate morality. Christians involved in politics violate the separation of church and state."

Do you vote? When you vote for someone, are you expecting your candidate to pass laws reflecting your point of view? Wouldn't that essentially be forcing your views on others? How is that different from what you're troubled about here? Is it your view that only nonreligious people should be allowed to vote or participate in politics, or did I misunderstand you? Where specifically in the Constitution are religious people excluded from the political process because of their spiritual convictions? Don't all laws force a morality of some sort? Can you give me an example of legislation that does not have a moral element underlying the law?

I want you to notice several things about these responses. First, each is a question. My initial response in a situation like this is not to preach about my view or even disagree with theirs. Rather, I want to draw them out, to invite them to talk more about what they think. This takes a lot of pressure off me because when I ask a question, the ball is back in their court. It also protects me from jumping to conclusions and unwittingly distorting their meaning. The more they talk, the more information I have to work with to maneuver in the conversation.

> Asking questions enables you to escape the charge, "You're twisting my words." A question is a request for clarification specifically so you don't twist their words. When I ask a clarification question, my goal is to understand a person's view (and its consequences), not to distort it.

Second, each of these questions is an invitation to thoughtful dialogue. Each is an encouragement to participate in conversation in a reflective way. Though my tone is relaxed and cordial, my questions are pointed enough to challenge the person to give some thought to what he's just said.

Third, these are not idle queries. I have a particular purpose for each question. With some, I'm simply gathering information ("Do you vote?"). Others, you might have noticed, are subtly leading; the questions are meant to make a point by indicating a problem with the other person's thinking ("Wouldn't that essentially be forcing your views on others?").

Each of the questions I have suggested occurs to me because I have a plan. I know that getting into conversations about spiritual matters is not easy, especially if someone's guard is up. It's not unusual to get tongue-tied, not knowing what to say. This is complicated by the fear of getting in over your head—or worse, of offending someone. We need some help.

Our first tactic is a handy solution to that problem. That's why I use it more than any other. It makes it easy for even the most timid person to engage others in a meaningful way, because it provides a step-by-step guide—a virtual game plan—to help you ease into a conversation.

Our first maneuver might be called the queen mother of all tactics because it's so flexible and adaptable. It's easily combined with other moves you will learn later. It's the simplest tactic imaginable to stop a challenger in her tracks, turn the tables, and get her thinking, a virtually effortless way of putting you in the driver's seat of the conversation.

It's simply called Columbo.

TAKE A TIP FROM LIEUTENANT COLUMBO

The Columbo tactic is named after Lieutenant Columbo, a brilliant TV detective from a bygone era who had a clever way of catching a killer.

The inspector arrives on the scene in disarray, his hair unkempt, his trench coat rumpled beyond repair, his cigar wedged tightly between stubby fingers. Columbo's pencil has gone missing again, so his notepad is useless until he bums a pen off a bystander.

To all appearances, Columbo is bumbling, inept, and harmless. He couldn't think his way out of a wet paper bag, or so it seems. He's stupid, but he's stupid like a fox because the lieutenant has a simple plan that accounts for his remarkable success.

After poking around the crime scene, scratching his head and muttering to himself, Lieutenant Columbo makes his trademark move. "I got a problem," he says as he looks around, rubbing his furrowed brow. "There's something about this thing that bothers me." He pauses a moment to ponder his predicament, then turns to his suspect. "You seem like an intelligent person. Maybe you can clear it up for me. Do you mind if I ask you a question?"

The first query is innocent enough (if the lieutenant seems threatening, he'll scare off his suspect), and for the moment he seems satisfied. As he turns on his heel to leave, though, he stops himself. Something has just occurred to him. He turns back to the scene, raises his index finger, and says, "Just one more thing."

But "just one more" question leads to another. And another. Soon they come relentlessly, question after question, to the point of distraction and, ultimately, annoyance.

"I'm sorry," Columbo says to his beleaguered suspect. "I know I'm making a pest of myself. It's because I keep asking these questions. But I'll tell ya," he says with a shrug, "I can't help myself. It's a habit."

And this is a habit you want to get into.

The key to the Columbo tactic is to go on the offensive in an inoffensive way with carefully selected questions that advance the conversation. Never make a statement, at least at first, when a question will do the job.

ADVANTAGES OF ASKING

There are dozens of fun ways to do this, and with a little practice it can become second nature. Hugh Hewitt, a nationally syndicated radio talk show host, is a master of this technique. In his wonderful little book *In, But Not Of*, a primer for Christians wanting to thoughtfully engage the culture, Hewitt advises asking at least a half dozen questions in every conversation.[1] It's a habit that offers tremendous advantages.

You may have learned the hard way that a frontal assault is rarely the best approach when navigating sensitive issues with resistant people. Your sincere questions, though, provide a number of benefits and will move you forward without risking a direct confrontation.

For one thing, sincere questions are friendly and flattering. They invite genial interaction by focusing on something the other person cares a lot about: herself and her ideas. "When you ask a question, you are displaying interest in the person asked," Hewitt writes. "Most people are not queried on many, if any, subjects. Their opinions are not solicited. To ask them is to be remembered fondly as a very interesting and gracious person in your own right."[2]

> Sometimes the little things have the greatest impact. Using simple leading questions is an almost effortless way to ease spiritual topics into a conversation if they haven't already come up, without seeming abrupt, rude, or pushy. Questions are engaging and interactive, probing yet amicable. Most important, they keep you in the driver's seat while the other person does all the work.

Second, you'll get an education. You'll leave a conversation knowing more than when you arrived. Sometimes that information will be just what you need to make a difference. When a young Christian asked me to recommend a book on Buddhism, I followed my own advice and asked why he wanted the book. He told me he wanted to bone up on the basics of that religion so he could witness to his Buddhist friend.

That was the information I needed. I told him not to bother with the book. Instead, I said, ask the Buddhist. Sit down over coffee and let him give the tutorial. It would be a lot easier, he'd be learning the specifics of his friend's convictions (instead of some academic version), and he'd be building a relationship with him at the same time.

Third, questions allow you to make progress on a point without being pushy. Since questions are largely neutral, or at least seem that way, they don't sound preachy. When you ask a question, you aren't stating your view, so you have nothing to defend.

Once, during a dinner party at the home of a well-known comedian, I got into a spirited conversation with the actor's wife about animal rights. I had serious reservations about her ideas, but I didn't contradict her directly. Instead I asked questions meant to expose some of the weaknesses I saw in her view.

Eventually, she began to challenge what she thought were my views. I pointed out I'd never stated my beliefs. I'd only been asking questions. Since I was probing instead of pressing a point, strictly speaking, I had no turf to protect. I didn't mind answering for my views, but up to that point they had not come up. I was off the hook.

> It may have occurred to you that using questions is the perfect solution to engaging controversial issues in the workplace, where spiritual discussions are often discouraged, especially if your views are Christian. Questions offer a low-key way of maneuvering without opening you to the charge of proselytizing.

There's a further benefit here. Questions buy you valuable time when you're not quite sure what to do next. They can help you move forward in the conversation even though the path is not obvious. The pressure is off. You can relax and enjoy the conversation while you wait for an easy opening.

Finally, and most important, carefully placed questions put you in the driver's seat of the conversation. "Being an asker allows you control of situations that statement-makers rarely achieve," Hewitt notes. "An alert questioner can judge when someone grows uneasy. But don't stop. Just change directions.... *Once you learn how to guide a conversation, you have also learned how to control it.*"[3]

Questions can be casual conversation starters providing a simple, friendly way to get the ball rolling in a discussion, like it did for me with the witch in Wisconsin. They can give you important information and allow you to make progress without being pushy. They can buy you valuable time, giving you a breather by letting the other person talk when you don't know where to go next. They can help you to indirectly and gently exploit a weakness or a flaw in another's view. Most important, though, when you're asking the questions, you're in charge, yet in a nonthreatening way.

It might have occurred to you that Jesus used this method frequently. When facing a hostile crowd, he often asked questions meant to either challenge his audience or silence his detractors by exposing their foolishness. "Show Me a denarius. Whose likeness and inscription does it have?" (Luke 20:24). "Was the baptism of John from heaven or from men?" (Luke 20:4). "Which is easier, to say to the paralytic, 'Your sins are forgiven'; or to say, 'Get up, and pick up your pallet and walk'?" (Mark 2:9).[4]

In none of these cases was Jesus speaking idly. He understood the power of a well-placed query. Whenever Jesus asked a question, he had a purpose. In the same way, the Columbo tactic is most powerful when you have a plan.

There are three basic ways to use Columbo. Each is launched by a different kind of question.[5] These three steps compose the game plan I use to tame the most belligerent critic. Sometimes I simply want to *gather information*. Other times, I ask a question to *reverse the burden of proof*—to encourage the other person to give the reasons for his views. Finally, I use questions to *make a point* by leading the conversation in a specific direction.

INITIATING THE GAME PLAN

In the next chapter, I will introduce you to the first step in our game plan. Before I do, though, I want you to be clear on exactly how the game plan works.

When you follow any reliable plan to accomplish an important goal, once you commit yourself to it, you forget about the goal and focus instead on the individual steps forward. You concern yourself with one step at a time. If the plan is a good one, the goal will take care of itself.

The same is true with our tactical game plan. When you find yourself in a conversation you hope will make a difference for Christ (the goal), I do not want you to be thinking about where you might end up down the road. That is a distraction you do not need, one that is likely to cause you confusion or anxiety that will only make your effort more difficult.

When you initiate your tactical game plan, then, do not concern yourself with anything but the first step. Do not worry about what comes next, partly because until you've taken the first step, you have no idea what the next step will look like. Forget about the endgame. Do not think about harvesting. You do not know whether there is a harvest ahead or even a good opportunity to garden.

I personally do not believe that every encounter is a divine appointment. Sometimes no fertile opportunity presents itself. You'll discover whether there's any spiritual potential quickly enough once you do your initial spadework.

Since at the beginning of an encounter, you have no idea what you're facing, the first and only thing I want you to think about at this point is one single goal—the first step of our game plan. Here it is: gather information.

WHAT WE LEARNED IN THIS CHAPTER

We started the chapter with a challenge. I gave you the opportunity to consider what you would say in the ten-second window of time available for you to respond to some standard challenges you might encounter as a Christian ambassador. Then I began to outline a simple plan as a guide to direct your steps. This plan is called Columbo.

The Columbo tactic is a disarming way to go on the offensive with carefully selected questions that productively advance the conversation. This approach has many advantages. Questions can be excellent conversation starters. They are interactive by nature, inviting others to participate in dialogue. They are neutral, protecting you from getting preachy, helping you make headway without stating your case. Questions buy valuable time. Finally, they are essential to keeping you in the driver's seat of the conversation.

Next, we learned there are specific purposes for the questions we ask. The first purpose of Columbo is to gain information. The second is to reverse the burden of proof. The third is to make a point.

Finally, I introduced you to the game plan concept. I pointed out that once you give proper attention to planning any enterprise, you then focus all your attention on the individual step at hand. The destination will take care of itself. At the beginning of any conversation, then, focus on one thing and one thing only: gathering information. In the next chapter, I will tell you how to do that effectively.

Chapter 4

COLUMBO STEP 1

Gathering Information

W hen Lieutenant Columbo shows up at a crime scene, he needs some basic facts to help him get his bearings. He needs a general feel for the situation before he can decide what his next move is going to be. That's why the first thing he does is gather information.

In the same way, you'll need more information before you know the best way to proceed in any conversation. You have no idea what you're facing or what possibilities lie ahead until you get the lay of the land. Your initial probes, then, will be friendly, open-ended queries.

The best way to start is with casual dialogue and general questions, drawing the person out by showing sincere interest in him and his ideas. If spiritual issues are not on the table yet, don't jump into them immediately. Relax and take your time. The more you let your friend talk, the more genial your interaction will be. It's more pleasant for him, and it's less work for you.

Your initial goal is to gather as much information from the other person as you can before you move on. You want him to talk as much as possible about his own convictions first. This approach gives you the best chance of "making the most of the opportunity," as Paul put it in Colossians 4:5.

If I sense an opening to something more spiritually significant, then I'll move gently in that direction—always using questions, though.

I want to tell you of a conversation I had that shows how crucial this first step can be. I once had a chat with a young professional named John who was sitting next to me on a flight. When he learned the purpose of my trip, he informed me he was not a Christian and none of his friends were either. John then added, "I used to be a Christian, but I'm not one anymore."

Let me stop here and ask you a question. Do you think that particular detail was important for me to know? Can you see how that little bit of information would make a big difference in the course I set for the conversation to follow? Sure you can. But there was more.

"Actually," John added, "I used to be a preacher's kid."

That surprised me. "How did you used to be a preacher's kid, John? Did your dad die?"

"No, my dad didn't die," he answered. "He's just not a preacher anymore. In fact, he's not even a Christian anymore."

Yikes! Was *that* important information for me to know? Do you think there might be a little emotional baggage getting in John's way here? There sure was. As I asked more questions and let him talk, he began to unload about the bad experiences he'd had with Christians and the church. It was not a pretty picture.

Think about the importance of what I was able to learn in the first few moments of our chat because I asked questions and listened. As John talked, a picture of his spiritual landscape began to form in my mind, and I realized his landscape was littered with landmines.

Do you see now how critical it was for me to gather information before I moved forward? Can you imagine what would have happened if I'd jumped blindly into a gospel presentation before letting him talk? *Been there, done that,* he would have thought, *and it hurt.*

Instead I took my time. I asked questions for clarification. I paid attention to his answers. I probed carefully with genuine interest in him and his painful experience. And because I'd been listening instead of preaching, I was able to maneuver around the hazards.

I think you can see why gathering information is the most important first step in any encounter. Whenever you get stuck in a conversation, always ask a question to get more details, then let the other person talk. Let him explain, clarify, defend—even attack. Don't get defensive. Just listen carefully. That's your first step.[1]

THE BEST FIRST QUESTION

Would you like a model question that will help you get going? Here's the one I use: "What do you mean by that?"

This question provides a natural opening to further dialogue, and it puts no pressure on you. It's delivered in a mild, genuinely inquisitive fashion. It's a simple, effortless way to use Columbo, like with these examples:

- "Do you believe in evolution?" What do you mean by "evolution"? There's more than one kind. Which one do you have in mind?
- "What about all the evil in the world?" What do you mean by "evil"? What makes bad things bad?
- "Do you take the Bible literally?" That depends on what you mean by "literally." What specifically were you thinking of?
- "Science has proved there is no God." Really? Precisely how did science do that?
- "Abortion is okay because a fetus is a human but not a person." Really? What's the difference between the two?

Your first Columbo question has tremendous advantages. To begin with, this question immediately engages the nonbeliever (or believer, if the topic is an in-house theological one) in an interactive way, making it an excellent conversation starter. When I noticed the jewelry worn by the witch in Wisconsin and asked, "Does that star have religious significance?"—a variation of "What do you mean by that?"—it led to a productive interaction.[2]

> Sometimes your first question will be directed at a specific statement or topic of discussion. Other times, the question will be more open-ended. As the dialogue continues, gently guide the conversation into a more spiritually productive direction with additional questions, if you can.

When you get into the habit of gathering information first, you'll sometimes discover that the additional clarity that results from your questions is all that's needed to parry an objection.

When someone says to me, "Reincarnation was originally part of Christian teaching but was taken out of the Bible in the fourth century," I ask them to explain how that works (a variation of our first Columbo question). The devil, as they say, is in the details of such a challenge.

How does someone remove select lines of text from tens of thousands of handwritten documents that had been circulating around the Mediterranean region for more than three hundred years? This would be like trying to secretly remove a paragraph from all copies of yesterday's *New York Times*. It can't be done.

Your first question almost always uncovers valuable information you wouldn't have received if you hadn't asked. Many objections flourish because of the muddled thinking that results from lack of clarity. Your first question often eliminates that obstacle by forcing the person to be precise about what he means.

WHY CLARITY WORKS

There are three reasons why gathering information is important. First, you don't want to misunderstand the person you're talking with. Second, you don't want to misrepresent him. Third, you don't want him to misunderstand himself.

Regarding the first, some questions or challenges are so vague, it's hard to know what to do with them. It makes no sense to move forward if you're confused or unclear about what is being said. The claim, "Everything is relative" is wildly ambiguous. It should never pass without a request for clarification. Questions like, "What do you mean by 'relative'?" or, "Is *everything* relative?" or, "Would that apply even to your statement?" are all in order.[3]

Other challenges are more complex. They contain a number of specific issues jumbled together that you may need to tease apart first with further questions.

Sometimes people claim that God is not necessary to explain morality because evolution can do the job. Since our survival depends on shared ethics (the argument goes), it's clear to see how natural selection working with a social-contract (our tacit agreement to adhere to values that ensure our survival) could account for morality. No God needed.

But this explanation hopelessly conflates two distinct notions. The first is Darwinian evolution, which by definition can explain morality only in terms of genetically determined physical traits selected for survival (though one wonders how the rest of the animal kingdom seems to have endured so well without it). The second is the "evolution" of an intelligently designed social code that a civilization developed as it moved from a primitive nuclear stage, with each local group fending for itself, to a social-contract stage, enabling all to live together in relative safety and harmony.

These are different issues: one a genetic accident, the other a thoughtful intention. In a situation like this, you'll need to probe gently with questions to clear up the confusion, then deal with each possibility on its own terms. "How exactly does that work?" would be a good question to begin clarifying the claim.

This first step of the game plan is especially helpful when people raise a direct objection to Christianity. When I ask clarification questions about the challenge, it forces the skeptic to be more specific and precise about her concern. I want my friend to spell out her view so clearly I will not misunderstand it.

The second reason you want to be clear on someone else's view is that if you don't understand that person's point, you may misrepresent it.[4] This is a serious misstep, even when done by accident. Instead of fighting the real issue (your opponent's actual view), you set up a lifeless imitation (a "straw man") that you then easily knock down. If you're guilty of using the straw man fallacy, you may find you have given a brilliant refutation of a view the other person doesn't hold.

Asking, "What do you mean by that?" helps you avoid these first two pitfalls.

> There are times when discretion is the better part of valor. If your wife calls you an idiot, don't ask, "What do you mean by that?" She might oblige by clarifying.

The third reason the question, "What do you mean by that?" (or some variation) is so useful is that it helps the other person to be more clear in her own mind about her view. I know this sounds strange, but there's a point here.

Sometimes the reason you are confused about another person's meaning is because she is confused too. She objects to Christianity for reasons she hasn't carefully thought through, and her objection flourishes because no one has challenged the lack of clarity that led to her muddled thinking in the first place. Your first question compels her—maybe for the first time—to be more precise.

Occasionally, your query will have a surprising effect. Sometimes critics charge into a conversation with their sails full of certitude and confidence, only to have the wind slip out of their sails when you ask this one simple question. They're becalmed, their self-assurance fading in the face of a question they were not prepared to answer. I've seen it time and again.

Don't be surprised, then, when you ask the question, "What do you mean by that?" and you get a blank stare and dead air in return. You ask for clarification, and many people simply do not know what to say.

There's a reason this happens: much of the time, people simply do not know what they mean.

I know that sounds surprising, but it's true. Even though people have strong opinions, they rarely reflect on their views. Often they're merely repeating slogans. When you ask them to flesh out their concern, opinion, or point of view, they're struck mute. They're forced to think about what they do mean, so be patient with the pause in the dialogue. You're doing them a favor by requesting clarification.

Asking questions is the simplest way to clear up confusion and deal with ambiguities. Your queries allow others to do more of the talking so you can do more of the listening, giving you a more precise picture of their point. Clarification questions also give you a chance to test the water without getting in over your head. They give you time to size up the situation and gather your thoughts.

"What do you mean by that?" is a question you can use with virtually every challenge—even daunting ones—leveled at you as a believer. Before you attempt to address any pushback, always ask for more information. You want to know exactly what the person thinks before you take any more steps forward.

> Be sure to pay attention to the response to your questions. If the meaning is still unclear, follow up with more queries. Say something like, "Hmm. How exactly does that work?" or, "Can you clarify that for me?" or, "I'm not sure what you're getting at." When you get more detail, feed the view back to them to make sure you got it right.

Don't underestimate the power of the question, "What do you mean by that?" Use it often. You can ask it in a variety of ways to stay engaged in productive, genial conversation while keeping the focus and the pressure on the other person, not on you.

TEN-SECOND WINDOW REDUX

In the previous chapter, I posed four scenarios for you to consider. Then I offered a series of questions I thought were appropriate responses to each one. My general goal was to use the Columbo tactic to get information, to buy time, and to steer things in a direction I thought might be productive. You may have wondered, though, why I chose the specific questions I did. Here was my thinking.

Challenge 1 was that it is not rational to believe in God. There is no proof.

I noticed that the challenge did not make clear what kind of God was being rejected. For some people, God is an old man with a beard sitting on a throne out in space somewhere. If that's the kind of God they don't believe in, then I agree with them. I don't believe in that kind of God either. Some reject the notion of a personal God but still believe in an impersonal god-force of some kind that animates the universe. Or it may turn out I'm dealing with a good, old-fashioned, naturalistic, materialistic atheist. In any case, I need more information before I can go forward.

Even when there seems to be little ambiguity, a clarification question—even a simple one—can break the tension of an awkward moment and buy you some time. It may even yield information you hadn't expected.

And be forewarned. When someone says there's no proof of God's existence, it's sometimes a trick. It may be a reasonable request for evidence, but often it's not. Unless you know in advance what kind of evidence would count (scientific data? historical documentation? philosophical arguments? revelation?) or what kind of proof would be satisfying (absolute proof? proof beyond a reasonable doubt? proof based on the preponderance of evidence? proof that's a reasonable inference to the best explanation?), you'll probably be wasting your time. If you're not clear on his criteria for proof, it will be too easy for an intellectually dishonest person to dismiss anything you offer. "Not good enough," is all he needs to say. "That's not proof."

The charge that belief in God is irrational is common but without basis. When anyone makes this assertion, I'm not going to let him off easily. I want him to tell me specifically how theism is at odds with good thinking. My Columbo question forces the person to spell out the problem instead of coasting on vague generalities.

Believing in leprechauns is irrational. Believing in God, by contrast, is like believing in atoms. The process is exactly the same. You follow the evidence of what you can see to conclude the existence of something you cannot see. The effect needs a cause adequate to explain it.

There is nothing irrational or unreasonable about the idea of a personal God creating the universe. A big bang needs a big Banger, it seems to me. A complex set of instructions (as in DNA) needs an author. A blueprint requires an engineer. A moral law needs a moral lawgiver. Each of these makes perfect sense. These are not blind leaps of faith but rather reasonable steps of intelligent reflection. Therefore the question, "Specifically, what is irrational about believing in God?" is completely in order.

I hope you see the benefit of this minimalist approach, at least as a starting place. When you first encounter an atheist, you could launch into something like the Kalam cosmological argument for God's existence—if you knew it, and if you understood it, and if you remembered it—but that would be premature, wouldn't it? Why make things hard on yourself? A question serves you much better initially.

Challenge 2 claimed that Christianity is basically the same as all other religions, love being the important common denominator. Further, it is wrong for Christians to tell others how to live or believe.

The challenger here presents another common objection to Christianity: religious pluralism, the idea that there is no one, true religion, but rather all religions are equally valid routes to God. My questions were meant to capitalize on a number of weaknesses in this view.

First, the comments show a naive understanding of other religions, which vary wildly in fundamental beliefs. For some—Buddhism, for example—God's existence is irrelevant to their ideology. As for love being the unifying element, it's an important feature of monotheistic religions like Judaism and Christianity but not of some nontheistic religions like animism.

Second, pluralism presumes that similarities between faiths are more important than differences. Think about it, though. Are aspirin and arsenic basically the same because they both come in tablet form? For some things, it's the differences that matter, not the similarities. Religion is one of them.

Third, as a suggested response, I offered, "What do you think Jesus' attitude was on this issue?" since it's clear that Jesus was not a pluralist.[5] As an observant Jew, Jesus held to the Ten Commandments, foremost among them the first: the Lord is God, and we owe fidelity to him alone; all other religions are distortions and deceptions. The early followers of Christ were first called "Christians" in Antioch by others (Acts 11:26). Their name for themselves was simply "the Way" (Acts 9:2; 19:9, 23; 22:4; 24:14, 22)—not "a way" or "one of the ways" or "our way" but *the* Way.

Finally, did you notice that the challenger's minimal theology (the essence of Jesus' teaching is love, not telling other people how to live or believe) does not allow him to escape his own charge? He has his own theological convictions—love, not judgment—that he thinks should govern how other people think and believe.

This, of course, is a judgment itself. That's why I asked, "Isn't telling people to love one another just another example of telling them how they should live and believe?" I offered an indirect challenge couched in the form of a question.[6]

Challenge 3 said we shouldn't take the Bible too seriously, because it was only written by men, and men make mistakes.

The key word here is *only*. There are two problems with this statement. Notice first that the statement itself presumes what it's attempting to establish, that the Bible is only a human document and not divinely inspired. Since this is the very question at issue, the attempt is subtly circular.

There's a more fundamental problem, though: the presumption that any work written by a human being is always riddled with error. It's clear, though, that even without God's help, fallible people can still get their facts right. Our libraries are filled with books written by mere mortals who seem capable of accuracy, insight, and wisdom. If this is true of so many others, why not of Paul, Peter, John, or Luke?

You might be thinking this is not compelling evidence for biblical inspiration, and you'd be right, but it is not meant to be. It's meant only to show that human involvement is not evidence against inspiration, since human authorship doesn't necessarily result in human error.

Remember, my goal is modest. All I want to do is put a stone in the person's shoe. I want to get him thinking. I want him to consider listening to Jesus in Scripture first before dismissing him. If I can open that door for him just a little, I have accomplished something important. Here's why I say that.

Most people who believe that the Bible is God's Word came to this conviction not through argument but through encounter. When soldiers were sent to arrest Jesus midway through his ministry, they returned empty-handed. Why had they disobeyed orders? Because they had listened. "Never has a man spoken the way this man speaks," they said (John 7:46). Jesus didn't start his discourse with reasons why people should believe his words. Instead he simply spoke the truth, and it immediately resonated with many in the crowd.

I came to believe that the Bible is God's Word in the same way I suspect you did. I read it and was moved by it. I encountered the truth firsthand and found it compelling.

If you want skeptics to believe in the Bible, don't get into a tug-of-war with them about inspiration. Instead, invite them to engage Jesus' words firsthand, then let the Spirit do the heavy lifting for you.[7]

So when someone says the Bible was only written by men, I ask questions to encourage that person to treat Jesus, for the moment, like any other teacher. I want him to listen to the words of Christ first, then draw conclusions. That's why I keep copies of John's gospel in my travel bag. With some conversations, I'll offer one as a gift, suggesting, "It might be best to let Jesus speak for himself." Once my new friend has read a bit, any further reasons I give for biblical authority will have the soil they need to take root.

Challenge 4 stated three different objections: it's wrong to politically force views on other people, Christians involved in politics violate the separation of church and state, and morality cannot be legislated.

It's pretty easy to see the problem with the first point. Those who are sensitive about forcing viewpoints have no business participating in a legislative process that does this very thing. That's why I asked the question, "Do you vote?"

Regarding the separation of church and state, the First Amendment restricts the government, not the people (read it). It ensures that the government will not give special favor to any specific religious sect or denomination. It does not prevent religious people with religious convictions from being part of the political process.

As to legislating morality, Aristotle famously observed that all law rests on a necessary foundation of morality. If the government's use of force is not in the service of the common good, then its actions are illicit. Put simply, morality is the only thing you *can* legislate. Anything else is simply a raw exercise of power.

That's the first step in our game plan: gathering information. See how easy it is? And look at what you accomplish. First, you immediately engage the nonbeliever in an interactive way. Second, you show a genuine interest in the other person's view. Third, you urge him to think more carefully about what he does mean. Fourth, you get a free education. Finally, there's no pressure on you. You're in the driver's seat.

Since the first step of your game plan is so simple, why not start by easing yourself into the shallow end of the pool, spending the next few weeks merely being a student of others' views? Use your Columbo question to draw them out, show genuine concern for their ideas, and help them explain their views with clarity. If there is any ambiguity in their answers, ask more clarifying questions, using some form of "What do you mean by that?" You'll be amazed at what God will do with that one innocent question.

WHAT WE LEARNED IN THIS CHAPTER

First, we learned there are specific purposes for the questions we ask. The first purpose of Columbo is to gather information. It's the initial step of our game plan.

The question, "What do you mean by that?" (or some variation) is a great one to get you going. It clarifies the person's meaning so you don't misunderstand or misrepresent it. It also immediately puts you in the driver's seat of the conversation.

This question does something else that's important. It forces the other person to think more carefully about what he does mean when he tosses out a challenge. Instead of settling for statements that are ambiguous or vague, ask him to clearly spell out his objection or concern. Your request may stall him out for a moment, but that's okay. Be patient with the pause in the conversation and let him think a bit.

We looked at four specific challenges to see how this approach works. I then explained in some detail my rationale for the questions I asked of the challenger so you could see how the Columbo tactic allows you to maneuver safely in conversation.

Finally, I encouraged you to ease into your tactical game plan by being a student of others' views for the next few weeks, using some form of the question, "What do you mean by that?"

That question is your first step in managing conversations. Use it often. In the next chapter, we will add another step to our game plan—the second use of the Columbo tactic.

Chapter 5

COLUMBO STEP 2
Reversing the Burden of Proof

S ome people think Christians are the only ones who need to answer for their views. Of course, we should be able to give reasons for what we think is true. But we're not the only ones. Others need to give an accounting too.

It's not unusual, though, for people to forget they have this responsibility. At times, they seem to think that all they have to do is tell a really good story and they've done their job.

You might call this maneuver "bedtime story."[1] A critic conjures up a tale meant to put your view or your argument to rest. It's a way of explaining away your point of view with an opinion but with no substantiating evidence. Bedtime storytellers often start with the phrase, "Oh, I can explain that," and then spin their yarn.

But this will not do. They might as well have started with, "Once upon a time." There is a difference between an opinion and an argument. An opinion is just a point of view. An argument, by contrast, is a point of view supported by reasons (more on this in a moment). Skeptics often give the first but not the second. When you understand this distinction, your job as an ambassador will be much easier.

If you've watched any reruns of *I Love Lucy* (or if you're old enough, like me, to remember the first runs), you might recall Ricky Ricardo saying, "Lucy, you've got a lot of 'splainin' to do." Ricky's statement applies here too. People on the other side of your opinion have a lot of 'splainin' to do themselves, and it's your job to get them to do it.

Many challenges to Christianity thrive on vague generalities and forceful but vacuous slogans. How do we help others be more explicit about the reasons for their views? How do we keep them intellectually honest? The second step of Columbo is the answer. It's the second part of our game plan. I call it reversing the burden of proof.

The burden of proof is the responsibility someone in the conversation has to give evidence for a view. Who has that responsibility? The person who makes the claim bears that burden. If you say something is so, especially if it's controversial, then you have a responsibility to tell why you think it's so.

> The natural impulse for more aggressive Christians is to take up a challenge and attempt to prove the other person wrong. Don't do it. If you try, you're just giving him a free ride.

It's not your job to refute every story a skeptic can spin or every claim he can manufacture. If he makes the claim, then it's his responsibility to give reasons why anyone should take his claim seriously. Don't allow yourself to be thrust into a defensive position if you're not advancing a view. Place the burden of proof where it belongs—on the one who is making the claim. No more free rides. That's your rule from now on.

Let me give you an example of what I mean.

COSMIC CONFUSION

Once I was a guest on a top-rated secular radio station in Los Angeles. The topic was intelligent design versus evolution. When a caller invoked the big bang to argue against a creator, I pointed out that the big bang actually works in my favor. Then I used my "a big bang needs a big Banger" line. This always gets a laugh, but it's also a clever way to make a commonsense point: all effects need causes adequate to explain them.

The caller disagreed. The big bang doesn't need God, he asserted. "You could start with a base of nothing," he began, "and you could say that there was nothing but an infinite, continuous moment, until one tiny, little, insignificant thing happened: a point happened in the nothingness."

Now, I know what you're thinking. How do you start with nothing and then end up with something? How do you get a point in the nothingness? Hardly a "tiny, little, insignificant thing." If your bank account has no balance, there's no sense checking the statement every month to see if you've earned interest.[2] The thought apparently did not occur to the caller, however. Facts, as C. S. Lewis once noted, can be inconvenient things.

"This requires no intelligence," he continued, "so no intelligent God had to intervene. All we need is a tiny imperfection in the perfect nothingness that expanded and became increasingly complex, and soon you have galaxies and planets."

"You're right about one thing," I responded. "When you start with, 'You could say that . . . ,' you can spin any yarn you want. But then comes the hard part: giving reasons why anyone should take your science fiction story seriously. It's not my job to disprove your something-from-nothing fairy tale. It's your job to prove it. You haven't done that. You haven't even tried."

I refused to let him tell a ridiculous tale and then toss the burden of proof back into my lap. I did not give him a free ride.

You might have heard the phrase "throw down the gauntlet" and wondered what it means. A gauntlet was an armored glove worn by medieval knights. When a knight threw his gauntlet into the arena, it was a challenge to another knight to take up the gauntlet and square off for a fight.

The caller on this radio show had thrown down his gauntlet and then expected to walk off with the prize without a struggle. This happens all the time. But I wasn't going to let him off that easily, and neither should you. For too long, we have let others contrive fanciful challenges and then sit back and watch us squirm.[3] Those days are over. Again, no more free rides. If they tell the story, let them defend it. They need to offer an argument, not merely tell a tale.

These stories often have great rhetorical power. They have the ability to psychologically unsettle you and undermine your confidence in your point of view. But every story has to be put to the test. Critics need to have more than a good imagination. They need reasons. That's the way arguments work.

A HOUSE WITHOUT WALLS

An argument is a specific kind of thing. Think of an argument like a simple house, a roof supported by walls. The roof is the conclusion, and the walls are the supporting ideas. By testing the walls, we can see whether they are strong enough to keep the roof from tumbling down. If the walls are solid, the conclusion (the roof) rests securely on its supporting structure. If the walls collapse, the roof goes flat and the argument is defeated.

Some arguments are not really arguments at all. Many people try to build their roof right on the ground. Instead of erecting solid walls (the supporting ideas that hold the conclusion up), they simply make assertions and then pound the podium, or verbally pound you.

An argument is different from an assertion, though, as I mentioned earlier. An assertion simply states a point. An argument adds supporting reasons why anyone should take the point seriously. The reasons, then, become the topic of mutual discussion or analysis. But if there are no reasons, there's little to discuss. Opinions by themselves are not proof. Intelligent belief requires justification.

Roofs are useless when they are on the ground. No one can live in a house without walls. In the same way, an assertion without evidence is not very useful.

> Don't let someone flatten you by dropping a roof on your head. Make him build walls underneath his roof. Ask him for reasons or facts to support his conclusions.

I frequently get calls on my radio show/podcast from people who think they are giving me an argument, when all they are doing is forcefully stating a view. This move may sound compelling at first, and their story may even seem plausible. But there is a difference between giving an explanation and giving evidence why the explanation is a good one. Your job is to recognize when the roof is lying flat on the ground and simply point it out. But how?

THE SECOND COLUMBO QUESTION

How do you reverse the burden of proof when the other person is making the claim? You do it Columbo style—with a question. Here it is: "How did you come to that conclusion?"[4] This question effectively shifts the burden of proof onto the challenger, where it belongs.

This is a gentler variation of "Where did you get your facts?" Though it's similar in content, it has a kinder, more genial tone, since it charitably assumes the critic has not just told a story or made an unsubstantiated claim but has done some thinking.

Remember, this is a model question. You can also ask, "Why do you say that?" "What are your reasons for holding that view?" "What makes you think it happened that way?" or, "I'm curious—why does that idea seem compelling to you?"[5] Questions like these give a person a chance to express his rationale, if he has any. They will also give you more material and time to work with in addressing his concerns.

> The first Columbo question helps you know what a person thinks. The second question helps you know why he thinks the way he does. It charitably assumes he has actually come to a conclusion, that he has reasons for his view and not merely strong feelings about it.

By the way, don't be surprised if you get dead air again when you ask someone for reasons. Most critics are eager to attack your faith but are not prepared to defend their own. They have never thought much about their views, so they can't offer you intelligible reasons for believing them, as surprising as that sounds. So be prepared for blank stares just like with your first Columbo question.

Caught off guard, some will admit they don't have any reasons for their view, which is a remarkable confession. This frank admission always prompts another question from me: "Why would you believe something you have no reason to think is true?"[6] Notice that this is just a variation of our second Columbo question. See how simple that is?

The question, "How did you come to that conclusion?" accomplishes something vital. It forces the people you're in conversation with to give an account of their beliefs. Christians should not be the only ones who have to defend their views.

Reject the impulse to counter every assertion someone manufactures or to refute every tale spun out of thin air. Instead steer the conversation to put the burden of proof back on the other person. Make him give his reasons, not just his point of view. It's not your job to defeat his claim. It's his job to defend it.

This step of the Columbo tactic trades on a very important notion: an alternate explanation is not a refutation. Here's what I mean. It's not uncommon for someone to trot out their I-can-explain-that opener, then conjure up a story that supports her view. You can see right away, though, that giving an explanation is not the same as giving an argument or refuting someone else's argument. She has to do more. She has to give some kind of accounting of why she thinks her story is sound.

Oxford biologist Richard Dawkins wrote a landmark work titled *The Blind Watchmaker*. Notice the way he explains how flight might have evolved: "How did wings get their start? Many animals leap from bough to bough, and sometimes fall to the ground. Especially in a small animal, the whole body surface catches the air and assists the leap, or breaks the fall, by acting as a crude aerofoil. Any tendency to increase the ratio of surface area to weight would help, for example, flaps of skin growing out in the angles of joints. From here, there is a continuous series of gradations to gliding wings, and hence to flapping wings."[7]

Of course, explanations like this abound in textbooks on evolution and may sound like good ones to a Darwinist. These kinds of fanciful tales are meant to parry objections, and this particular one has a good track record. This is partly because it sounds plausible enough at first (if it didn't, it wouldn't be appealing) and partly because it shields the Darwinian paradigm from a certain kind of criticism.

Don't misunderstand me. Starting with a hypothetical explanation is not in itself the difficulty. Science, forensics, and normal day-to-day problem-solving trade on this ability all the time. Imagining what might have taken place may be a legitimate first step. It is not the last one, though, because a story doesn't settle anything. More is required.

In the case of flight, Dawkins's breezy account obscures two obstacles. First is the need for a massive infusion of new genetic information—at just the right time and in just the right balance—to accomplish the prodigious structural changes physically needed for flight. Second is the instinctual, sensory, psychomotor alterations required for the kind of flight that evolution could take advantage of. To overcome these serious hurdles, Dawkins needs to show the detailed and precise evolutionary pathways in specific cases of flight (birds, for example).[8] This he does not do.

Explanations like Dawkins's are common in Darwinian circles. They are known derisively by critics as "just so stories," after Rudyard Kipling's book of that title—a children's book with chapters like "How the Leopard Got His Spots" and "How the Camel Got His Hump." But stories like these pop up outside of Darwinism too. Make sure you are not lulled to sleep by them.

There are three questions you should always ask whenever someone offers an alternate explanation: Is it possible? Is it plausible? Is it probable?

First, is it *possible?* Some options seem unworkable on closer examination. In chapter 4, I questioned the view that the teaching of reincarnation was secretly removed from the Bible sometime during the fourth century. Such editing would require deleting selected lines of text from tens of thousands of handwritten New Testament documents that had been circulating around the Roman Empire for more than three hundred years. This could not happen. It's simply not possible.[9]

The "point in the nothingness" assertion about the causeless big bang I mentioned earlier in this chapter fails for the same reason. As one wit put it, from nothing, nothing comes.

Second, is it *plausible?* Is it reasonable to think something like this might have taken place, given the evidence? Many things are possible that are not plausible. It is possible that I would have liver for dinner tonight. Nothing, in principle, prevents that from happening. It is not plausible, however. The reason is simple—I hate liver. Therefore no one would ever be justified in thinking liver would be on my dinner plate at suppertime.

So whenever you hear, "Well, I can explain that," look closely to see whether there's any evidence that the alternative offered describes what actually took place. It may be theoretically possible, but is it plausible? Does any reliable evidence point to that alternative?

Third, is it *probable?* Is it the best explanation, considering the competing options? The person you're talking with must be able to show why his view is more likely than the one you are offering. For this he needs reasons. Why is his explanation a better one than yours?

Here's the basic critical-thinking principle: when it comes to weighty matters, go with the odds-on favorite, not the long shot, especially when so much is riding on the decision. It may seem plausible to some that monkeys banging on typewriters long enough could eventually pound out the works of Shakespeare, but that doesn't mean we're justified in thinking a baboon wrote *Hamlet.* I'm still convinced Shakespeare did that.

This is why your second Columbo question, "How did you come

to that conclusion?" is so powerful. It helps you handle outlandish speculations and bizarre alternate explanations by placing the burden of proof where it belongs—on the shoulders of the one making the claim.

> Reversing the burden of proof is not a trick to avoid defending our ideas. When we give opinions, we have to answer for them, just like anyone else. We have a responsibility, but so do they. That's my point.

So if you find yourself stymied in a discussion, you may be looking for an argument that isn't there. It may be a bedtime story or an unsubstantiated assertion. Simply ask yourself, *Did he give me an argument, or did he just give me an opinion?* If the latter, then say, "Well, that's an interesting point of view, but what's your argument? How did you come to that conclusion? Why should I take your point seriously? Please take a moment and give me some of your reasons." When he answers you, be alert to the differences between what is possible, what is plausible, and what is probable, given his evidence.

There are only a few exceptions to the burden-of-proof rule, and they are usually obvious. We are not obligated to prove our own existence, to defend self-evident truths (circles are not square), or to justify the basic reliability of our senses. The way things appear to be are probably the way they actually are, unless we have good reason to believe otherwise.[10] This principle keeps us alive every day. It doesn't need defending.

The second step of our game plan is not an evasive ploy on our part. Rather it's a legitimate way to ward off extreme or unfounded confidence in an unreasonable view, or extreme and unfounded doubt of a reasonable option.

An atheist once asked me if it was possible I could be mistaken about my beliefs. "Possible? Of course it's possible," I admitted. "I'm not omniscient. Plus, I've actually been wrong a few times in my life."

I pointed out, though, that this knife cuts both ways. If my admission weakens my case, it weakens his case too, since atheists aren't omniscient either.

I don't think it weakens anybody's case, though, which is why I'd never use this line against an atheist. I'm not threatened by the challenge, and I don't threaten others with it, since it accomplishes nothing for either side.

Just because it's possible to be mistaken about something that seems obvious, that does not mean it's reasonable to think we are. This is the skeptic's error. Do not be taken in by it.

Ask, "How did you come to that conclusion?"—or some variation—often. If there is any ambiguity in any answer, ask more questions. Have them spell things out. The question is a fair one. It's engaging and conversational; it's probing but still amicable. And it keeps you in the driver's seat while the other person does the work he is responsible for.

Remember, you don't have to swing for the fences. You don't even have to get on base, in my opinion. You just need to get into the batter's box, and your first two Columbo questions will get you there. Ask them often, then watch and see what the Holy Spirit does.

WHAT WE LEARNED IN THIS CHAPTER

First, we learned the second step of our game plan—the second use of the Columbo tactic. It's based on the fair expectation that people offer good reasons for the important things they think are true. Instead of giving our critics a free ride by letting them make assertions they expect us to refute, we make them defend their own beliefs—or unbelief, as the case may be.

I call this move reversing the burden of proof. In any dispute, the person who advances an opinion, claim, or point of view has the job of defending it. It's not your duty to prove him wrong. It's his duty to prove himself right. Our second Columbo question, "How did you come to that conclusion?" (or some variation) does the job.

The question is powerful for two good reasons. It ensures you understand the reasons for the other person's view (if there are any), and it gets the other person thinking about the legitimacy of his view.

Second, we learned how a basic argument is structured. Opinions are not proof. A person giving a real argument does more than just state a belief. She supports her belief with evidence and reasons, much like the walls of a house support its roof. Roofs are useless when they're on the ground, and opinions are harmless when they lack justification.

When someone says to you, "The Bible's been changed so many times," or, "You don't need God to have objective morality," or, "There's an infinite number of universes, and ours just happens to be the one that looks designed," don't retreat in silence. Instead just raise your eyebrows and say, "Oh? How did you come to that conclusion?"

It's not enough for someone to contradict your view by simply telling a story. An alternate explanation is not a refutation. The new option must be not only possible, or even plausible, but also more likely (all things considered) than the idea you are offering.

Chapter 6

TWO RELIABLE RESCUES

Your first two Columbo questions are vital to keeping you in the driver's seat while your tactical game plan unfolds. They can also be handy, though, to get you out of tight spots you may get maneuvered into.

You might find yourself in two specific circumstances in which you are awkwardly on the defensive, with the other person in the driver's seat taking you places you did not intend to go and were not prepared to handle. I call these situations the Professor's Ploy and Getting Out of the Hot Seat.

When you find yourself with your back against the wall, how do you turn the tables, regain your balance, and steer the conversation in a more profitable direction? In both cases, Lt. Columbo comes to your rescue.

THE PROFESSOR'S PLOY

I mentioned earlier that the Columbo tactic is a good one to use in the workplace. It's also a good one to use in the classroom, but there is a potential pitfall.

Some professors are on a crusade to crush the confidence of any Christian who wanders into their lecture hall, and they're not afraid to admit it. One student told me that on the first day of class, his professor asked all the Christians to raise their hands. With a sniff, he said, "You won't be Christians when I get through with you."

Professors like this one are fond of using their bully pulpit to bully Christians, taking potshots at them every chance they get. "The Bible is just a bunch of fables and fairy tales," they might say, even if the class has nothing to do with religious issues. Some well-meaning believers won't take this lying down. They'll raise their hands, take up the challenge, and attempt a head-to-head duel with the professor.

Don't make this mistake. It's right-hearted but wrongheaded. The approach rarely works, because it violates a fundamental rule of engagement: never make a frontal assault on a superior force in an entrenched position. An unwritten law of nature seems to govern exchanges like these: the man with the microphone wins. The professor always has the strategic advantage, and he knows it. It's foolish to get into a power struggle when you're outgunned.

There's a better way. Don't disengage. Instead use your tactics. Raise your hand and ask a question. For starters, you might ask, "Professor, can you give us a little more detail on what you mean? What kind of fable are you talking about? Do you think nothing in the biblical documents has any historical value? Is everything in the book a fanciful invention of some sort? What's your opinion?" Notice that these are all creative variations of our first Columbo question, "What do you mean by that?"

Let the professor explain himself. As a good student, listen carefully to his response. Take notes. Ask further clarification questions if necessary. If he falters in any way, the other students will notice. If he has trouble making his ideas clear, it will become obvious he's not thought carefully about his challenge.

When you're satisfied you have a clear take on his view, raise your hand again and ask him how he came to his conclusions. Ask him to explain the line of evidence that convinced him not to take seriously anything in those ancient records. Make the teacher—the one making the claim—shoulder the burden of proof for his assertions. This allows you to stay engaged while deftly sidestepping the power struggle.

Your interaction may go smoothly. Then again, the professor might suspect you're a Christian carefully sandbagging to gain an advantage by maneuvering with questions to make a point (which would be true). If he does, he might try to turn the tables by calling you out, using a distractive ploy to derail your efforts. This is the pitfall I warned about.

"You must be one of those fundamentalist Christians," he might say, "who thinks the Bible is the inspired Word of God, every jot and tittle." Looking at his watch, he continues. "Okay, I'm a fair man. We have a little extra time. Why don't you stand up and explain to the rest of the class why you think the Bible is not a bunch of fables but rather the infallible Word of God? Go ahead."

Think for a moment about what the professor has just done. In one quick move he has cleverly shifted the burden of proof onto you, the student. This is illicit—as you now know—since you have not made any claim. He is the one advancing a view. It's up to him to defend it. He's the teacher, after all.

Do not take the bait. Falling into this trap is nearly always fatal. The professor is trying to get you to do his job. Don't let it happen.

Instead when you find yourself facing any form of the you-prove-me-wrong challenge, politely shift the burden back where it belongs—on the person who made the claim.

"Well, professor," you might say, "you don't know my view, since I haven't offered it. For all you know, I'm on your side. More to the point, my view is irrelevant. It doesn't really matter what I believe. Your ideas are on the table here, not mine. I'm just a student trying to learn. You're the instructor. All I'm doing is asking for clarification of your ideas and wondering whether you have good reasons for them."

If he gives an answer, thank him for explaining himself and either ask another question or let it go for the time being. You've done the best you can under the circumstances.

The Professor's Ploy is the attempt any person makes to shift the burden of proof for his claim onto someone else. The professor (in this case) demands that students defend views they have not expressed, sidestepping his own responsibility to give an account of his beliefs.

Do not be afraid to question your professors. Challenge them on your terms, though, not theirs. And do it with grace, respect, and tact. You don't have to be the expert on every subject. You don't have to have all the answers. You can still be effective even when you know very little, if you ask the right questions.

Whenever anyone—professor or otherwise—makes a controversial claim and then says, "You prove me wrong," don't play their game. Do not let them make you do the work they should be doing. If you keep the burden of proof on the person making the claim, it takes the pressure off you but still allows you to direct the conversation.

Note this important principle: you are in control of your side of the conversation. You don't have to allow yourself to be dragged into a compromising position you do not want to be in. Don't be nasty or defensive, but don't allow yourself to be bullied. When you stay in question mode, you're in the safety zone.

GETTING OUT OF THE HOT SEAT

There is a second tough situation that your first two Columbo questions can help you manage. Sometimes you'll be in persuasion mode in a conversation, only to discover you're facing an aggressive challenger you are not equipped to handle.

Maybe the other person knows more about the issue than you do. Maybe you're not quick enough on your feet to keep up with a fast talker in an intense discussion. In any case, you're out of your depth and you know it. You're in the hot seat, and it's not a pleasant place to be. I want to teach you a move that will get you out.[1]

Before I do, though, I want to ask you a question. When you find yourself overwhelmed by the flow of information coming at you or outmaneuvered by a clever challenger, who is in the driver's seat of the conversation at that moment? Not you, that's for sure, which is why you feel so uncomfortable.

In this situation, the tactical approach really shines. Columbo questions can help you manage the conversation even when you're outmatched and in over your head. They enable you to maneuver out of an awkward circumstance someone else has steered you into and buy yourself some thinking time.

When you're in the hot seat, forget about trying to answer the challenges offered or respond to the points made. You already know you're not up to that task. Instead use the other person's energy to your advantage by practicing a little of what I call conversational aikido.

Aikido is a clever approach to self-defense that uses an opponent's forward inertia in your favor. In this situation, that means letting them talk but directing their efforts in a way that nullifies the attack and benefits you.

Here's how it works. When you feel overmatched and overwhelmed in a conversation, immediately shift from persuasion mode to fact-finding mode. Don't continue to argue your case. Instead, using your first two Columbo questions, become a student of the other person's view by asking for clarification and for reasons. Say something like this:

> Boy, it sounds like you know a lot more about this than I do, and you've raised some interesting points. My problem is that this is all new information for me. I wonder if you could do me a favor. I really want to understand your points, but you need to slow down a bit so I get them right. Would you take a moment to carefully explain your view and also your reasons for it to help me understand better?

When you respond this way,[2] it buys you valuable time. It also shows that you're not afraid of the other person and you're interested in taking his view seriously. So make sure you understand the ideas. Write them down if you need to. When all your questions have been answered, end the conversation by saying these magic words: "Thanks. Now let me think about it. Maybe we can talk more later."

These words—now let me think about it—are like magic because once you say them, you free yourself from any obligation to respond further at the moment. All the pressure is gone, since you've already pleaded ignorance. You have no obligation to answer, refute, or reply once you've admitted you're outgunned and need to give the issue more thought.

Now who is in the driver's seat? You are, of course. You're relaxed and listening, a student, not a challenger. You have deftly but graciously turned the tables. You have sidestepped a challenge you cannot answer and defused the confrontation. The pressure is off, but you're still engaged.

Think for a moment how useful this approach can be. Instead of trying to resist the force of another's attack, you step aside and let her have the floor. You invite her to make her case slowly and clearly so you'll have an opportunity to fully understand her point.

What do you do next? You do what you said you were going to do: you *think* about it. Do your homework—on your own, at your leisure, when the pressure is off. Research the issue, maybe even enlisting others in the process, and come back better prepared next time.

You might even want to start a notebook. Open a computer file and record the question and its details from your notes. Then begin to craft a response based on your research. Review what you've written. Rehearse your response out loud a few times or role-play it with a friend. If your discussion was part of a chance meeting, you may not be able to revisit the topic with the same person. But when the issue comes up with someone else, you'll be ready. You'll own that question.

When you face a new challenge, start another entry and go through the same steps. You'll be surprised how soon your expanding notebook will cover the basic issues. There aren't that many.

The key here is to get out of the hot seat but still stay engaged. Your maneuver deftly shifts control of the conversation back to you while shifting the spotlight and the pressure back on him. It's not retreat; it's just a different type of engagement. It greatly reduces your anxiety level, strengthens your confidence, and gives you an education so that you can be more effective next time around.

If you take this approach, no egos are at stake, so there are no losers. You're simply asking the more aggressive person to give you his best shot. Essentially, you're inviting him to do what he wanted to do in the first place—beat you up. You're just giving him the opportunity to do a complete job.

So let me ask you a question. Is there any Christian you know—even the most retiring, shy, bashful, timid, or reserved—who is unable to do this? Is there anyone who cannot say, "You want to beat me up? Okay. Just do it slowly and thoroughly, please." Anyone can do this. It's easy. This little technique enables even the most skittish Christian to tame a tyrant.

NARRATING THE DEBATE

I'll finish this chapter by offering a tip. It's a simple way to bring clarity to a discussion or pull the curtain back on someone who is illicitly dodging your point or distorting the argument in some way.

Many people you talk to will struggle when you turn the tables by asking them to give evidence for their claims or by using questions to expose their bad thinking. When a person has not thought much about his assertions, avoiding your questions may be his only recourse. He may try to change the subject or reassert his point in other ways.

When this happens, it may be helpful for you to narrate the debate. Take a moment to step outside of the conversation, in a sense, and describe to your friend the turn the discussion has just taken. This will help him (and others listening) to see how he's gotten off course. You can say something like this:

> I want you to notice the turn our talk just took. First, you made a fairly controversial statement, and I asked you a couple of questions about it. So far, you haven't answered them. Instead you've

taken off in another direction. Before we move on to a new topic, would it be okay with you if we finish the old one? I really am interested in your response.

Sometimes, though, there's a different problem. The person you're talking with may not be interested in truth at all. Instead he's maneuvering for a score in an intellectual jousting match, especially if others are listening. He's substituting slick rhetoric and subtle distractions or distortions for intelligent points. If you're alert, you might catch him at his verbal sleight of hand and gracefully call him on it.

Here's an example of calmly narrating a common ad hominem attempt[3] in a discussion about religious pluralism.

Did you notice what just happened? I raised a question about the legitimacy of your idea that all religions lead to God, and you responded by calling me a name—a bigot, to be precise. You changed the subject. We were talking about an issue, and then you attacked my character. Why did you do that?

During a radio conversation with a popular internet atheist, the atheist consistently tried to represent my views in the most unattractive way possible, distorting them so they'd be more vulnerable to his attacks. This, of course, is an example of a straw man fallacy, and I called him on it by narrating his maneuver. "I want others to notice what you just did. You asked me a question, and I gave you my answer. You then gave a distorted summary of my view for the listeners. I pointed out it was a misrepresentation. Then you said, 'Well, that's the way I interpret your view.' So even though you know you got my view wrong, you're still going to cling to your own interpretation. Okay. I just want everyone to be clear on what you're doing."

When you're dealing with an evasive or intellectually dishonest person, don't let him get off the hook by dodging the issues or distorting the argument. Narrating the debate keeps the other person honest while keeping the conversation cordial. Encourage him to clarify himself. Call him on any false moves he's made. Forcing him to face the music may be the first step toward a change of mind, either his or that of others listening.

> When a cherished view is at stake, it's not unusual for people to raise empty protests—objections that sound worthwhile but simply can't be defended once examined. Narrating the debate often exposes a lack of substance behind the bluster.

WHAT WE LEARNED IN THIS CHAPTER

First, we learned how to deal with the Professor's Ploy, a common move used by others to sidestep the burden-of-proof responsibility for their claims. Two important principles guide us here. One, do not allow yourself to get caught in a power play when you're over-matched. Instead use your tactics. Two, refuse to shoulder the burden of proof when you have not made the claim. Shift that responsibility back where it belongs—on the other person. Don't let a bully put you on the defensive. You're in charge of your side of the conversation.

Next, we learned how to use Columbo to get ourselves out of the hot seat. When you find you're overmatched by a fast talker in an intense discussion, practice a little verbal aikido by shifting from argument mode to fact-finding mode. Immediately become a student of the other person's ideas. Ask probing clarification questions instead of trying to win your case. Then use the magic phrase, "Let me think about it." Once you understand the other person's point of view, work on the issues later, on your own, at your leisure, when the pressure is off.

Finally, I introduced a concept to you that I call narrating the debate. It's a way of summarizing in clear terms the illicit moves the other person in the conversation has made, such as avoiding an issue or offering cleverly-worded deceptive or distorted reasoning.

Chapter 7

COLUMBO STEP 3

Using Questions to Make a Point

U p until now, we have talked about using the Columbo tactic in a very particular way. We have used friendly questions to gather two types of information: a person's view and her reasons for it. One of the advantages of this approach, I noted, is that it's largely a passive enterprise. We put nothing on the line, so there is no pressure. There's nothing for us to defend, so there is no risk.

The third use of Columbo takes us more on the offensive, yet in an inoffensive way. We still use questions to keep our risk levels low and our comfort levels high. Here, though—since our queries have a different purpose—we ask a different kind of question, sometimes called a leading question.

As the name suggests, leading questions lead the other person in the direction we want them to go. In the third step of our game plan, you are going to use questions to make a point. Think of yourself like an archer shooting at a target. Your questions are your arrows. The point you want to make is the target you want to hit. The target is key. If you're going to use questions to make a point, then you must be clear in your mind on what point you want to make.

Your target will be different in different situations. You may want to use questions to indirectly explain or advance your ideas. Your questions will be aimed at that target. Sometimes you will set up the terms of the conversation by using questions to put you in a more beneficial position for your next move. Other times your goal will be to undermine what you think is a bad argument or a flawed point of view. There's also a clever way to enlist your opponent as an ally to help you build the case against his view, always using questions.

In each of these situations, every time you ask a question and get a favorable response, your question accomplishes two things that a mere statement cannot. First, the person is telling you he understands the point. Second, he's telling you he agrees with it, at least provisionally, and is taking a step forward with you in the thinking process.

Ultimately, we want to win people over to our point of view, but we don't want the conversation to feel like we're forcing our opinions on them. Instead we want to persuade them. When the steps to a conclusion are unambiguous, straightforward, and reasonable, it's much easier for someone to follow along with us on the journey, because he can see the route clearly. He can even retrace it on his own if he wants to. With each question, we lead him closer toward our destination.

> When you get approval for each successive link in the process of reasoning, you move the conversation in the direction you have in mind. In that way, you carefully guide the other person to your conclusion. Remember, you're in the driver's seat.

There are different ways this third use of Columbo works out in application. Generally, your leading questions will be used to inform, persuade, refute, or set up the terms of the discussion. Let me show you some specific examples of how this approach plays out in actual conversations.

TELL THEM SOMETHING THEY ALREADY KNOW

Sometimes the questions that are most powerful and persuasive are the ones that alert people to what they already know.

This was true of Shannon, an American college student living in Germany whom I met on a train from Normandy to Paris. Shannon had been raised in a Christian home, had been educated at a Christian college, and had what she described as a strong relationship with the Lord. Still, she was perplexed by the idea that others were lost apart from trust in Christ.

"What about someone who believes in God?" she asked. "What about the person who is sincerely following his own religion and trying to be the best person he can be?"

I hear these kinds of questions from non-Christians all the time. But I also hear them with surprising frequency from people who consider themselves believers. I suspected Shannon already knew enough to answer her own question. She simply had not put the pieces together.

"Why should anyone become a Christian in the first place?" I asked. "You and I are Christians. What benefit does putting our trust in Jesus give us?"

"Jesus saves us," she answered.

"From what?"

"He saves us from our sins."

"Right. You might say we have a spiritual disease called sin, and Jesus did something on the cross that heals the disease."

She nodded.

"Can simply believing in God heal that disease?"

After thinking a moment, she said, "No."

"Can trying our best to be a good person heal it, or being really religious, or even being sincere? Can any of those things forgive our sin?"

She shook her head. No, none of those things in themselves could take away our guilt.

"We'd still be dying from our spiritual disease, wouldn't we?" I said. She agreed.

Then I just connected the dots for her. "If religion or sincerity or doing our best cannot save you and me, then how can any of those things save someone else? Either Jesus rescues us by taking the punishment for our sin on himself, or we are not rescued and have to pay for our own crimes. It's no more complicated than that."

I want you to notice three important things about this conversation.

First, I gave Shannon no new information. I simply reminded her of things she already knew but had not related to her concern. Second, I did it almost entirely with questions. There is a third detail, though, a hitch that may not have occurred to you.

Remember from chapter 1 that the first responsibility of an ambassador is knowledge—an accurately informed mind. Knowing that people need to trust in Jesus for salvation or face judgment is not enough. If that's all we communicate to them—if we don't give an accurate sense of why Jesus matters—then God seems petty, pitching people into hell simply because of what seems to outsiders to be an incoherent detail of Christian theology.

And that's the hitch: you have to know *why* Jesus is the only way before it is helpful to say *that* he is the only way. Without that knowledge, the third step of Columbo will not help you on this issue.

TURNING THE TABLES

Columbo can also help you get out of a different kind of tough situation. Sometimes you may need to use questions to set up the conversation in a way that is most favorable to you.

I had a friend who was a deeply committed Christian woman whose boss was a lesbian. That in itself isn't the problem. My friend had the maturity to know you can't expect non-Christians to live like Christians. Her difficulty was that her boss wanted to know what she thought about homosexuality. That was awkward.

> If you are placed in a situation in which you suspect your convictions will be labeled intolerant, bigoted, narrow-minded, or judgmental, use Columbo to turn the tables.

When someone asks for your personal views about a controversial issue, preface your remarks with a question that sets the stage—in your favor—for your response. Here's how I suggested my friend answer the disconcerting request made by her employer.

> You know, this is actually a very personal question you're asking. I don't mind answering, but before I do, I want to know if it's safe to offer my views. So let me ask you a question first: do you consider yourself a tolerant person or an intolerant person on issues like this? Is it safe to give my opinion, or are you going to judge me for my point of view? Do you respect diverse points of view, or do you condemn others for having convictions that differ from your own?

You see what I'm doing, of course. I am leveraging the other person's values in my favor. Regardless of how inconsistent the politically correct crowd often is, they will still strongly affirm their "tolerant" values when asked. If you first set the stage for your conversation in this way, then when you give your point of view, it's going to be difficult for anyone to call you intolerant or judgmental without looking guilty too.

This line of questioning trades on an important insight: there is no neutral ground when it comes to the tolerance question. Everybody has a point of view they think is right, and everybody passes judgment at some point or another. The Christian gets pigeonholed as the judgmental one, but everyone else is judging too, even people who consider themselves tolerant and open-minded.

I call this the passive-aggressive tolerance trick.[1] The key to disarming this trick is knowing that everyone thinks his beliefs are true.

Let me say this again, since it is so easily missed: every person in every discussion is convinced that his own opinions are correct. He may not know they are correct, but he certainly believes they are. That's why he believes what he believes. If people didn't think their beliefs were true, they wouldn't believe them. They'd believe something else and think that was true instead.

Here's how to use Columbo to trade on that insight. When you are labeled intolerant by someone, simply ask, "What do you mean by that?" This, of course, is our first Columbo question.

Though I already have a pretty good idea of what the person means when he says I'm intolerant, when I ask the question, "What do you mean by that?" it flushes out his definition and sets the stage—in my favor—for the next two questions. Here's how it looks.

"You're intolerant."

"Can you tell me what you mean by that? Why would you think I'm an intolerant person?"

"Because it's clear you think you're right and everyone who disagrees with you is wrong. That's intolerant."

"Well, you're right, I do think my views are correct. Of course, it's always possible I'm mistaken, and we could talk about that if you like. But what about you? You seem to be disagreeing with me. Do you think your views are right?"[2]

"Yes, of course I think I'm right. But I'm not intolerant like you."

"That's the part that confuses me. Why is it when I think I'm right, I'm intolerant, but when you think you're right, you're just right? What am I missing here?"

Of course, *I'm* not missing anything in this exchange; he is. His move is simple name calling.[3] When someone labels you as intolerant, it's no different than calling you ugly. The first is an attack on your character. The second is an attack on your looks. Neither is useful in evaluating the merits of the idea you both were discussing. Each of you thinks he's right. Only one person, though, is being publicly faulted for it—you.[4] That's the tolerance trick.

> The quickest way to deal with a personal attack is to simply point it out with a question. When someone goes after you rather than your argument, ask, "I'm a little confused at your response. Why did you change the subject? Even if you're right about my character, could you explain to me what that has to do with this issue?"

EXPLOITING A WEAKNESS OR A FLAW

You might have noticed something unique about how I dealt with the tolerance trick. My questions went beyond positioning myself in a more favorable way in our conversation. This time I also used Columbo questions to challenge the other person's ideas.

Once you have gained a clear understanding of what a person thinks and why he thinks it (using Columbo 1 and 2), you can use Columbo questions to subtly expose a weakness or a flaw you might see in his view or to gently uproot difficulties or problems you detect. It's the approach I was using with the witch in Wisconsin (chap. 1) when I asked her if it was okay to kill the toddler who had been conceived by incest.

I stumbled upon a wonderful example of this while reading *Icons of Evolution*, the fine critique of Darwinism by Jonathan Wells. The following dialogue is an example of one student's gentle use of the third step of the Columbo tactic.

Teacher: Okay, let's start today's lesson with a quick review. Yesterday I talked about homology [how different organisms show remarkable similarity in the structure of some of their body parts].

Homologous features, such as the vertebrate limbs shown in your textbook, provide us with some of our best evidence that living things have evolved from common ancestors.

Student (raising hand): I know you went over this yesterday, but I'm still confused. How do we know whether features are homologous?

Teacher: Well, if you look at vertebrate limbs, you can see that even though they're adapted to perform different functions, their bone patterns are structurally similar.

Student: But you told us yesterday that even though an octopus eye is structurally similar to a human eye, the two are not homologous.

Teacher: That's correct. Octopus and human eyes are not homologous because their common ancestor did not have such an eye.

Student: So regardless of similarity, features are not homologous unless they are inherited from a common ancestor?

Teacher: Yes, now you're catching on.

Student (looking puzzled): Well, actually, I'm still confused. You say homologous features provide some of our best evidence for common ancestry. But before we can tell whether features are homologous, we have to know whether they came from a common ancestor.

Teacher: That's right.

Student (scratching head): I must be missing something. It sounds as though you're saying that we know features are derived from a common ancestor because they're derived from a common ancestor. Isn't that circular reasoning?[5]

Here's another example of how to use Columbo to expose a weakness or a flaw. Let's revisit the conversation with our professor from chapter 6. There we learned to avoid being taken in by what I call the Professor's Ploy by making the professor bear the burden of proof for his claims instead of letting him push that burden back on us.

I suggested pressing the professor for reasons justifying his view—in this case, that the Bible is just a bunch of myths and fables. Suppose he answered, "I know the Bible is a myth because it has miracles in it" (a common line of thinking for materialists[6]). This bit of valuable information sets up the next series of questions.

Student: And why does that mean the Bible is myth or fable?

Professor: Because miracles don't happen.[7]

Student: How do you know miracles don't happen?

Professor: Because science has shown that miracles don't happen.

Now, I happen to know that science has shown nothing of the sort, nor can it. Since science only measures natural causes and effects, it's not capable of ruling out supernatural causes, even in principle.[8] Armed with this information, I can now ask the decisive question: "Professor, would you please explain to us exactly how the methods of science have disproved the possibility of supernatural events?"

The professor has no place to go at this point because no such scientific proof exists. Disproving the nonnatural is outside the province of science. Science has never advanced any empirical evidence to show that supernatural events cannot happen. Instead, according to the dictates of naturalistic philosophy, science (and the professor) has assumed a priori—prior to looking at the evidence—that miracles are impossible.[9] Thus any alleged historical reference to supernatural signs must be either a myth or a fable. Your simple question and the long silence that follows it do all the work necessary to make your point: the professor is assuming something he ought to be giving evidence for instead.

> One of the advantages of the Columbo tactic is not having to assert something you want someone else to believe. You aren't taking the burden of proof on yourself. Instead you accomplish your goal in an entirely different and more powerful way. You use questions to make the point for you.

PUTTING THE PIECES ON THE TABLE

I addressed the controversial issue of why Jesus is the only way when the question came up during a book promotion at a local Barnes and Noble bookstore. I met a man that evening who didn't understand why he, a Jewish person, needed Jesus. He believed in God and he was doing his best to live a moral life. It seemed to him that those were the important things—how he lived, not what he believed. Here is how I used Columbo questions to lead him to a proper understanding of the cross.

"Let me ask you a question," I began. "Do you think people who commit moral crimes ought to be punished?"

"Well, since I'm a prosecuting attorney," he chuckled, "I guess I do."

I got a little lucky here, since I had no idea what his profession was. Even so, most folks have a basic intuition that people ought to pay for the bad they do and not get off scot-free. With my first question, then, I was relying on his moral common sense.

"Good. So do I," I said, agreeing with him. "Now, a second question: have *you* ever committed any moral crimes?" This question was more personal, but since our conversation was friendly, he wasn't put off.

After pausing a moment, he nodded. "Yes, I guess I have."

"So have I," I offered candidly, agreeing with him again. "But that puts us both in a tight spot, doesn't it? We both believe people who do bad things should be punished, and we both believe we've done bad things." I waited a moment for the significance to sink in. "Do you know what I call that?" I asked. "I call that bad news."

In less than sixty seconds, I had accomplished something remarkable with my two questions. I was able to get the attorney to put important pieces of my line of thinking on the table for me.

I didn't have to convince this man he was a sinner. He was telling me. I didn't have to convince him he deserved to be punished. He was telling me. Of course, he wasn't thinking of sin and judgment when he walked into the Barnes and Noble. My questions, though, brought these commonsense intuitions to the surface so I could use them to make my point.

Now that we agreed on the problem, it was time to give the solution.[10] Here is where the knowledge part of the ambassador equation is so vital.

"This is where Jesus comes in," I continued. "We both know we're guilty. That's the problem. So God offers a solution: a pardon, free of charge. But clemency is on his terms, not ours. Jesus is God's means of pardon. Here's why. He personally paid the penalty in our place. He took the rap for our crimes. No one else did that. Only Jesus. Now we have a choice to make. Either we take the pardon and go free, or we turn it down and pay for our crimes ourselves, such as they are. Either Jesus pays or we pay. That's the simple equation. The choice is up to us."[11]

In this conversation, I handled an awkward question by combining two things: my knowledge of what Jesus accomplished on the cross and the Columbo tactic. My questions helped me lead the attorney, step by step, to an answer to his question.

There was something more going on, though, a subtle maneuver I used with the attorney, and with virtually every person in the conversations cited in this chapter, that gave me a leg up in the discussion: he was helping me make my case.

I mentioned just a bit ago that Columbo can be used in a clever way to enlist your opponent as an ally to help you build your case against his view. It's a move that's central to using Columbo to make a point.

Think about it. The attorney's question was about the singular role Jesus plays in salvation. Answering his question accurately required talking about sin, guilt, and judgment—not pleasant topics. There are two ways I could have approached that task.

First, I could have started by simply stating the facts—we're all sinners, including him, and we all need forgiveness to save us from judgment, and so on—all the details that must be in place to make Jesus' singular sacrifice intelligible. The liability is, of course, that each step invites objections that could stall us out, bogging us down in disputes about the particulars that would keep us from ever getting to the explanation. Every piece I'd try to put *on* the table, the skeptic could immediately try to take *off* the table.

The second way would be to use Columbo, which is what I did. I asked questions to get the attorney to put the important facts on the table for me. This approach was powerful because I didn't have to persuade him of some foreign concept or controversial idea. I merely connected the pieces I had helped him lay on the table for me, just by using questions. Once he affirmed those important points, it would be very hard for him to dispute them later on.

Of course, to make an ally out of your opponent, you have to know how to answer the challenge you're facing. Then you need to think about what pieces you need to make your point. Finally, you need to formulate questions that invite your challenger to place those pieces on the table for you.

Jesus did this very thing in Luke 7:41–47. He described a theoretical situation and asked Simon, his dinner host, for an assessment. He then used the Pharisee's answer to make his powerful point about forgiveness: he who is forgiven much, loves much.

Let's say you want to make the point that the existence of God is the only adequate explanation for the existence of objective morality in the world.[12] Here's a series of questions I designed to solicit the skeptic's cooperation.

> Do you believe there is real evil in the world? Is the evil you described objective evil or just things that happen that don't fit your fancy?[13] Do you think some kind of standard is necessary for you to distinguish good from evil, right from wrong? That standard, then, can't be inside us (relativism) but must be outside us (objectivism). Is that right? Where do you think that external, objective moral standard comes from?

There's more I could add, but I think you get the point. Notice that with this approach, you're laying a foundation for your point by first trying to establish some common ground between you and your friend. Openings like, "Do we agree that . . . " or, "Would you agree with me that . . . " show your willingness to side with them when you agree, while using the point of agreement to build to your conclusion. It's one of the most powerful ways I know to use Columbo to make a point.

FINDING THE FLAW

As I've pointed out, the last step of Columbo—using questions to expose a weakness or a flaw—is more demanding, because it requires some insight into what has gone wrong with a person's point of view. You have to be able to see some weakness in his argument before you can expose it. But how do you find the flaw?

There is no special formula for making this discovery. You just have to be alert. In the process of conversation, you may notice some weakness, liability, or contradiction that can be exposed and exploited. The key is to pay close attention to the answer to the question, "How did you come to that conclusion?" Then ask yourself if the person's conclusion makes sense in light of the evidence he gives.

Remember, an argument is like a house whose roof is supported by walls. In this step of Columbo, you want to find out whether the walls (the reasons or evidence) are strong enough to hold up the roof (the person's point of view).

Look, observe, reflect. Maybe your friend's comments have tipped you off to some problem with his view. Is there a misstep, a non sequitur,[14] a fallacy, or a failing of some sort? Can you challenge any underlying assumptions that might be faulty? Whatever flaw you discover, be sure to address the problem with a question, not a statement.

STUMPED OR STALLED OUT?

As I mentioned earlier, the third use of Columbo requires information the first two Columbo questions do not require. You need to know the specific direction you want the conversation to go, the precise purpose you want to accomplish with your leading questions. Do you want to use your questions to clarify a point, convey new information, expose a weakness? You have to know which target to aim at before you can continue.

This skill takes time to develop, though, so don't be surprised or discouraged if you find yourself stalled out at first. It's not always easy to flush out the error in someone's thinking or to maneuver in conversation by using questions instead of statements. It takes practice, but in time you'll improve. In part 2 of this book, "Finding the Flaws," I will give you a batch of tactics that will make it easier for you to root out and expose bad thinking.

If you find you don't have the resources to go further in a discussion, or if you sense the person is losing interest, don't feel compelled to force the conversation. Let the encounter die a natural death, and move on. Consider it a fruitful, interactive learning experience nonetheless.

Remember, as an ambassador for Christ, you don't have to hit a home run in every conversation. You don't even have to get on base. As I mentioned earlier, sometimes just getting up to bat will do. Your first two Columbo questions—"What do you mean by that?" and,

"How did you come to that conclusion?"—will help you get in the game. The rest will come with time and with the experience you'll gain from having personal, real-life, face-to-face conversations.

> We may spend hours helping someone carefully work through an issue without ever mentioning God, Jesus, or the Bible. This does not mean we aren't advancing the kingdom. It is always a step in the right direction when we help others to think more carefully. If nothing else, it gives them tools to assess the bigger questions that eventually come up.

INNOCENT AS DOVES

I mentioned at the beginning of the chapter that the third use of Columbo takes us on the offensive. The danger, of course, is that we become offensive when we go on the offensive. These are two different things. Yes, we want to be able to point out weaknesses in a view (go on the offensive). But we don't want to seem pushy, condescending, or smug (be offensive). How do we avoid that pitfall?

Jesus offered this advice: "Be shrewd as serpents and innocent as doves" (Matt. 10:16). I think one of the things he had in mind was that we should be clever in our maneuvering yet remain innocent in our manner. Lt. Columbo was polite to a fault, being careful never to offend his suspects while still disarming them with well-placed questions.

Here's how Jesus' insight might apply to our tactical game plan. Sometimes the best way to disagree with someone is not to face the issue head-on but to soften the challenge by using an indirect approach. You can cushion your third use of Columbo a couple of ways.

For one, think about softening your dissent a bit by using a question to suggest an alternative. Use the phrase, "Have you ever considered . . ." to introduce your concern, then offer a different view that gently questions the person's beliefs or confronts what you think is a weakness in his view. Here are some examples.

- "Have you ever considered that if the Bible was merely written by men, it would be hard to account for fulfilled prophecy? How would you explain that?"
- "Have you ever considered the difficulty involved with adding something like the teaching on Jesus' divinity to every existing handwritten copy of the New Testament circulating in the Roman world by the fourth century? How is this physically possible?"
- "Have you ever considered that the existence of evil is actually evidence for the existence of God, not against it?"[15]
- "Have you ever considered that if abortion is okay, it's going to be hard to condemn infanticide, since the baby's location—inside the womb (abortion) or outside the womb (infanticide)—is the only difference between the two? How can mere location be relevant to the baby's value?"
- "Have you ever considered that if Jesus was wrong about being the only way of salvation, it's difficult to call him a good man, a prophet, or a wise religious teacher? What do you think about that problem?"

Another way to soften your challenge is to phrase your concern as a request for clarification. Begin by asking, "Can you clear this up for me?" or, "Can you help me understand this?" Then offer your objection in a way that gently challenges the belief or confronts the weakness you think you see in the point of view. Consider the gentle approach of the following questions.

- "Can you clear this up for me? If Jesus' divinity was an invention of the church in the early fourth century, how do you explain all the references to a divine Christ in Christian literature written before that time?"

- "Can you help me understand this? If there is no evidence that life came from nonlife—that life spontaneously arose from inanimate matter to kick off the sequence of evolution—and there is much evidence against it, how can we say that Darwinian evolution is fact?"[16]
- "Can you help me with something that confuses me? How does having a 'burning in the bosom' about the Book of Mormon give adequate evidence that this book is from God, when people have similar reasons—a strong internal conviction from God in response to prayer—for rejecting it?"
- "Can you clear this up for me? If homosexuality is truly natural, then why did nature give homosexual men bodies designed for reproductive sex with women and then give them desires for sex with men? Why would nature give desires for one type of sex but a body for another?"

One of the reasons this approach is so attractive is that it shows respect for the person you disagree with. First, you make an effort (with your first two Columbo questions) to understand her viewpoint. Next, you ask, "Do you mind if I ask a couple of questions about what you've told me?" or, "Would you consider an alternative or be willing to look at another angle if there were good reasons for it?" By soliciting permission to disagree, you make the encounter more amicable. You also stay in the driver's seat.

There is one more way to soften your approach that, strictly speaking, may not involve Columbo (because it doesn't always use a question). Even so, it may serve a valuable tactical purpose. You may find yourself in a situation where either you can't think of a question or it would seem awkward or contrived to use a question rather than simply state your view.

In these circumstances, you need a genial way to introduce your point. Here are some recommendations you might want to consider.

- "Let me suggest an alternative, and tell me if you think it's an improvement. If not, you can tell me why you think your option is better."
- "I wouldn't characterize it that way. Here's what I think may be a better or more accurate way to look at it. Tell me what you think."
- "I don't think that's going to work, and I'd like to suggest why so you can consider it. Is that okay with you?"
- "I'm not sure I agree with the way you put it. Think about this . . ."

Here's another way to purchase a little more protection for yourself in your conversations. When you introduce your point with, "It's my understanding that . . ." or, "This is the way it seems to me," and then explain your position and invite a response, you indicate you are provisional in your claims. Yes, you have convictions, but they are open to discussion and, potentially, revision.

Qualifying your comments this way not only is an implicit act of humility but also gives you a margin of safety. It may turn out that you've missed something your friend will uncover in the process of conversation. If you discover that your ideas are compromised in some way, this could be embarrassing if you expressed them in a dogmatic way to begin with. Further, qualifying your comments gives you a little psychological liberty to adjust your views. Ironically, when you are somewhat provisional, your points often sound more persuasive.[17]

WHAT WE LEARNED IN THIS CHAPTER

In this chapter, we learned how to employ Columbo to take us in an entirely new direction. We discovered that in addition to being useful for gathering information or reversing the burden of proof, questions can be effective ways to lead someone in the direction we want them to go. Such leading questions often work better than statements to explain our view, to set up the discussion in a way that makes it easier for us to make our point, to indirectly expose a flaw in another's thinking, or to soften our challenge to a person's view.

Unlike the first two uses of Columbo, this one requires knowledge of some kind. When we know what we want to accomplish (inform, persuade, set up the terms, refute), we can use leading questions to achieve our purpose. Using Columbo can also be a clever way to enlist your opponent as an ally to help you build your case.

If someone's thinking is flawed, the key to finding the error is to listen carefully to the reasons and then ask yourself if the conclusions follow from the evidence. Point out errors by using questions rather than statements. You might soften your challenge by phrasing your concern as a request for clarification or by suggesting an alternative with the words, "Have you considered . . ." or, "Can you clear this up for me . . ." before offering your ideas. This approach creates a genial atmosphere for your conversation, plus it provides you with a margin of safety when sharing your views.

Skill at Columbo is something you will develop over time, so if you stall out at first, don't be discouraged. Instead of trying to force a conversation you don't have the resources to pursue, simply move on, knowing that you have done the best you can for the moment while trusting God to do the work necessary to begin changing the other person on the inside.

Chapter 8

PERFECTING COLUMBO

We have spent quite a bit of time focusing on a single tactic. I have taken this time because Columbo is so important. It is central to every tactic that follows.

If you've been practicing what we've covered, you've already discovered how handy Columbo can be. You're learning how to advance the dialogue for spiritual ends without seeming pushy. You're realizing that asking simple questions is an almost effortless way to have courteous conversations with others even though you might strongly disagree with their ideas.

You may have noticed, however, that it's difficult to be clever on command. Sometimes it's hard to think of new things on the spur of the moment. You may be able to get conversations started, but then you get bogged down.

Perfecting any new skill takes time and practice. If you were just beginning to learn a sport, such as tennis, some of your time would be spent practicing the basics (a forehand, a volley). Then you would get feedback from someone else who could help you refine your strokes.

Similarly, as you begin to implement your tactical game plan using Columbo, you might wonder if there is something you can do to improve your technique, a way to practice before the pressure is on. In this chapter, I would like to coach you in specific ways to improve your Columbo skill.

IMPROVING YOUR FOOTWORK

Initially, you will not be quick on your feet with responses like the ones in the examples I have given in previous chapters. Instead you may find that your best ideas come when your head is clear and you are not under pressure to respond immediately. In any encounter, there are two times when the pressure is off: before the conversation begins and after it's over. Those are perfect times to focus on improving your technique.

Peter reminds us to always be "ready to make a defense to everyone who asks you to give an account for the hope that is in you" (1 Peter 3:15). There are three things you can do to ready yourself to respond. You can *anticipate* beforehand what might come up. You can *reflect* afterward on what took place. And in both cases, you can *practice* the responses you think of during these reflective moments so you'll be prepared for the next opportunity.

First, think about conversations you might have in the future about your convictions and try to anticipate obstacles that may come up. Then think of Columbo questions you can use for those challenges so you have them ready in advance. Work on an issue or question that people frequently ask you about or one that has stumped you in the past. Brainstorm a handful of straightforward response questions that might put you in the driver's seat of those conversations. Imagine what it would look like to have a dialogue using your questions.

> Always try to anticipate comebacks or counterarguments the other side might raise. Take these rejoinders seriously, stating them fairly and clearly, even convincingly. Then refute them in advance. When they do come up, you'll be ready.

In my national radio debate with atheist and *Skeptic* magazine founder Michael Shermer, I knew he was going to ask me, "Who created God?" because Shermer always asks it in debates (I'd done my homework), even though he should know better. I give this straight-forward answer to the question in *The Story of Reality*: "The question presumes that God was created, but no one believes that, certainly not Christians, so this is not a question any theist has to answer. An eternal, self-existent Being has no beginning, so he needs no creator. This doesn't prove such a Being exists, of course. It only shows that those who believe in God do not have to answer inappropriate questions about his origin."[1]

Since I knew Shermer would ask this question, and since I knew how to answer it, I was able to craft a response and practice it beforehand so I was ready for it when it came up. Here's what I said: "Michael, *you* don't believe God was created, because you don't believe in God. *I* don't believe God was created, because I believe God is eternal. *Nobody* in this conversation believes God was created. So why are you asking, 'Who created God?'"

So the first thing you can do to improve your Columbo technique is to plan and practice in advance. This small bit of preparation takes a little effort but can be very effective. When you face the challenge, the response will be right at your fingertips.

Here's a second way to improve. After each encounter, take some time for self-assessment. I've made it a habit to immediately reflect on how I could have been more effective. It has become second nature to me. *How did I do?* I ask myself. *Could I have asked different questions or taken the conversation in another direction? What were my missteps? How could I do better next time?* With the pressure off, alternatives occur to me.

This is where the Ambassador Model from chapter 1 comes in handy. When I ask myself about the three skills of an ambassador—knowledge (an accurately informed mind), wisdom (an artful method), and character (an attractive manner)—I have something specific to focus on. Did I know enough about the issue, or do I need to brush up on something for next time? Could I have maneuvered with more tactical wisdom in the conversation? Was my manner attractive? Did I act with grace, kindness, and patience?

You can do the same thing. Ask yourself how you could have phrased your questions more effectively or conducted yourself differently in the conversation. If a friend was with you during the encounter, enlist her help. How did she, as a bystander, think you were coming across?

This kind of assessment is not hard at all and can be a lot of fun.[2] When you go back and think about an encounter, you prepare yourself for future opportunities. The next time around, these new ideas will quickly come to mind.

Finally, when you think of a new idea or approach, practice it out loud. I do this constantly. I try to anticipate the twists and turns my new tack might take and how I would respond to possible comebacks. If I think of something, I role-play my side. Often I'll write down my thoughts or record them so I can review them later.[3] If I'm with a friend, I ask him to role-play with me. He may think of moves on either side of the conversation that haven't occurred to me. Also, when we work on it together, we both learn from the experience.

Sometimes I practice this way when I'm alone in the car, listening to talk radio. After hearing a few comments by the host or a caller, I turn the volume down and then pretend it's my job to respond to what was said. It's almost like being on live radio, except if I say something foolish, no one hears.

Practice like this increases your practical experience. It places you in an actual dialogue in a way that is safe. When these issues come up in real-life encounters, you'll be ready since you've already rehearsed your responses.

I prepare this way when I'm interviewed on radio or TV or when I'm in a campus debate or a public crossfire situation. It may sound to listeners like I'm clever or quick on my feet, but often this is not the case. Usually, my answers are not spontaneous at all, even when the conversation takes what seems like an unpredictable turn. If I've anticipated the move and prepared for it, I'm not caught by surprise.

This is the same way political candidates prepare for televised debates or comedians prepare to be "spontaneously" funny on late-night talk shows. You will probably never be in a situation quite like theirs, but that doesn't mean you can't learn from their methods.

> If you want to improve your Columbo skill, remember this important truth: even people who don't usually like taking tests don't mind them at all when they know the answers to the questions.

As you work on developing your proficiency, I think you will discover something I have learned. Preparation will increase your confidence, but eventually you must engage. Interacting with others face-to-face is the most effective way to improve your abilities as an ambassador.

WHAT I LEARNED FROM MY MISTAKES

In real-life situations, you're going to make mistakes. Improving your tactical skill, then, means you'll have to get used to benefiting from your blunders. Let me tell you a (somewhat) embarrassing story of how I learned that the hard way.

I'd just finished teaching Columbo at a church service one Sunday morning. Under the cover of the pastor's closing prayer, I quickly ducked down the center aisle to be in a position to greet people at the door as they exited the church. A young lady was already there waiting for me, though, hand extended.

"I'm a Christian," she announced, "and a Buddhist and a pagan."

"Well, it sounds to me like you don't know very much about those religions," I shot back.

Before I go further, let me ask you: did I engage her confused theology with a thoughtful question? No. I slighted her intellectual integrity with a thoughtless insult. The words of my sermon were still bouncing around the interior of the church, and I had already abandoned my own advice.

Fortunately for me, she didn't react to the put-down. Instead she calmly said, "Well, I think I do know a bit about those religions, and I don't see a problem."

Coming to my senses, I offered the question I should have asked to begin with. "What do you think Jesus would have said about your statement?"

"Oh, I think he would be fine with it," she said.

I had no time for a follow-up because the throng exiting the sanctuary quickly carried her away. It wasn't until my self-assessment time later that I thought of a second question I might have asked if I'd had one more shot: "Can you show me in the Gospels any specific thing Jesus said that would give you the impression he'd be okay with someone saying they were a Christian and a Buddhist and a pagan?"

Of course, this question would have put her in a pinch, since Jesus said nothing to support her view. Quite the opposite. Jesus was a Torah-observant Jew, not an all-roads-lead-to-Rome pluralist.

No, I wasn't quick enough on my feet that morning to meet the challenge the young lady offered. Instead I blundered badly. My self-assessment afterward, though, gave me something for the future. Next time this issue comes up, I'll be ready with a couple of good questions.

Let me give you some more examples of things I wish I would have said during a conversation but didn't think of until after I'd worked through the steps I've described.

In chapter 3, I mentioned a conversation I had with an actor's wife about animal rights. Here is how that evening ended. As I stood at the door, thanking the hosts, I asked one last question about our discussion. It's a question I ask all animal rights advocates if I get the opportunity: "Where do you stand on abortion?" I had no intention of arguing further. I just wanted to know her views, for the record. To my way of thinking, the answer to this question is a measure of an animal rights person's intellectual and moral integrity.

She gave me the same answer I have received from virtually every person I have asked who holds her views. "I'm pro-abortion," she said. Then she clarified. "I'm not actually *for* abortion. I just don't believe any unwanted children should be allowed to come into the world." I thanked her for her candid answer and departed.

Driving home, I couldn't help thinking about her final comments. I was sure I had missed an opportunity, but what was it? Suddenly I realized what was wrong with her response. Not wanting to bring unwanted children into the world may be a legitimate reason for contraception, but it has nothing to do with abortion. When a woman is pregnant, the child is already in the world. The human being already exists; the baby is just hidden from view inside her mother's womb. This woman's response assumed that before making the journey down the birth canal, the baby did not exist.

This weakness could be exploited with a question. I could have responded to her comment by asking, "Do you think unwanted children ought to be allowed to stay in the world?" The answer to this question will always be yes, unless someone wants to affirm infanticide, something I'm sure this woman would never do. The door is now open to a final query, the leading question that properly frames the debate: "The issue with abortion, then, isn't whether the child is wanted but whether a woman already *has* a child when she is pregnant, isn't it?"[4]

Here's another example of an opportunity I missed. Once, in a dorm lounge at Ohio State University, a student asked me about the Bible and homosexuality. When I cited some texts, he quickly dismissed them. "People twist the Bible all the time to make it say whatever they want," he sniffed.

I don't recall my specific response to him that evening. I do remember, though, that I was not satisfied with my answer. On the drive back to my hotel, I gave the conversation a little more thought. I realized it made little sense to argue with his comment. What he said was uncontroversial. People do twist Bible verses all the time. It's one of my chief complaints. Something else was going on, however, and I couldn't put my finger on it at first.

Suddenly it dawned on me. The student's point wasn't really that some people twist the Bible. His point was that *I* was twisting the

Bible. Yet he hadn't demonstrated that. He had not shown where I'd gotten off track with the passage I'd used to address his concern. Rather he didn't like my point, so he dismissed it with a some-people-twist-the-Bible dodge.

I quickly wrote out a short dialogue using questions (Columbo 1 and 2) intended to surface that problem. I also tried to anticipate his responses and how I would use them to advance my point (Columbo 3).

Here is what I came up with.

Student: People twist the Bible all the time to make it say whatever they want.

Me: Well, you're right about that. It bugs me too. But your comment confuses me a little. What does it have to do with the point I just made about homosexuality?

Student: Well, you're doing the same thing.

Me: Oh, so you think *I'm* twisting the Bible right now?

Student: That's right.

Me: Okay. Now I understand what you're getting at, but I'm still confused.

Student: Why?

Me: Because it seems to me you can't know that I'm twisting the Bible just by pointing out that other people have twisted it, can you?

Student: What do you mean?

Me: I mean that in *this* conversation, you're going to have to do more than simply point out that people in *other* conversations twist the Bible. What do you think that might be?

Student: I don't know. What?

Me: You need to show that I'm actually twisting the verses I've offered you. Have you ever studied the passages I mentioned?

Student: No.

Me: Then how do you know I'm twisting them?

A word of caution here. Once you learn Columbo, you'll realize how incapable most people are of answering for their views. The temptation will be strong to use your tactical skill like a club. Don't give in to that urge. Your goal is not to embarrass them but to show them their error and get them thinking. You want to put a stone in their shoe, not drop a rock on their head.

> As a general rule, go out of your way to establish common ground. Whenever possible, affirm points of agreement. Take the most charitable read on the other person's motives, not the most cynical one. Treat them the way you would like others to treat you if you were the one in the hot seat.

Initially, you will not be quick on your feet with responses to challenges. Your best ideas will come afterward, when the pressure is off. Make note of them. Practice them out loud. Try to anticipate the rejoinder and what your counter will be. It will really pay off. Next time around, you'll be ready.

A WORD ON STYLE

There are two basic executions of the Columbo tactic. The first is the bumbling approach of Lieutenant Columbo himself—halting, head-scratching, and apparently harmless. This tack should be easy for most of us because that's often how we feel when we're trying to gain a foothold in a conversation. The second is more confrontational and aggressive. It's the technique a lawyer uses in a courtroom.

The style you adopt in any conversation will depend on your goal. Do you want to persuade the other person, or do you want to refute him? Persuasion comes across as more friendly, because your goal is to win the person, not necessarily to win the argument. By contrast, lawyers want to win the argument. To convince the jury, they must refute the defendant.

Since my goal is usually to persuade, in most conversations I adopt the genial approach of Lieutenant Columbo. I soften my challenge by introducing my questions with phrases like, "I'm just curious," "Something about this thing bothers me," "Maybe I'm missing something," or, "Maybe you can clear this up for me."

Sometimes, though, my purpose is not to persuade the person I differ with but to persuade the ones who are listening. This is the situation I face in a debate. I realize there is little hope of winning my opponent. The audience, however, is generally more open-minded. If I can prove my challenger wrong, I might win many of those who are on the fence, as long as I mind my manners. Harshness never plays well with an audience.

In informal debates, I can use either style, depending on the situation. If someone is squaring off with me when others are listening in, I might choose a refutation style for the sake of the bystanders. This is especially true if my challenger is belligerent and I have little confidence he will be moved. Prudence dictates that I refute him and persuade the crowd. If I were a student in class, I'd usually have a better chance of influencing the other students than I'd have of persuading the professor. Even so, I would probably take a more indirect, laid-back approach as an act of courtesy toward the instructor.

WHAT WE LEARNED IN THIS CHAPTER

In this chapter, we focused on refining your tactical effectiveness as a Christian ambassador by exploring three ways you can improve your skill at Columbo.

First, try to anticipate objections you might face, and then think of questions in advance. This allows you to formulate responses before the pressure is on.

Second, take some time for self-assessment after each encounter. Ask how you could have phrased questions more effectively or conducted yourself differently in the conversation. Enlist a friend in the process, especially if he was with you during the dialogue.

Finally, if you think of anything new, work out the details in advance. Write your ideas down, construct a tactically sound dialogue, then role-play your response—and potential pushbacks from the other side—out loud, by yourself or with a friend.

Chapter 9

TURNABOUT

Defending against Columbo

The proper use of Columbo depends to a large degree on the goodwill of the person using it. The purpose of our questions is not to confuse but to clarify—to clarify the issues in the discussion, to clarify our point, or to clarify some error we think the other person has made.

You might discover that you are not the only one who can use questions to navigate tactically in conversations. Others—including those who disagree with you—may know how to do this too, and some are skilled at it.

What do you do, then, when someone else begins to use Columbo against you, especially when you suspect that his motives are not so noble? How do you respond when you think another person's questions are intended to trap, manipulate, or humiliate you?

In this chapter, I want to show you how to defend against the different ways Columbo can be used against you. I will also be relating an extended conversation I had with a waitress at a Seattle restaurant, because it's a good example of how the various elements of Columbo come together in a single encounter.

Before I speak to the broader issue of defending against Columbo, let me make a clarification. There should be no risk when someone asks us either of the first two Columbo questions. We welcome the opportunity to clarify our views and then give our reasons for what we believe. The danger we need to guard against is the misuse of the third application of Columbo—leading questions meant to make a point against us.

The key to protecting yourself from what may be a Columbo ambush is to remind yourself of an important principle I mentioned earlier: you are in complete control of your side of the conversation. You have no obligation to cooperate with anyone trying to set you up with leading questions. Simply refuse to answer them, but do so in a cordial way.

Politely respond to unwelcome queries by saying, "Before we go further, let me say something. My sense is that you want to explain your point by using questions. That confuses me a bit because I'm not sure how I should respond. I think I'd rather you simply state your view directly. Then let me chew on it for a moment and see what I think. Would that be all right with you?"

Notice, this is an abbreviated version of the maneuver discussed in chapter 6 to get you out of the hot seat. Your response forces the other person to change her approach. She can still make her point, but you avoid being trapped in the process.

There are other circumstances where Columbo can be used against you that are not so easy to neutralize because the questions are loaded or subtly deceptive. The key once again is to remind yourself of who is in control of your side of the conversation—you are. This mentality helps steel you to be firm when you face a verbal bully. In my experience, I've encountered two varieties of this kind of questioning.

CHOPRA'S CHALLENGE

I faced the first version of misleading questioning in a national TV debate with bestselling New Age author Deepak Chopra, who asked me a question you will inevitably be asked. It's one of the most important questions anyone can ask, but it's also one of the most difficult to answer, for two reasons. First, the correct answer—a simple yes—is wildly politically incorrect. Second, that simple answer would also be wildly misunderstood by the average person.

Dr. Chopra was counting on both working in his favor when he put the question to me this way: "You're saying that people who don't believe just like you are going to hell?"

Someone once said if you word the question right, you can win any debate. Dr. Chopra's challenge was a classic case in point. A simple yes would have been the correct answer (properly qualified[1]) but would have sent a distorted message, as you'll see in a moment. Further, Chopra's words subtly suggested that I thought hell was the punishment people deserved for disagreeing with me.

Obviously, Dr. Chopra's question was not meant to clarify a theological point. Instead, in the gamesmanship of the moment, his challenge was intended to discredit me with the audience. If I had answered directly—"Yes, people who do not believe just like me are going to hell"—the debate would have been over. Chopra's query would have succeeded in painting me with an ugly stereotype. Viewers would not have heard Jesus offering reprieve and rescue from a judgment they each will face. Instead they would have heard conceit and condescension from a fundamentalist wishing hell on anyone who didn't see things his way. That's the distortion. And that's the danger of dealing with a question worded that way.

In Chopra's case, I decided to sidestep his challenge rather than try to resolve such a delicate issue with a sound bite. I simply said, "No, that's not the point I'm making here. I'm making a different point."

Notice the way I took charge of my side of the conversation by politely refusing to walk into Chopra's trap. I did not deny the substance of the question. I deflected it. It simply would not have been productive to try to tease out the nuances of an answer with the limited time we had on TV, especially with Dr. Chopra crouched and ready to spring at any perceived misstep.

Instead I stayed in the driver's seat, using his question as a springboard to make the point that I wanted to make, one I thought was strategic to my purposes.[2] I had to be alert, though. Questions like Dr. Chopra's are not innocent ones.

TACTICS FOR ATHEISTS

The second variety of deceptive questioning you need to be warned about is much more subtle and therefore much more dangerous. An entire book has been written to help atheists rattle you with questions meant to create unwarranted doubt about your convictions.

More and more atheists are taking tactical cues from atheist philosopher Peter Boghossian, who has written a book titled *A Manual for Creating Atheists*. It is essentially a tactics book for atheists, and the purpose of the book is to help other atheists make an atheist out of you.

Boghossian calls his approach Street Epistemology. His strategy is unique, though, since he has no interest in making the case in favor of atheism or against any particular religious claim. It's not necessary. If he can use questions simply to plant a seed of doubt about the legitimacy of your faith, then he's satisfied. This is the same gardening concept I discussed earlier, but now it's being used by an atheist.

Boghossian's Street Epistemologists are dangerous not because they're right but because they're very clever and they're very nice. They are friendly and noncombative, and ask lots and lots of questions challenging your faith, since they're convinced your beliefs have no basis in fact.[3]

The questions Boghossian teaches atheists to ask are not meant to clarify, though. They are meant to stupefy.[4] They are often hypotheticals—"What if . . ." kinds of questions—that unsuspecting Christians answer without reflection, not realizing they're being ambushed.

Boghossian gives a personal example of how he did this in a conversation with a Mormon security guard[5] who appealed to creation as evidence for God, making the argument that if the universe began to exist, then a creator God must exist.

> **PB:** Well, if the universe always existed, then it wasn't created. If it wasn't caused, what would that mean?
>
> **SG (pausing):** That there's no God?
>
> **PB:** Yup. That's what it would mean.[6]

Of course, it would mean nothing of the sort, and Boghossian knows that, since he's a philosopher. The technical error in his argument is called denying the antecedent in a conditional syllogism, but you can readily see for yourself that even if the universe always existed—which almost no one believes anymore, because of overwhelming scientific evidence to the contrary—it still wouldn't rule out God. The universe, being contingent and not self-existent, could still depend on a self-existent God for its eternal existence.[7]

Using a clever hypothetical linked to a question, the philosopher had duped the security guard, who, Boghossian admitted, "looked horrified and scared."[8] The atheist was elated, though: "I tried to hide my joy, show my approval, and acknowledge our success."[9]

Boghossian had taken advantage of a Mormon's philosophic and scientific naivete by feeding him a fallacy. He then patted himself on the back, since even though his reasoning was awful, he'd accomplished what he'd set out to do—ravage the Mormon's confidence, regardless of the truth.

Once again, your best defense with people like this is to politely refuse to play the question game. The moment you feel like the questions might be designed to manipulate you, stop the conversation and ask for clarification before you go any further. Here's how that might look, in brief, in Boghossian's encounter with the Mormon.

> **PB:** Well, if the universe always existed, then it wasn't created. If it wasn't caused, what would that mean?

SG: I'm not clear on what you're getting at. What do you think it would mean?

PB: That there is no God.

SG: Really? How does that follow?

Notice, your response here forces the questioner to make his point and defend it instead of his question getting you to make his point for him.

Here's another example, this time of a question put to me by a Boghossian disciple.

Atheist: If there were no hell, would you still be a Christian?

This query seems innocent enough on the surface. Of course we wouldn't be "Christian," strictly speaking, if there were no hell. There would be no need for Christianity if there were no need for hell.

It's a trick question, though, cleverly designed to diminish Christianity to a "carrots and sticks" enterprise by suggesting that believers become Christians merely to get the carrot of heaven and avoid the stick of hell. No threat of the stick, no reason to believe. Faith is reduced to creaturely pleasure-or-pain self-interest and nothing more.

But that's not at all what the Christian has in mind with his answer. To be fair, some Christians may believe this way, but those who understand the fullness of God's purpose do not.

Clearly, there would only be no hell if there were no sin, which would mean there would be no need for a Savior and thus no need for Christianity proper. Even so, we would still want the kind of friendship with God he intended for us at the first, before the fall precipitated the problem that both hell and a Savior (Christianity) were meant to resolve.

Here is what the atheist misses. We have not been rescued for some *thing*—a pleasant place called heaven—but for some *one*.

We have been saved for the intimate, personal, loving relationship that God desired to share with us from the beginning, even before there was a need for a place called hell, where justice would be satisfied.

The problem with the Christian's innocent response is that—though true as far as it goes—it is distorted by the atheist. The Christian means one thing, but the questioner gives it a different twist, pressing his deceptive point and catching the believer by surprise. The atheist poses a hypothetical ("If there were no hell . . ."), and the Christian walks into a rhetorical trap.

Instead the believer should have requested clarification. Here are a couple of examples of what I have in mind.

> **Atheist:** If there were no hell, would you still be a Christian?
>
> **Christian:** I'm confused by your question. Are you asking, would I still trust Christ to die and save me from hell if there were no hell? That makes no sense. Or are you asking, would I still want to be with Christ forever if there were no hell to avoid? What exactly is your point with the question?

Or . . .

> **Christian:** That is an interesting question that's not occurred to me before, so I'm not going to give you a quick answer. I need to think about it a bit, because a hasty answer may give you the wrong impression. What do you think is at stake here?

Generally speaking, when an atheist presses you with questions you're not sure how to answer, always ask for clarification. Here are some more examples.

- Help me out here. What specifically are you are getting at with your question?

- There are probably a number of ways to answer that, depending. What do you have in mind?
- Of course, any person can be mistaken about what he believes. So could I. I'd have to consider conflicting evidence, though. Where are you headed with these questions?
- Sure, I'd change my mind if I had no good reasons to believe what I do and good reasons to believe something else. What do you suggest?
- What evidence would cause me to change my mind? I'm not sure I can tell you in advance. I'd have to consider particular objections. What were you thinking?
- You asked how I would know if I were delusional. I have no reason to think I'm experiencing delusions. Why would you think I am? And why would you label an inaccurate belief a delusion? You've had inaccurate beliefs, haven't you? Does that make you delusional too?

When the atheist offers a response, listen carefully, assess thoughtfully, and answer slowly, if at all. Don't worry if you can't answer all the questions he asks about your faith. As I said, Street Epistemologists are clever. They're prepared with particular questions you may not be able to respond to in a clear way at the moment. No worries. Don't be afraid to say, "I'll have to give that some thought."

WHEN A QUESTION IS NOT A QUESTION

Sometimes you will be asked a question that is not a question at all. Instead it is a challenge in disguise. Consider this comment made to me by a UCLA graduate student: "What gives you the right to say someone else's religion is wrong?"

This is the kind of remark that can catch you off guard, leaving you slack-jawed and dumbfounded. There's a reason for your confusion. Even though the statement is worded like a question, you're pretty sure it isn't one. Instead it's a vague challenge of some sort masquerading as a question. Now what?

People ask questions for various reasons. Sometimes they ask a question because they're curious or confused. They want information they think you can provide. Other questions are rhetorical, tossed out simply to stimulate thinking or move the conversation forward. No response from you is necessary, nor is one expected.

"What gives you the right?" is different. It's not really a question at all. There's no curiosity involved. Instead it is a statement disguised as a question, a kind of goal line stand meant to stop you in your tracks. "Who are you to say?" is another example, along with its cousin, "Who's to say?"

These challenges can easily put you on the defensive, because it's pretty clear they are not requests for information, nor are they harmless probes. The question from the UCLA student was in that category. It wasn't rhetorical, nor was it a mere pursuit of facts. It was a challenge. She was making a point with a question, but what was it?

> "Who are you to say?" kinds of questions are cheap shots because they don't really communicate anything meaningful. They just stop you in your tracks. Like the phrase, "That's just your interpretation," they are attempts to silence you, not attempts to appeal to you for clarification or legitimate justification.

The best way to navigate in this situation is simply to point out that the question is confusing. Our trusty "What do you mean by that?" is perfect here. You might say, "I get the impression you think I've made a mistake. Where did I go wrong?" This will force the person to rephrase her question as a statement, which is what you want.

In my case, I told the UCLA student her question confused me. Did she really want to talk about rights? Did she really want to know what my credentials were or what authority I had to speak on these things? Clearly not.

Anyway, I wasn't laying claim to any authority, nor was I promoting my pedigree, academic or otherwise. The only rights I was appealing to were rational rights. I was offering an argument. It stands or falls on its own merits, not on my authority as the one offering a point of view.

> Who's to say? Ultimately, the person who has the best reasons is in the best position to say what's true and what's false. This is the way sound thinking has always worked. Anyone disagreeing with this truism will quickly offer his reasons why it's wrong, immediately defeating his point.

I wanted the student to think about what she was really saying with her question, then to rephrase it in the form of a statement. The most important thing to remember about these questions is that behind them lurk strong opinions that are vulnerable to challenge if they can be flushed out into the open. That's what I was after.

For example, "What gives you the right to say someone else's religion is wrong?" can be restated as, "No one is justified in saying one religious view is better than another." "Who's to say?" means, "No one could ever know the truth about that," or, "One answer is just as good as another." "Who are you to say?" usually means, "You're wrong for saying someone else is wrong." This last one is obviously contradictory, but you might not notice that problem if the claim remains hidden behind a question mark.

Each of these is a strong assertion. And each is open to challenge, which is my point. Remember, the person who makes the claim bears the burden of proof.

The statement-question has power only when it's allowed to be played. If you force the implicit claim to the surface with your questions meant to clarify the issue, the objection loses its luster, and you can address the real point lurking in the shadows.

SHEEPISH IN SEATTLE

Once in a restaurant in Seattle I got into a chat about religion with the waitress serving my table. My general comments in favor of spirituality were met with an approving nod, but a shadow of disapproval crossed her face when I mentioned that some religious beliefs seemed foolish to me.

"That's oppressive," she said, "not letting people believe what they want to believe."

Now, much could be said about this challenge. Notice that she took my judgment of certain religious beliefs as a threat to personal liberty. I ignored that problem, though, and zeroed in on a more fundamental flaw.

"Do you think I'm wrong, then?" I asked, using a variation of the first Columbo question.

At this, she balked, unwilling to commit the same error she had just accused me of making. "No . . . I'm not saying you're wrong. I'm just . . . trying . . . trying to understand you," she faltered.

I chuckled. "It's okay if you think I'm wrong. Really, it doesn't bother me. I just wonder why you don't admit it. Look, if you don't think I'm wrong, then why were you correcting me? And if you do think I'm wrong, then why were you oppressing me?"

Of course, *I* didn't think her comment was oppressive, but now I was playing her rules against her. Boxed in, she hesitated for a moment, then changed the subject. "All religions are basically the same, after all."

It was a parry—a stock retort. I suspect it had worked for her before, and now she was trying it on me. But I noticed something about the comment. She had just made a claim, and it was up to her to support it. It was time for another Columbo question.

"Religions are basically the same? Really? In what way?" I asked.

My question had a remarkable effect. I was amazed at the impact those simple words had on her. Her jaw fell slack, and her face went blank. She didn't know what to say. She had obviously not thought much about the details of various religions. If she had, she'd have known there are significant differences. Why the empty claim, then, if she had no idea of its truth? I suspect she'd gotten away with it before, stonewalling Christians who didn't know enough to ask for clarification.

Finally, after a long pause, she came up with one similarity. "Well, all religions teach you shouldn't kill people; you shouldn't murder."

In point of fact, many religions aren't concerned with morality at all. A distinctive of the great monotheistic religions is their concern about ethical conduct, but that's not a standard feature of religion. All religions are not basically the same. Instead of lecturing her about it, though, I used my questions.

"Consider this," I said. "Either Jesus is the Messiah or he isn't, right?"

She nodded. So far, so good.

"If he isn't the Messiah," I continued, "then the Christians are wrong and the Jews are right. If he is the Messiah, then the Jews are wrong and the Christians are right. So one way or another, somebody's right and somebody's wrong. Under no circumstances can both religions be basically the same, can they?"

It was a straightforward line of thinking that should have yielded an uncontroversial conclusion. Yet she ignored my question, regrouped, then continued. "Well, no one can ever know the truth about religion."

This is another assertion that should never go unchallenged, so I calmly asked, "Why would you believe that?"

The turnabout caught her by surprise. She was used to asking this particular question, I suspect, not answering it. I was violating the rules, asking her for a reason for her beliefs, and she wasn't prepared for the role change.

I waited patiently, not breaking the silence, not letting her off the hook. Finally, she ventured, "But the Bible has been changed and translated so many times over the centuries, you just can't trust it."

Notice two things about this response. First, she had changed the subject once again. The alleged corruption of the Bible has nothing to do with the possibility of knowing religious truth. Even if the Bible vanished from the face of the earth, some knowledge of God could still be possible, at least in principle. Second, her dodge was in the form of another claim, an assertion that it was her job to defend, not my job to refute.

"How do you know the Bible's been changed?" I asked. "Have you studied the transmission of the ancient documents of the text of the Bible?"

Once again, the question stalled her. "No, I've never studied it," she finally said. This was a remarkable admission, given her confident contention just moments before. But she didn't seem the least bit bothered.

I didn't have the heart to say what I might have said in a case like this: "Then you're saying you are reasonably certain about something you know nothing about." I might have added, "If you've never studied this, how do you know the Bible has been changed as you say?"

Instead I simply told her I had studied the question extensively, and the academic results were in. The manuscripts are accurate to nearly 99 percent precision. The Bible hasn't been changed.[10]

She was surprised. "Really?"

By this point, the waitress was running out of comebacks. She had watched her options evaporate one by one and was getting uncomfortable. "I feel like you're backing me into a corner," she complained.

I wasn't trying to be unkind to her or to bully her intellectually. I had listened to what she said and taken her points seriously. Yet with each claim she made, I asked fair questions she had no answers for. Apparently, she'd never given any thought to the opinions she held with such confidence—a problem I encounter repeatedly with all sorts of people I talk with. She was dumbfounded by the challenges and felt boxed in.

This young lady was like so many I have met. She knew all the popular slogans, but when fair Columbo questions eliminated foolish options, the truth began closing in on her. This dear person was speechless, not because I was clever but because, I suspect, she'd never had to defend her responses before.

When she says to Christians, "Your narrow views are oppressive," or, "The Bible's been changed so many times," or, "All religions are basically the same," they retreat in silence. They haven't been taught to simply raise their eyebrows and say, "Oh? What do you mean by that?"

Critics rarely are prepared to defend their "faith." They have seldom thought through what they believe and have relied more on generalizations and slogans than on careful reflection.

To expose their error, take your cue from Lieutenant Columbo. Scratch your head, rub your chin, pause for a moment, then say, "Do you mind if I ask you a question?" Like the emperor and his imaginary clothes, all it takes is one person to calmly say, "You're naked," and the game is up. That's the power of Columbo.

If you remember only one thing from part 1 of this book, remember this: whenever you get in a tough spot, always ask questions.

WHAT WE LEARNED IN THIS CHAPTER

In this chapter, we learned how to defend against the Columbo tactic when someone uses it against us. Remind yourself that you are in control of your side of the conversation. Politely refuse to answer the person's leading questions. Rather ask him to simply state his point and his reasons for it so you can give the issue some thought.

If you think you're being ambushed with a question, slow down and ask for clarification. Find out specifically what he is getting at with his question. Don't feel obligated to answer queries if you don't know where they're leading.

We also learned to be alert for questions that are not really questions at all but assertions in disguise ("Who are you to say?"). When you encounter this situation, point out that the question is confusing. Then ask the person to rephrase it in the form of a statement. Or simply ask your first Columbo question, "What do you mean by that?"

We finished with an example of a conversation I had with a waitress to give you an idea of how the different elements of the game plan work together harmoniously in a real-life exchange.

PART TWO
FINDING THE FLAWS

Chapter 10

SUICIDE
Views That Self-Destruct

Someone once said that if you give a man enough rope, he'll hang himself. Our next tactic is based on the tendency of many erroneous views to self-destruct. Such ideas get caught in their own noose and quickly expire.

Commonly known as self-refuting views, these ideas defeat themselves. Like the sign in the restaurant saying, "Authentic Italian food served the traditional Chinese way," or the tabloid headline that reads, "Woman gives birth to her own father," views that commit suicide are often obvious.

Here is another example from a philosophy student's T-shirt. The front sported the caption, "The statement on the back of this shirt is false." The back of the shirt read, "The statement on the front of this shirt is true."

There is no need to expend energy addressing views that are bent on destroying themselves. They die by their own hand, saving you the trouble. If an atheist tells you he knows God doesn't exist because God told him so in a vision, your work is already done.[1] All you need to do is point out the problem and quietly watch the view commit hari-kari.

IF IT'S TRUE, IT'S FALSE

Here's how self-refutation works. Every statement is about something. The sentence, "Cats chase rats," is about cats. Sometimes statements include themselves in what they refer to. The statement, "All English sentences are false," is about all English sentences, including itself.

In this last case, you can immediately see a problem. The statement has within it the seeds of its own destruction. If all English sentences are false, then the English sentence declaring it so must also be false, and if false, then it is easily and appropriately dismissed. Because it cannot satisfy its own standard, it falls on its own sword.

When statements fail to meet their own criteria of validity, they are self-refuting. Even when they seem true at first glance (and many do), they still prove themselves false. The minute the words are uttered, the claim fails. Here are some conspicuous examples I have encountered over the years.

- "There are no absolutes." (Is this an absolute?)
- "No one can know any truth about religion." (And how did you come to know that truth about religion?)
- "You can't know anything for sure." (Are you sure about that?)
- "Talking about God is meaningless." (What does this statement about God mean?)
- "You can know truth only through experience." (What experience taught you that rational truth about knowledge?)
- "Never take anyone's advice on that issue." (Should I take your advice on that?)
- "I am the only one here who is not unique." (Think about it . . .)

The Suicide tactic works because of a rule of logic you are already familiar with, even if you're not familiar with its name. It's called the law of noncontradiction. This law reflects the commonsense notion that contradictory statements cannot both be true at the same time.[2]

All suicidal views either express or entail contradictions. They make two different claims that are at odds with each other: A is the case and A is not the case. Obvious contradictions are often funny because we readily see the absurdity built into them.

- "I used to believe in reincarnation. But that was in a former life."[3] (I don't believe in reincarnation. I do believe in reincarnation.)
- "Nobody goes there anymore. It's too crowded." (It's not crowded. It is crowded.)
- "I wish I had an answer to that, because I'm tired of answering that question." (I don't know the answer to that question. I do know the answer to that question.)
- "I really didn't say everything I said."[4] (I did not say it. I did say it.)
- "This page intentionally left blank." (This page is blank. This page is not blank.)
- "You're in rare form, as usual." (Your performance is rare. Your performance is not rare.)
- "These terrorists have technology we don't even know about." (We know about things we don't know about.)

When an idea or objection violates the law of noncontradiction in a straightforward fashion, I call it Formal Suicide.

To determine whether a view has suicidal tendencies, first pay attention to the basic idea, premise, conviction, or claim. Try to identify it. Next, ask if the claim applies to itself. If so, is there a conflict? Does the statement fail to live up to its own standards? Can it be stated in the form A is the case and A is not the case? If so, it commits suicide.

This procedure may sound a bit cumbersome at first, but in practice it's an almost instantaneous process if you're paying attention and know what to watch for. Here's another way of looking at it. If exactly the same reasons in favor of another's view (or against your own) defeat the reasons themselves, then the view is self-defeating.

The final step is easy. Simply point out the contradiction, using a question when possible. When someone says, "There is no truth," ask, "Is that statement true?"

> It might have occurred to you that Columbo and Suicide work well together. If you notice that a person's viewpoint self-destructs, point it out with a question rather than a statement.

Challenges designed to show that a view is contradictory are always lethal if they can be sustained. The argument against God based on the existence of evil is popular because it trades on a presumed contradiction. This gives it unstoppable force if it succeeds.[5] When a view commits suicide, it cannot be revived, because there is no way to repair it. Even God cannot give life to a contradictory notion.[6] Philosophers say such views are "necessarily false." They cannot be true in any possible way. Because they are dead on arrival, defending them is a lost cause.

You might wonder why anyone would believe self-refuting ideas. Very few people knowingly affirm contradictions (though some are so evident, you wonder how they could be missed). When contradictions are implicit, though, embedded in a larger idea, they are harder to see. This is the reason why people are taken in by them.

We know that the claim, "My brother is an only child," is false because the concept of brother entails having a sibling. When Yogi Berra counsels, "Always go to other people's funerals, otherwise they won't go to yours," we chuckle. A person cannot pay his last respects at your funeral if he's dead.

Though these two contradictions are easy to spot, they are different from the explicit examples I've given. Here the contradictions are under the surface. Implicit contradictions are sometimes difficult to identify because they are hidden.

For the remainder of the chapter, I want to walk you through popular notions that are implicitly self-refuting, so you can see how the Suicide tactic works. In each case, the problem is not immediately obvious. Every one of these fails, though, through contradiction. They are sunk before they ever set sail.

IS TRUTH TRUE?

I have already pointed out that the postmodern claim, "There is no truth,"[7] invites an obvious question: "Is the claim that there is no truth itself a true statement, or is it false?" If false, then false. If alleged true, then false again.

This fact became painfully obvious in my debate with noted academic Marvin Meyer. I defended the resolve, "Objective truth exists and can be known," while Dr. Meyer took the opposing side.

I want you to notice something about formal disputes like these. To debate, Dr. Meyer must argue against one view and in favor of another. The argument takes a very particular form: the view he opposes (mine) is false; the view he promotes (his) is true.

This is what took place during our debate. With grace and considerable skill, the professor pointed out the failings of my perspective. Aristotle, it turns out, was wrong; Derrida was right. Mr. Koukl is mistaken; Professor Meyer is correct.

Do you see the problem here? Dr. Meyer marshaled an array of facts, truth, and knowledge for the purpose of persuading his audience that facts, truth, and knowledge are all sophisticated fictions.

In the course of the debate, I pointed out this liability to the audience. I mentioned that Dr. Meyer was forced by the nature of debate itself to make use of the very thing he was denying in the debate, dooming his effort to failure. Merely by showing up, Dr. Meyer had implicitly affirmed the resolve I was defending, effectively conceding the debate to me before it even began.

I further pointed out to the audience that every vote cast for Dr. Meyer as the winner of the debate meant the voter had been persuaded that Dr. Meyer's view was (objectively) true and mine was (objectively) false. Therefore every vote for my opponent was really a vote for me.

The audience laughed, but the point wasn't lost on them. This wasn't because I was clever. It was because the view Dr. Meyer was defending was obviously false, a fact that couldn't be missed once the problem was carefully clarified.

The "Christian" version of postmodernism fares no better, even though baptized with religious language. The following example from a Christian college professor was related to me by a student from her class.

"Are any of you in this room God?" The professor scanned the audience slowly, looking for takers. No hands went up.

"God knows 'TRUTH,'" she continued, writing the word in all capital letters on the board. "All truth is God's truth. God *is* truth. But you are not God. Therefore you only know 'truth.'" She then scrawled in lower case this secondary and substandard take on reality next to the superior version that is forever out of reach of mere humans.

She paused for a moment, letting her point sink in, then closed. "Have a nice day," she said and dismissed the class.

It was a brilliant piece of rhetorical wizardry. Students were too busy taking notes and worrying whether this would be on the test to think carefully about what had been stolen from them or the ruin this foreshadowed for their faith.

The professor's assertions teemed with confusion. What does TRUTH mean? Omniscience? That couldn't be her meaning. That God knows everything and we do not is a trivial observation—hardly a revelation, even for college freshmen.

Did she mean we can't know things in the way that God knows them, that we don't see the world the way he does? Again, not particularly profound.

No, the professor was seeking to undermine the conviction that human beings can know something like absolute truth—knowledge they can count on. She was saying that instead we mortals inhabit a kind of knowledge twilight, where the outlines of reality are vague and indistinct, robbing us of all confidence that anything we think we know is actually so.

The professor seemed blind to her point's suicidal tendencies. The following response makes this failure obvious (note the questions).

> Professor, I'm confused about your comments. Is this insight you've offered true or false? I don't think you'd knowingly teach us something false, so you must think it's true. And that's what confuses me. What kind of truth would that be? It couldn't be "TRUTH," because you're not God. So it must be "truth." But if this is just your personal perception of reality, why should any of us take you seriously? We have our own perceptions. Since according to you, none of us has TRUTH, who's to say who is right and who is wrong when it comes to the nature of truth itself? Can you clear this up for me?

Paul warned us not to be taken "captive through philosophy and empty deception, according to the tradition of men, according to the elementary principles of the world, rather than according to Christ" (Col. 2:8). Yet captivity abounds, even in places God intended to be a refuge from such error.

CAN GOD MAKE A ROCK SO BIG HE CAN'T LIFT IT?

This kind of challenge is called a pseudo-question. It's like asking, "Can God win an arm wrestling match against himself?" or, "If God got in a fight with himself, who would win?" or, "Can God's power defeat his own power?"

The question is nonsense because it treats God as if he were two instead of one. The comparative phrase "stronger than" can be used only when two subjects are in view, like when we say Bill is stronger than Bob, or my left arm is stronger than my right arm. Since God is only one, it makes no sense to ask if he is stronger than himself. The question proves nothing about any deficiency in God, because the question itself—"Can God's omnipotence defeat his omnipotence?"—is incoherent.

"GOD DOESN'T TAKE SIDES"

This reprimand comes up every election cycle. I once saw a full-page ad in the *Los Angeles Times* lecturing one side of the political spectrum on this very point. The assertion is self-defeating, though, as illustrated in the following conversation.

> "You think God is on your side, but you're wrong. God doesn't take sides."
>
> "Let me ask you a question. In this disagreement we're having on whether God takes sides, what do you think God's opinion is?"
>
> "I just told you. God is against taking sides."
>
> "Right. So in our dispute, God would agree with you, not me."
>
> "That's right."
>
> "He would *side* with you in this issue, then. I guess God does take sides after all."

Note the contradiction: God doesn't take sides. God does take sides. The assertion is self-defeating. Not surprisingly, the ad went on to campaign for its political view as the moral high ground, compounding the error.

TO ERR IS HUMAN

A common attack on the Bible goes like this: Men wrote the Bible. People are imperfect. Therefore the Bible is flawed and not inspired by God.

Remember our rule for discovering suicidal statements: If exactly the same reasons in favor of another's view (or against your own) defeat the reasons themselves, then the view is self-defeating. The presumption that if man is capable of error, he will err applies also to this very argument against inspiration.

Consider this exchange.

"You think the Bible must be flawed because people make mistakes."

"Yes, that's the way it seems to me."

"I'm curious—why do you think you are an exception to that rule?"

"What do you mean?"

"Well, you don't seem to think you've made a mistake in your judgment about the Bible. But you're a flawed human being too."

"Of course I am. But I didn't mean that people always make mistakes."

"If people don't always make mistakes, though, you can't rule out the Bible just because people wrote it, can you?"

> It's not enough to dismiss the Bible simply by noting that men wrote it. This in itself proves nothing. It doesn't follow that if people are capable of error, they always will err. Taken at face value, this objection is self-refuting.

C. S. Lewis cites a related example. In response to the Freudian and Marxist claim that all thoughts are tainted (either psychologically or ideologically) at their source, he writes, "If they say that all thoughts are thus tainted, then, of course, we must remind them that Freudianism and Marxism are as much systems of thought as Christian theology. . . . The Freudian and the Marxian are in the same boat with all the rest of us and cannot criticize us from the outside. They have sawn off the branch they are sitting on. If, on the other hand, they say that the taint need not invalidate their thinking, then neither need it invalidate ours. In which case they have saved their own branch, but also saved ours along with it."[8]

Statements like, "Everyone's view is a product of his own prejudices," or, "All your so-called facts are only beliefs dictated by your cultural biases," falter for the same reason. Are these views themselves merely a product of prejudice or cultural bias? If so, why take them seriously?

"ATMAN IS BRAHMAN AND BRAHMAN IS ATMAN"

Hinduism as a religious view also seems compromised by contradictory notions. The pantheistic monism at the heart of some versions of this Eastern religion teaches that reality as we know it is an illusion— *maya*—of which each of us is part.

This Hindu concept that the world is an illusion contradicts the idea that I can know that I am a player in the illusion. Implicitly, it claims that I am not a real self and that I am a real self at the same time. Thus this central doctrine of Hinduism self-destructs.

> If I am an illusion, how could I know it? How could I possess true knowledge that I do not exist? (I think, therefore I ain't?) Do people in a dream know they are imaginary? Does Charlie Brown know he is a cartoon character?

One escape route people have tried in order to avoid this problem is to claim that the law of contradiction is a Western notion that doesn't apply in Eastern thought like Hinduism. Eastern thinkers are comfortable with contradiction, so they say.

This problem, though, has nothing to do with what people are comfortable with. It has to do with how reality is structured. People may be comfortable with all sorts of unusual things. This may tell you something about psychology, but not about reality.

Computers work on a binary system of zeros and ones. Because of the law of noncontradiction, we are able to keep these two distinct. It doesn't matter whether the computer is in the Eastern Hemisphere or the Western Hemisphere or whether the person at the keyboard is Christian, Hindu, Taoist, animist, or atheist. The computer works regardless because reality is still structured according to the law of noncontradiction, even if people from other cultures are psychologically confused on this point.

THEISTIC EVOLUTION: DESIGNED BY CHANCE?

Some people suggest that God used evolution to design the world. They are motivated, I think, by two impulses. The first is a desire to affirm the Bible. The second is a conviction that the standard Darwinian model has merit. Thus they declare both true.

These two notions, however, seem incompatible to me. It may sound reasonable for God to use evolution, but if you look closer, I think you will see the problem.

Suppose I wanted a straight flush for a hand of poker. Either I could pull the cards out of the deck individually and design the hand, or I could shuffle the cards randomly and see if the flush is dealt to me. It would not make any sense, though, to "design" the hand by shuffling the deck and dealing. There's no way to ensure the results. (I guess if I were really clever, I could make it look like I was shuffling the deck when in reality I was stacking it, but that would be a deceitful kind of design called cheating.)

In the same way, either God designs the details of the biological world, or nature shuffles the deck and natural selection chooses the winning hand. The mechanism is either conscious and intentional (design) or unconscious and unintentional (mutation and natural selection). Creation has a purpose, a goal. Evolution is accidental, like a straight flush dealt to a poker rookie.

The idea that something is designed by chance is contradictory. Like trying to put a square peg in a round hole, it just doesn't fit.[9]

"ONLY SCIENCE GIVES RELIABLE TRUTH"

This modern slogan seems reasonable at first glance. Many people think knowledge begins and ends with the scientific method, and anything not confirmed by science is mere opinion and unsubstantiated belief. This view is called scientism. However, those who hold this view will be surprised to know that it commits suicide. Consider this dialogue.

"I don't believe in religion."

"Why not?"

"There is no scientific evidence for it."

"Then you shouldn't believe in science either."

"Why not?"

"Because there is no scientific evidence for it."

I might have moved a little too quickly on that one, so let me expand a bit. I noticed first that the slogan, "Only science gives reliable truth," is a statement about truth that also purports to be true, so it includes itself in what it refers to (in the same way that the statement, "All English sentences are false," includes itself). Next, I simply applied our basic test for Suicide by asking, "Can the statement satisfy its own requirement?"

I quickly realized it could not. Since there is no scientific evidence proving that science is the only way to know truth, the view self-destructs. I then used Columbo to point out the flaw.[10]

The next time someone dismisses you with the "Only science gives reliable truth" canard, ask if he wants you to take his statement as fact or as unsubstantiated opinion. If fact, ask what testable scientific evidence led him to his conclusion. As it turns out, this claim is not a fact *of* science. It is a philosophical assertion *about* science that itself cannot be proven by any scientific method and would therefore be unreliable according to this approach.

RELIGIOUS SUICIDE

The notion of religious pluralism, that all religions are equally true or valid, is also self-refuting. There are two ways to demonstrate this.

First, if all religions are true, then Christianity is true. Yet a central claim of classical Christianity is that other religions are false when taken as a whole. Clearly, Jesus was not a pluralist.[11] Either Christianity is correct that Jesus is God's Messiah for the world and that other religions are deceptions, as Scripture teaches, or Christianity is false and some other view is true. In no case, though, can all religions be true and valid.

Second, when you think about it, religions give diverse pictures of what reality is like. Some forms of Hinduism teach that God is impersonal. Islam, Judaism, and Christianity teach that God is a personal being. In Buddhism, the question of God is irrelevant. In their central teaching about God, then, these religions are at odds with each other.

In classical theism, death is final, followed by either eternal reward or eternal punishment. In Eastern religions, death is a door the soul passes through many times as it works out its karma in reincarnation. Some religions teach that reprobates are destroyed while the righteous live on.

Can you see the problem? When someone dies, they might go to heaven or hell, or they might be reincarnated, or they might simply turn to dust, but they can't do them all at the same time.

Some religions are clearly mistaken on details central to their worldview. Every one of them could be wrong on every single point, in principle, but they cannot all be right. Note, this is not bigotry; it's simple math. Taken at face value, then, religious pluralism commits suicide.

YOU ARE WHAT YOU EAT?

I once saw a sign in a restaurant that read, "You are what you eat." I pointed out to the waitress that if we are what we eat, then we couldn't be something until we eat something. But we can't eat something unless we are something. Therefore it's not true that we are what we eat.

The waitress, unschooled in the finer points of self-refuting arguments, looked at me and said, "You'll have to talk to the manager."

WHAT WE LEARNED IN THIS CHAPTER

First, we learned that we do not always have to do all the work when dealing with an argument or a challenge. Sometimes a view defeats itself. The tactic we use to expose this tendency is called Suicide.

Suicidal views have within them the seeds of their own destruction because they express contradictory concepts. They refute themselves. That's why they are called self-refuting.

Views that violate the law of noncontradiction are necessarily false. This means that nothing can be done to fix them. They are beyond repair in this world or any world. If a view entails contradiction—for example, "All English sentences are false"—there is no hope of reviving it. For this reason, the presence of contradiction is a decisive defeater of any argument or point of view.

We also learned how to recognize and respond to self-destructive statements. First, pay attention to the basic premise, conviction, or claim. Next, ask if the claim applies to itself. If so, does it satisfy its own criteria, or is there an internal contradiction? If the exact same reasons in favor of another's view (or against your own) defeat the reasons themselves, then the view is self-refuting. If you discover a problem, use a question (Columbo) rather than a statement to point it out.

Finally, we learned how to respond to popular examples of ideas or objections that violate the law of noncontradiction in a straightforward fashion (Formal Suicide). Remember, many formal contradictions are not immediately obvious. Instead they are implicit, embedded in the larger idea. This makes them easy to miss. Even intelligent and educated people sometimes hold contradictory views without realizing it.

Chapter 11

PRACTICAL SUICIDE

In the previous chapter, we learned that once in a while, defending against an opposing view takes almost no work at all. Sometimes the easiest way to deal with another's objection is not to feed her more information but rather to show her that her point commits suicide.

We have already explored the concept I call Formal Suicide, when an idea or objection violates the law of noncontradiction in a straightforward fashion. However, some views that are not internally contradictory can be self-defeating in other ways. Practical Suicide, Infanticide, and Sibling Rivalry are terms I use to describe three other ways statements or arguments self-destruct. I will take up Practical Suicide in this chapter and discuss the other two in chapter 12.

PRACTICAL SUICIDE

Some points of view fail the pragmatic test. They simply cannot work in real-life application. When a person says, "I never say anything out loud," there is no logical contradiction, strictly speaking, just a practical one—he can't verbalize his conviction without refuting it. This type of suicide applies to a number of views people can believe but not promote without running into trouble.

You see the conflict immediately in the claim, "It's wrong to say people are wrong." Holding that it is wrong to find fault with others is not itself incoherent. I know that sounds odd, considering the wording. But when you think about it, the problem occurs only when you say the statement. You would be doing the very thing you say should not be done. This kind of inconsistency is self-defeating, because the person who voices this view contradicts his convictions.

Like most two-year-olds, my own little girl adopted a philosophy of "no" for a season. It was her answer to everything. I'd sometimes hear her alone playing in her room, absentmindedly stringing denials together with varying force and inflection, perfecting her technique like a piano virtuoso prepping for her next performance.

She was easy to trap, though. After a series of negatives, I'd simply ask, "Are you going to answer no again?" No matter what she answered, she'd be sunk. The philosophical subtlety was lost on her, but it should not escape you. There is no internal contradiction in a philosophy of "no." Once my daughter tried to practice her conviction consistently, though, she ran into trouble. This happens all the time, even with those who are old enough to know better.

> During a radio broadcast, I took exception to the theology of some televangelists. I was immediately challenged by a caller who said, "You shouldn't be correcting Christian teachers publicly on the radio."
>
> "Then why are you calling to correct me publicly on my radio show?" I asked.

Some Christians, convinced that arguing is contrary to Scripture, argue aggressively that arguments dishonor God and are of no use in persuading others. They reject apologetics because they think reason is not an appropriate tool for believers, then painstakingly list the reasons they think they're right ("I'll give you three good reasons why you shouldn't use reason").

This is the problem people face when they make the blanket

statement, "It's wrong to judge." Maybe it *is* wrong to make moral judgments in certain cases,[1] but using this rule in an unqualified way to condemn someone making a moral judgment is itself a breach of the principle.

When a caller to my radio show took me to task for condemning homosexuality, he soon found himself caught in his own net. The following conversation could be titled "Condemning Condemnation."

Lee: I'm not a homosexual, but I think it's wrong to condemn anybody for anything.

Greg: Why are you condemning me, then?[2]

Lee: What?

Greg: I said, why are you condemning me if you think it's wrong to condemn people?

Lee: I'm responding to the fact that a lot of Christians condemn people.

Greg: I understand. And it sounds like you're condemning me because I just condemned homosexuality as wrong.

Lee: Yes, I am. You are supposed to love everybody.

Greg: Wait a minute. You're not listening to yourself. You just said it's wrong to condemn people. And now you admit you're condemning me. So I'm asking, why are you doing the very same thing that you say is wrong when I do it? [Notice how I am narrating the argument here.]

Lee: No, I'm not. [Lee pauses as the light slowly begins to dawn.] Okay, let's put it this way. I'm not condemning you; I'm reprimanding you. Is that better?

Greg: Then my comments about homosexuals are simple reprimands as well.

I want you to notice two things about this exchange. First, it took Lee a few moments before he realized his error. This is not uncommon. Amazingly, some people never see it. When Lee finally came to his senses, his attempts at correcting his blunder were not helpful.

Second, since *I* saw the problem immediately, it wasn't difficult for me to come up with a question to press the issue until Lee caught on. I employed the third use of Columbo—using a question to make a point. In this case, I pointed out that his view was flawed, being contradictory in practice.

> Philosopher Alvin Plantinga calls this suicidal tendency the "philosophical tar baby." If you get close enough to use the idea on someone else, he says, you're likely to get stuck fast to it yourself.[3]

MORAL RELATIVISM SELF-DESTRUCTS

Moral relativists—those who deny universal, objective morality—are especially vulnerable to Practical Suicide. Whenever a relativist says, "You shouldn't force your morality on other people," I always ask, "Why not?"

What can he say now? He certainly can't respond, "It's wrong." That option is no longer open to him. It's a contradiction, like saying, "There are no moral rules; here's one." This response commits Practical Suicide.

If a relativist does say that forcing morality is wrong, I ask, "If you think it's wrong, then why are you doing it? Why are you pushing *your* morality on *me* right now?"

The only way out for a relativist—the only way for him to respond that's consistent with his relativism—is to say, "Pushing morality is wrong for me, but that's just my personal opinion and has nothing to do with you. Please ignore me."

C. S. Lewis observes, "Whenever you find a man who says he does not believe in a real Right and Wrong, you will find the same man going back on this a moment later. He may break his promise to you, but if you try breaking one to him he will be complaining 'It's not fair'. . . . A nation may say treaties do not matter; but then, next minute, they spoil their case by saying that the particular treaty they want to break was an unfair one. But if . . . there is no such thing as Right and Wrong . . . what is the difference between a fair treaty and an unfair one?"[4]

As I have written elsewhere, "A person can wax eloquent with you in a discussion on moral relativism, but he will complain when somebody cuts in front of him in line. He'll object to the unfair treatment he gets at work and denounce injustice in the legal system. He'll criticize crooked politicians who betray the public trust and condemn intolerant fundamentalists who force their moral views on others."[5]

I think this was Paul's point in Romans 2:1 when he wrote, "You have no excuse, everyone of you who passes judgment, for in that which you judge another, you condemn yourself; for you who judge practice the same things." Paul argued that those who set up their own morality are still faulted by the standards of their personal moral code.

That's Practical Suicide. When you see it happening, use a question to point it out. If someone says, "People should never impose their values on others," ask if those are *his* values (they are). Next, ask why he's seeking to impose them on others.

> Usually, a person cannot deny moral truth without immediately affirming it. The minute they say, "And it's wrong to push your morality on me," they have sunk their own ship.

"SEPARATION" SOVIET STYLE

In 1976, a decade before the Iron Curtain came down, I spent five weeks with three others in a clandestine mission operation in Eastern Europe and the former Soviet Union. There I encountered a memorable example of Practical Suicide.

When we crossed the border from Romania into Moldavia, we were stopped on the Soviet side and searched. Once the border guards found Bibles, they took our car apart, checking everywhere for religious contraband. Then the questioning began. Where did we get the Bibles? Why were we bringing them across the border? Who were they for? Didn't we know such activity was illegal? It went on for hours.

We knew that the Soviets claimed they had religious freedom. They also claimed to print Bibles for their own people. We also knew that both claims were false, which gave us an advantage in the conversation.

"Don't you have freedom of religion in the Soviet Union?" we asked, parroting the propaganda.

"Yes, of course we have religious freedom," the interpreter shot back with some indignation, "but we have separation of church and state."

Now, it wasn't clear to us how bringing Bibles across the border interfered with that principle. Yet it was the interpreter's stock reply to just about every objection we raised.

"It is forbidden to bring Bibles and other religious material into the Soviet Union," she continued. "In schools, we teach the children that there is no God. Only old people believe that. Our people are taught Marxist-Leninism. We don't allow any other propaganda. We have separation of church and state."

"But you print Bibles in the Soviet Union, right?" I asked.

"Yes, we do," she answered. "Our believers get all the Bibles they need."

"And you have religious freedom?"

"Yes, we have religious freedom, but we have separation of church and state."

"But we can't bring Bibles across the border?"

"No, we don't allow that propaganda in our country."

"The Bible is propaganda?"

"Yes."

"But you print Bibles in your own country."

"Yes."

"Now I'm confused," I remarked. "You say you have religious freedom, but we are not allowed to bring Bibles into your country because they are propaganda. Then you tell me you print Bibles in the Soviet Union."

She nodded in agreement to each point. I was surprised she couldn't see what was coming. "Then apparently your government is printing anti-communist propaganda right in your own country."

"No, you don't understand," she replied. "We have separation of church and state."

PROSELYTIZING PROHIBITED

Some years ago, the Southern Baptist Convention publicized its plans to direct its annual summer evangelistic outreach to Jews living in Chicago. It then encouraged Baptists to "pray each day for Jewish individuals you know by name that they will find the spiritual wholeness available through the Messiah."

The public reaction was immediate and severe. The director of the Jewish Anti-Defamation League said the campaign "projects a message of spiritual narrowness that invites theological hatred."[6] A consortium of religious groups in Chicago, including Christian denominations, issued a statement condemning the SBC, warning that the Baptists' evangelism in the Windy City would encourage hate crimes.

The grievances were aired on a national TV talk show where two enraged rabbis, one from New York and one from Chicago, confronted two remarkably calm Baptists. The substance of their complaint was this: Proselytizing should be reserved for people with no spiritual convictions. Jews already have a religion. It's the height of arrogance to suggest that they need a new one. Therefore Christians should make their appeals elsewhere. Essentially, the rabbis were saying, "Keep your spiritual opinions to yourself. Stop trying to change other people's religious views."

Do you see the problem here? The rabbis were incensed that Christians were trying to change the religious convictions of Jews. Yet their antidote was for the Christians to abandon their religious convictions about evangelism and adopt the rabbis' view—evangelize only those who have no religion.

In the heat of the moment, it probably did not occur to the Christians to simply ask, "If that's what you believe, then I don't understand why you are trying to change our religious beliefs right now. Why do you interfere when we're trying to obey Jesus' command to preach the gospel? Why don't you keep your religious views to yourself?"

Oddly, the Baptists were branded intolerant merely for planning to engage others in voluntary, thoughtful conversation about religion. Yet the rabbis who viciously condemned them on national television were considered tolerant and open-minded.

The claim, "It's wrong to try to change other people's religious beliefs," is usually an example of Practical Suicide. The idea itself is not incoherent. However, a person risks contradiction simply by trying to promote this conviction.

WHAT WE LEARNED IN THIS CHAPTER

In this chapter, we discovered that there is more than one way for an argument to self-destruct. Though some views are not internally contradictory—they do not fail through Formal Suicide—still, in practice they are self-defeating. The view can be believed but not acted on or promoted. Anyone advancing the opinion cannot avoid violating his convictions ("It's wrong to say people are wrong," for example).

I call this tendency Practical Suicide. Moral relativists are especially vulnerable to this problem, as are those who believe it's wrong to try to change another person's religious views.

Chapter 12

SIBLING RIVALRY AND INFANTICIDE

Arguments or points of view can self-destruct for a variety of reasons. We have already talked about two: Formal Suicide and Practical Suicide. Now I would like to introduce you to a couple more examples of Suicide that are not internally contradictory but are self-defeating in their own unique ways.

Sometimes a conflict arises when a person raises two objections that are at odds with each other. This Sibling Rivalry is easy to spot if you look for it. At other times, someone's view is built on a prior concept that turns out to disqualify the view itself. I call this Infanticide. Think of it like a deranged creature from a sci-fi movie that devours its own offspring. This kind of Suicide is more difficult to spot, but it is a powerful defeater nonetheless. In either case, if you look closely, you will discover that the hard work has already been done for you.

SIBLING RIVALRY

Occasionally in conversations you will notice something odd. You will hear a pair of objections voiced by the same person, but the complaints are logically inconsistent with each other. They are like children fighting between themselves, siblings in rivalry.

Since both objections cannot be simultaneously legitimate, your task is cut in half. A fair-minded person will surrender at least one when you identify the problem. Graciously point out the conflict, then ask which is the real concern. Sometimes this move effectively silences both objections because the person you are talking with realizes she has been unreasonable.

Is Gandhi in Heaven?

When I was in India, Christian apologist Prakash Yesudian told me of a conversation he had with a Hindu about Gandhi, who is much revered there. Notice how Prakash coupled Columbo with the Sibling Rivalry tactic.

"Is Gandhi in heaven?" the Hindu asked. "Heaven would be a very poor place without Gandhi in it."

"Well, sir," Prakash answered, "you must at least believe in heaven, then. And apparently you have done some thinking about what would qualify someone for heaven. Tell me, what kind of people go to heaven?"

"Good people go to heaven," he responded.

"But this idea of what is a good person is very unclear to me. What is good?"

In typical Hindu fashion, he replied, "Good and bad are relative. There is no clear definition."

"If that is true, sir, that goodness is relative and can't be defined, how is it you assume Gandhi is good and should be in heaven?"

Either Gandhi fulfills some external standard of goodness, thus qualifying for heaven, or goodness is relative and therefore a meaningless term when applied to anyone, including Gandhi. Both cannot be true at the same time.

Kavita

During that same trip, I had a discussion with a Hindu college student named Kavita. As I talked about Christianity, she raised a standard objection. "If God is as you say, how could he allow such suffering, especially for the children?" She gestured with a sweep of her hand as if to take in the collective anguish of Madras, which was great.

The first thing I pointed out was that God hadn't done this to India. Hinduism had. Ideas have consequences, and the suffering in Madras was a direct result of things Hinduism teaches and Hindus believe.

I then explained that it wouldn't always be this way. A day would come when all evil would be destroyed, and Jesus himself would wipe away every bitter tear.

"How could that be?" she objected. "Evil and good exist as dual poles. If you have no evil, it is impossible to have good. Each must balance the other out."

I noticed immediately that Kavita's response was at odds with her first question. "Let me repeat this reasoning back to you," I said, "and you tell me what you think of it."

She nodded.

"You ask, 'Why are innocent children starving in the streets?' I answer, 'Good and evil exist as dual poles. Children starve in Madras so kids in other parts of the world may be happy and well. The one balances the other out.' What do you think?"

When the point sank in, she was forced to smile. "Touché!" she replied.

The Quarrel

I encountered a clear example of Sibling Rivalry after an airing of *The Quarrel*, a film that explored the problem of God and the Holocaust. Producer David Brandes had asked me to help moderate a discussion with an audience about the moral issues raised in the movie.

From one side of the auditorium, a Jewish woman offered the idea that maybe God allowed the Holocaust as a punishment for Israel's wayward drift into secularism. Some Jewish thinkers have raised this possibility in light of the promised curses for apostasy recorded in Deuteronomy 28. The reflection prompted a sarcastic, "Well, that's a real loving God," from the other side of the theater.

I called attention to the conflict suggested by the second comment. Those who are quick to object that God isn't doing enough about evil in the world ("A good God wouldn't let that happen") are often equally quick to complain when God puts his foot down ("A loving God would never deliver judgment"). If God appears indifferent to wickedness, his goodness is challenged. Yet if he acts to punish sin, his love is in question. These objections compete with each other in most cases. They are siblings in rivalry. One or the other needs to be surrendered. Both can't be held simultaneously.[1]

Who Are You to Say?

Sibling Rivalry is the type of suicide moral relativists commit when they object to the problem of evil. This happened at a restaurant during a conversation with a waitress (I seem to get in a lot of discussions with waitresses).

At first the young lady talked like a relativist. Everyone has his own morality. Right and wrong is a private affair. Who's to judge? As our conversation ranged over other topics, though, the problem of evil came up. How could God exist when there is so much evil in the world?

I want you to notice something about the problem of evil. The entire objection hinges on the observation that evil exists "out there" as an objective feature of the universe. That is a serious problem for relativists, though.

According to relativism, when someone uses the word evil, he is expressing a personal preference. The sentence, "Premarital sex is wrong," means nothing more than, "I don't prefer sex outside of marriage," or, "Extramarital sex is wrong *for me.*" Strictly speaking, the person is not talking about sex at all. The relativist is talking about himself.

In that light, imagine how silly this conversation would sound.

"I can't believe in God."

"Why not?"

"Brussels sprouts."

"Brussels sprouts? What do brussels sprouts have to do with anything?"

"Did you ever taste those things? They're awful."

"I personally agree with you about the taste of brussels sprouts, but some people do like them. What does the fact that you don't like brussels sprouts have to do with God's existence?"

"I can't believe in a God who would create something that tastes so awful to me."

This kind of objection is trivial, of course. If relativism were true, talk of evil as an objection to God's existence would be nonsense. The complaint would mean nothing more than, "If God were really good, he wouldn't allow things that I don't like."

C. S. Lewis summed it up this way: "Of course, I could have given up my idea of justice by saying it was nothing but a private idea of my own [relativism]. But if I did that, then my argument against God collapsed too—for the argument depended on saying that the world was really unjust, not simply that it did not happen to please my private fancies."[2]

To say that something is evil is to say it is not the way it is supposed to be. This makes no sense unless things are supposed to be different. Yet this is what the relativist denies.

This waitress promoted two rival concepts at the same time—subjective morality and objective evil. The objections competed with each other. They were siblings in rivalry. G. K. Chesterton saw the problem more than a century ago: "[The modernist] goes first to a political meeting where he complains that savages are treated as if they were beasts. Then he takes his hat and umbrella and goes on to a scientific meeting where he proves that they practically are beasts. . . . In his book on politics he attacks men for trampling on morality, and in his book on ethics he attacks morality for trampling on men."[3]

The belief that objective good and evil do not exist (relativism) is in conflict (rivalry) with a rejection of God based on the existence of objective evil.

Just Doin' What Comes Naturally

If homosexuality is morally neutral because it's natural, then adoption by same-sex couples must be wrong because for homo-sexuals, parenthood would be unnatural by the same standard. The same principle governs both issues. If nature dictates morality,[4] and the natural consequence for homosexuals is to be childless, then it's unnatural and therefore immoral for homosexuals to raise children.

Artificial insemination of lesbians or adoptions by same-sex couples would be wrong by the logic of their own argument. This is a Sibling Rivalry type of suicide.

INFANTICIDE

I have saved Infanticide for last because it is the most difficult kind of suicide to understand. Let me start with an example. Think for a moment about how this simpleminded father closed a letter to his son in college: "Son, if you didn't get this letter, please let me know, and I'll send another. I made a copy."

This makes us chuckle for a reason. The son would have to receive the letter in order to ask for a copy, but then he wouldn't need it. If he never got the original, he wouldn't know to ask for a replacement. There is a certain dependency relationship in play here that is at the heart of Infanticide.

Sometimes an objection (the "child") is dependent on a prior notion (the "parent") that must be in place for the challenge to be offered. Saying, "Vocal cords do not exist," is not internally contradic-tory. But since it requires vocal cords to say it, making the statement results in contradiction. The parent concept (vocal cords) devours the child (the verbal claim there are no vocal cords). That's why I call this variation Infanticide.

If a claim cannot be made unless the parent concept on which it depends is true, yet the claim denies the parent concept, then the argument commits Infanticide. The child is destroyed by the parent it relies on.

Bowling and Badness

The most powerful example of Infanticide that I know of has to do with the problem of evil. We looked at one complaint by moral relativists related to evil that was compromised because of Sibling Rivalry. When moral objectivists (people who believe in real, universal morality) argue that God cannot exist because of evil, however, their view fails in a different way. It commits Infanticide.

> Surprisingly, instead of evil being a good argument *against* God, I am convinced it is one of the best evidences *for* God.

The first question the atheist must answer is, "What do you mean by 'evil'?" His impulse will be to give examples of evil (murder, torture, oppression). But that misses the point. Why call those things evil to begin with? One must first have some clear idea of what evil is before one can point to examples of it.

I want you to think about the concepts of good and bad for a moment. How do you know the difference between, say, a good bowler and a bad one? Only one thing matters in bowling. The person who knocks down the most pins wins. It's the score that counts.

Knowing the difference between mediocre and masterful in anything requires a way of keeping score. There must be some standard of perfection for you to measure a performance. In bowling, that standard is 300—every pin down in every frame (some people have done this). If you are a golfer, one stroke per hole—a hole in one with every swing—is golfing perfection (no one has ever done this).

Notice that even when perfection is not attainable (a golf score of 18 on an eighteen-hole course), a scoring system is still necessary to distinguish between excellence, mediocrity, and abject failure. In the same way, moral judgments require a way of keeping score to distinguish virtue from vice. This is the point I was making earlier about the failure of coupling moral relativism with a complaint about objective evil in the world. If there is no scoring system (relativism), there can't be any evil.

Earlier in the chapter, I observed that we use the word evil when we see things that are not the way they are supposed to be. We have a standard in mind—a moral scoring system of sorts—that allows us to recognize moral shortfalls. The reason we say some things are evil is that we realize they score low on the goodness scale, so to speak. If there were no standard, there could be no error. C. S. Lewis notes, "My argument against God was that the universe seemed so cruel and unjust. But how had I gotten this idea of just and unjust? A man does not call something crooked unless he has some idea of a straight line."[5]

This is the problem for the atheist. He must show where the moral scoring system comes from (the moral "straight line") that allows him to identify evil in the first place. Where is the transcendent standard of objective good that makes the whole notion of evil intelligible? Are moral laws the product of chance? If so, why obey them? What—or who—establishes how things are supposed to be?

Here's an insight that helps. A moral rule entails a command along with a duty to obey it. Both require minds. Ethicist Richard Taylor explains, "A duty is something that is owed . . . but something can be owed only to some person or persons. There can be no such thing as a duty in isolation. . . . The concept of moral obligation [is] unintelligible apart from the idea of God. The words remain, but their meaning is gone."[6]

There seems to be no good way to account for a transcendent standard of objective good—the moral rules that are violated by people who commit the evil in question—without the existence of a transcendent moral rule maker. In the movie *The Quarrel*, Rabbi Hersh challenges the secularist Chaim on this very point: "If there's nothing in the universe that's higher than human beings, then what's morality?

Well, it's a matter of opinion. I like milk; you like meat. Hitler likes to kill people; I like to save them. Who's to say which is better? Do you begin to see the horror of this? If there is no Master of the universe, then who's to say that Hitler did anything wrong? If there is no God, then the people that murdered your wife and kids did nothing wrong."[7]

A morally perfect God is the only adequate standard for the system of scoring that makes sense of the existence of evil to begin with. Since God must exist to make evil intelligible, evil cannot be evidence against God. The complaint commits Infanticide.

> Ironically, evil does not prove atheism. It proves just the opposite. There can be a problem of evil only if God exists. It is a problem only a theist can raise, not an atheist. When an atheist voices the concern, he gets caught in a suicidal dilemma.[8]

Notice that this difficulty is a little different from the Sibling Rivalry problem with evil, mentioned earlier. In that case, two incompatible contentions rested side by side: the first was that true evil does not exist because morality is relative; the second was that evil does exist, so God's existence is in question. When someone simultaneously holds that evil does and does not exist, there is an irreconcilable conflict—a sibling rivalry. One or the other has to go.[9]

With Infanticide, however, the notion of morality (with its corresponding concept of evil) rests on the prior foundation of God's existence. God seems to be necessary in order for any conversation about evil to be coherent. Thus it can never be used to refute God, because without him the objection would have no meaning.

Moral Atheists?

Christians who grasp that God is necessary for morality sometimes make a blunder. They mistakenly conclude that atheists cannot be moral. Michael Shermer, atheist editor of *Skeptic* magazine, fires back, "Look, I'm an atheist, and I'm moral."

Both the criticism and the response miss the point. The question is not whether an atheist can be moral but whether he can make sense of morality in a universe without God. Gravity still works even when people have no explanation for why it works.

The "why it works" question is what philosophers call the grounding problem. What grounds morality? What does it stand on? What explanation best accounts for a moral universe? What worldview makes the most sense out of the existence of evil or good?

Atheism is a physicalist system that does not have the resources to explain a universe thick with nonphysical things like moral obligations. Neither can some Eastern religions, by the way. If what we take as reality is really an illusion, as classical Hinduism holds, then the distinction between good and evil is meaningless.

Someone like the Judeo-Christian God must exist in order to adequately account for moral laws. If there is no God, then no conduct is actually good. One person's behavior (an atheist's) can mimic another person's behavior (a Christian's), but without an external standard—a scoring system—neither the atheist nor the Christian can be genuinely good (or bad, for that matter).

Theism solves the grounding problem for morality. It explains how even an atheist like Michael Shermer is genuinely capable of noble conduct: he still lives in God's world.

More Scientific Suicide

I want to revisit a problem that came up earlier. In chapter 10, I showed how the idea that science is the only source of reliable truth commits what I call Formal Suicide. However, this notion is doubly dead, because it commits Infanticide too.

The term *scientism* describes the view that science is the only reliable method of knowing truth about the world. Accordingly, "Everything outside of science is a matter of mere belief and subjective opinion," writes philosopher J. P. Moreland, "of which rational assessment is impossible."[10]

Here is how scientism commits Infanticide. Imagine you wanted to collect all knowledge in a box. Let's call it the Truth Box. Before any alleged truth could go into the box, it would have to first pass the scientific truth test (this is the claim of scientism).

The problem is that your knowledge project could never get started, because some truths would need to be in the Truth Box first before science itself could begin its analysis. The truths of logic and mathematics would have to be in the box, along with the truth of the basic reliability of our senses. Certain practical truths expressed as moral requirements—like "Report all data honestly"—would have to be in the box. The entire scientific method would have to be in the box before the method itself could be used to test the truthfulness of anything else.

None of these truths can be established by the methods of science, because science cannot operate in a knowledge vacuum. Certain truths—known through means other than science—must be in place before science can begin testing for other truths. Since the notion of scientism (the child) is inconsistent with the nonscientific presuppositions that make science possible (the parent), scientism as a comprehensive view of knowledge commits Infanticide.

Freedom, Reason, and Knowledge

It always strikes me as odd when people try to advance arguments for determinism. Here's why.

Determinists claim that freedom is an illusion. Each of our choices is fixed, strictly determined beforehand by the circumstances that precede it. All of our "choices" are inevitable results of blind physical forces beyond our control.

The problem with this view is that without freedom, rationality would have no room to operate. Arguments would not matter, since no one would be able to base beliefs on adequate reasons. One could never judge between a good idea and a bad one. One would hold beliefs only because he had been predetermined to do so.

That's why it's odd when someone tries to argue for determinism. If determinism were true, the person would have been determined to believe in it, with others just as determined to disagree. He would have to admit that reasons don't matter and that trying to think the issue through is a waste of time.

Although it is theoretically possible that determinism is true—there is no internal contradiction, as far as I can tell—no one could ever know it if it were. Every one of our thoughts, dispositions, and opinions would have been decided for us by factors out of our control.

Genuine knowledge, by contrast, is based on sound reasons, not deterministic reactions. Therefore arguments for determinism self-destruct. The parent (determinism) destroys the child (the argument for determinism).

THE TACTICAL GOAL OF SUICIDE

When I use any form of the Suicide tactic, I have a specific goal in mind. I want to show the person that there is a fatal inconsistency in her beliefs—a problem I think she would correct if she really understood it. Furthermore, the contradiction suggests that deep down she does not really believe everything she has said.

When she says, "There is no truth," she actually believes there are some truths but is doubtful about others (probably the one you are talking with her about). When she says, "It's wrong for you to push your morality on others," it's clear she doesn't think this is always wrong, only sometimes (probably in your case).

I think you can see how the Suicide tactic is not an end in itself but can be used as a bridge to further questions. What kind of evidence is adequate to give us confidence that something is true? Under what circumstances might we legitimately impose our morality on someone else? Do those circumstances apply here?

WHAT WE LEARNED IN THIS CHAPTER

We finished our look at the Suicide tactic by considering two final ways that views self-destruct: Sibling Rivalry and Infanticide.

Sometimes objections come in pairs that are logically inconsistent with each other. Like children fighting, they are in opposition, siblings in rivalry. Since they contradict each other, both objections cannot be legitimate complaints. At least one can be eliminated by pointing out the conflict.

Infanticide is a little more difficult to grasp. Sometimes an objection (the "child") is dependent on a prior notion (the "parent") that must be in place in order for the challenge to be offered. If a claim cannot be made unless the parent concept on which it depends is true, yet the claim denies the parent concept, then the parent kills the child, and the argument commits Infanticide.

We saw how this type of self-refutation applies to the problem of evil. Since God's existence is necessary to make the notion of evil intelligible, the existence of evil cannot be used as a proof that God does not exist. It indicates just the opposite. If evil exists, then good exists. If good exists, then God exists. Ironically, the existence of evil is powerful evidence for God, not against him.

Chapter 13

TAKING THE ROOF OFF

Some points of view, if taken seriously, don't actually commit suicide, but they work against themselves in a different way. When played out consistently, they lead to unusual—even absurd—conclusions.

To understand how this works, think of maps and highways. If you were visiting Los Angeles and wanted to go to Santa Barbara up the coast, someone might draw a map to guide you to your destination. If, however, you followed the instructions very carefully and took the highway they suggested but found yourself in Riverside, on your way to the desert, you would know something was wrong with the route you were given.

In a similar fashion, worldviews are like maps. They are someone's idea of what the world is like. The individual ideas making up a worldview are like highways leading to different destinations. If you use the map but arrive at a strange destination, either part of the map is inaccurate (the part about the highway you were driving on), or the map itself is the wrong one for the region.

I realize that this last option is not likely when you are talking about real maps. I doubt you would try to find your way around New York using a map of Chicago. But this kind of thing happens all the time with worldviews. Sometimes the roads are wrong on otherwise good worldview maps. At other times, worldview maps are inadequate for the actual terrain.

Keep this illustration in mind as we explore our next tactic. It is a method that helps you determine the accuracy of someone's map of reality—their worldview—by noting where the route on the map leads them.

> If you help someone see in advance that the route his map recommends will lead him off a cliff, he might consider changing his course. He might even discover he is using the wrong worldview map altogether and exchange it for one that is more reliable.

TAKING A TEST DRIVE

I learned the tactic of Taking the Roof Off from the writings of Francis Schaeffer. The tactic itself is simple. First, adopt the other person's viewpoint for the sake of discussion. Next, give his idea a test drive. Try to determine where you will end up if you follow his instructions faithfully. If you arrive at an odd destination, point it out and invite the person to reconsider the worldview route he has been taking.

Sometimes when you press an idea to its logical consequences, the result is counterintuitive or absurd. If you take a view seriously and apply it consistently and it leads to disaster, you are on the wrong route. Something must be wrong with your map if this is the place you end up.

This tactic makes it clear that certain arguments prove too much. It forces people to ask if they can really live with the kind of world they are affirming. Those who are intellectually honest will think twice about embracing a view that ultimately leads to irrationality, incoherence, and absurdity. That is too high a price to pay.

Taking the Roof Off is also known as *reductio ad absurdum* (or simply *reductio*). This is a Latin phrase that means to reduce a point to its absurd conclusion or consequence.

WHY *REDUCTIOS* WORK

When I was a young Christian, I read Francis Schaeffer's *The God Who Is There*. Schaeffer argued that Christians have a powerful ally in the war of ideas: reality. Whenever someone tries to deny the truth, reality ultimately betrays him. As Schaeffer pointed out, "Regardless of a man's system, he has to live in God's world."[1]

Human beings are made in the image of God and must live in the world God created. Although culture shifts, human nature remains the same. Ideas change, but ultimate reality does not.

> Every person who rejects the truth of "the God who is there" is caught between the way he says the world is and the way the world actually is.

This dissonance—what Schaeffer called the "point of tension"—is what makes Taking the Roof Off so effective. Any person who denies the truth of God's world lives in a contradiction. On the outside he claims one thing, yet deep inside he believes something else because he cannot escape the truth that God has imprinted on his soul (Rom. 1:19). To protect himself from considering the consequences of this conflict, he subconsciously erects a defense, a deceptive cover, a roof. He's in denial. Our job is to remove that roof, expose the fraud, and deprive him of his false sense of security. In Schaeffer's words, "Every man has built a roof over his head to shield himself at the point of tension. . . . The Christian, lovingly, must remove the shelter [the roof] and allow the truth of the external world and of what man is to beat upon him. When the roof is off, each man must stand naked and wounded before the truth of what is. . . . He must come to know that his roof is a false protection from the storm of what is."[2]

Regardless of our ideological impulses, deep inside each of us lives a commonsense realist. Those who are not realists are either dead, in an institution, or sleeping in cardboard boxes under the freeway.

Knowing this gives us a tremendous advantage. The key to dealing with moral relativism, for example, is realizing that for all the adamant affirmations, no one really believes it, and for a good reason: if you start with relativism, reality does not make sense.

It is significant that those who want to practice relativism never want relativism practiced toward them. Schaeffer tells of an encounter with a Hindu student at Cambridge who had been vigorously condemning Christianity.

"Am I not correct in saying," Schaeffer asked, "that on the basis of your system, cruelty and noncruelty are ultimately equal, that there is no intrinsic difference between them?" The Hindu nodded. To his alarm, a student who understood the implications of this view took a kettle of boiling water and held it above the Hindu's head, repeating, "There is no difference between cruelty and noncruelty."[3] The Hindu turned on his heel and walked out.

In a very real sense, every person who denies God is living on borrowed capital. He enjoys living as if the world is filled with morality, meaning, order, and beauty, yet he denies the God whose existence makes such things possible.

> When you start with theism—"In the beginning, God"—these destinations make complete sense. When you start with materialism, though—"In the beginning, the particles"—that route takes you over a cliff of absurdity and despair.

ROOF REMOVAL, STEP BY STEP

Taking the Roof Off is not complicated if you follow these three steps.

First, reduce the person's point of view to its basic argument, assertion, principle, or moral rule. This might take a moment of reflection. Ask yourself what the person's specific claim is. The first step of Columbo ("What do you mean by that?") comes in handy at this point. State the idea clearly (write it out if you need to). If this is part of a conversation, check with the person to make sure you got her view right. You might say, "Let me see if I understand you correctly," then repeat the point as clearly as you can.

Second, mentally give the idea a test drive to see where it leads. Ask yourself, *If I follow this principle consistently, what are the consequences? What implications might it have for other issues? Does it take me somewhere that seems wrong, counterintuitive, or absurd?* The answers to these questions may not be immediately obvious but often become clear later, after you have given the issue some thought.

Third, if you find a problem, point it out. Invite the other person to consider the implications of her view and the absurd end it leads to. Show her that if she applies her view consistently, it will take her to a destination that seems unreasonable. Therefore something about her original view needs to be modified.

Mother Teresa once appealed to the governor of California to stay the execution of a vicious double murderer. She reasoned that since Jesus would forgive, the governor should forgive.

Though the intentions were good, the argument itself proves too much, as our tactic demonstrates. When applied consistently, this view becomes a reason to forgo any punishment for any crime, because one could always argue, "Jesus would forgive." Emptying every prison does not seem to be what Jesus would advise, since great evil would result. Capital punishment might be faulted on other grounds, but not on this one. Here is the analysis.

> **Claim:** If Jesus would forgive capital criminals, then it is wrong to execute them.
>
> **Taking the Roof Off:** On this reasoning, it would be wrong for government to punish any criminal, because one could always say, "Jesus would forgive." This seems absurd, especially when Scripture states that the purpose of government is to punish evildoers, not forgive them.[4]
>
> **Therefore:** Even though Jesus might forgive murderers, that does not mean it is wrong for the government to punish them.

Here's another example. Typically, social conservatives in this country have opposed granting marriage licenses to same-sex partners. A common response to that opposition is, "That's the same thing people said about interracial marriage." The assumption is that since people were wrong to oppose interracial marriage, they must be wrong to oppose same-sex marriage.

To take the roof off, first ask what the core argument is. In this case, it's a little tricky, but I think this sums it up: We were wrong in the past on one marriage question (interracial marriage). Therefore we are wrong in the present on a different marriage question (same-sex marriage). The following dialogue demonstrates the flaw in this logic.

"I don't think same-sex unions should be endorsed by the government."

"You know, people said the very same thing about interracial marriages. They were wrong then, and you are wrong now. Same-sex marriage is right."

"So you think the government should approve of homosexual unions?"

"Of course."

"But people said the government should approve slavery too. They were wrong then, and you are wrong now. Same-sex marriage is wrong."

Here's the breakdown.

Claim: Because people were wrong in the past on one issue, they are wrong in the present on a different issue.

Taking the Roof Off: Since the government was wrong in endorsing slavery in the past, it would be wrong for them to endorse same-sex marriage in the present. This is absurd because the same kind of reasoning produces contradictory results: same-sex marriage is wrong, *and* same-sex marriage is right.

Therefore: It is not sound to argue that just because people were wrong in the past about interracial marriage, they are now wrong about same-sex marriage.

The only way out of this problem is to show a similarity between interracial marriage and same-sex marriage that is relevant to the issue of government endorsement. There is none.

Jesus used the Taking the Roof Off tactic in an argument with the Pharisees. Notice how he reduced the Pharisees' reasoning to its logical and absurd conclusion: "The Pharisees . . . said, 'This man casts out demons only by Beelzebul the ruler of the demons.' And knowing their thoughts Jesus said to them, 'Any kingdom divided against itself is laid waste; and any city or house divided against itself will not stand. If Satan casts out Satan, he is divided against himself; how then will his kingdom stand? . . . But if I cast out demons by the Spirit of God, then the kingdom of God has come upon you'" (Matt. 12:24–26, 28).

Here's how the tactic played out.

Claim: Jesus casts out demons by the power of Satan.

Taking the Roof Off: If Satan is the source of Jesus' power, then Satan is casting out Satan, destroying his own kingdom. This is absurd.

Therefore: Jesus' power must come not from Satan but from God, who opposes Satan. Those who oppose Jesus, then, are opposing God, not Satan.

Each of the following vignettes tackles a common challenge by using Taking the Roof Off. Notice how many ways this technique can be used. It is flexible because people frequently hold beliefs that lead to absurd consequences.

BORN A BASHER?

It's been common to justify one's "sexual orientation" by an appeal to nature. Some people think the claim, "I was born this way," is all that's needed to stem moral criticism of their behavior. But why settle for this approach? Why think the state of nature is an appropriate guide to morality?

The basic argument can be summed up this way: anything that is natural is also moral. Same-sex sexual orientation is natural for gays (the claim goes).[5] Therefore same-sex sexual orientation is moral. What happens when we go down that road?

I once asked a radio caller who used this reasoning regarding homosexuality if the same rationale would justify gay bashing. If scientists isolated a gay bashing gene, would violence toward homosexuals be acceptable? Hardly. If there really were a gay bashing gene, the correct response would be to fight its influence, not surrender to it.

Seventeenth-century philosopher Thomas Hobbes noted famously that life in an unregulated state of nature is "solitary, poor, nasty, brutish, and short." Morality protects us from the brutality of living in a world where people act out their natural impulses. Animals always do what comes naturally.

Since living according to nature would result in all kinds of barbarism, how does it make sense to invoke the natural state of things to justify anything? The difference between just doing what comes naturally and principled self-restraint is called civilization. Morality that counters one's natural inclinations rather than approves them is our only refuge from a life that is "solitary, poor, nasty, brutish, and short."

Here's how the *reductio* looks.

Claim: Any "natural" tendency or behavior is morally acceptable.

Taking the Roof Off: If gay bashing (or any other vice) comes naturally for someone, it must be okay. This is obviously wrong.

Therefore: Even if an impulse is natural, that does not mean it's moral. No "sexual orientation" can be justified this way.[6]

CHALK ONE UP FOR GOD

You may have heard a story of an atheist philosophy professor who performs a parlor trick each term to convince his students that there is no God.[7] "Anyone who believes in God is a fool," he says. "If God existed, he could stop this piece of chalk from hitting the ground and breaking. Such a simple task to prove he is God, and yet he can't do it." The professor then drops the chalk and watches it shatter dramatically on the classroom floor.

If you meet anyone who tries this silly trick, take the roof off. Apply the professor's logic in a test of your own existence. Tell the onlookers you will prove you don't exist.

Have someone take a piece of chalk and hold it above your outstretched palm. Explain that if you really existed, you would be able to accomplish the simple task of catching the chalk. When he drops the chalk, let it fall to the ground and shatter. Then announce, "I guess this proves I do not exist. If you believe in me, you're a fool."

Clearly, this chalk trick tells you nothing about God. The only thing it is capable of showing is that if God does exist, he is not a circus animal who can be teased into jumping through hoops to appease the whims of foolish people.

TROTTING OUT THE TODDLER

Virtually every argument in favor of abortion could equally justify killing newborns if pressed to its logical conclusion. If it's acceptable to take the life of an innocent human being on one side of the birth canal, why forbid it on the other side? A seven-inch journey cannot miraculously transform a "nonhuman tissue mass" into a valuable human being.[8]

When someone justifies abortion by saying, "Women have the

right to choose," use a version of Taking the Roof Off called Trotting Out the Toddler. Ask if a woman should have the right to kill her one-year-old child for the same reason.[9] Since both an unborn child and a one-year-old are human beings, the same moral rule should apply to each. The logic of choice, privacy, and personal bodily rights endangers newborns, not just the unborn.[10]

At the University of New Mexico, a student said we should abort children to save them from future child abuse. Former Stand to Reason speaker Steve Wagner "trotted out the toddler" in response. "Should we also kill two-year-olds to save them from future child abuse?"

"I hadn't thought about that," the student said. And that's the point. People don't think about the logical implications of their ideas. It's our job to help them see where their ideas logically take them.

CLIMATE CONTROL

A chorus of voices have charged that Christians, through their moralizing about homosexuality, are promoting a climate of hate. The phrase of choice is "less than." By claiming that homosexuality is wrong (they say), Christians demote homosexuals to a "less than" status, making them the object of scorn, hatred, and physical abuse.

The flaw in this logic becomes obvious when you take the roof off. In Los Angeles, a radio talk show host—himself a homosexual—noted that this kind of thinking would make Alcoholics Anonymous responsible every time a drunk gets beat up in an alley.[11]

Such a tactic is equally dangerous to those who use it. If moralizing causes hate, and hate leads to violence, are those who demonize Christians for condemning homosexuality also guilty of hate-mongering? It simply does not follow that moral condemnation of homosexuality encourages gay bashing, any more than moral condemnation of "bigoted" Christians encourages violence against believers.

The Taking the Roof Off tactic clearly demonstrates that this kind of attack is really about protecting personal preferences, not promoting moral principles.

"FAITH" VERSUS FACTS

Some people think that facts and knowledge undermine true faith.

The reasoning goes like this. Hebrews 11:6 says, "Without faith it is impossible to please God" (NIV). Faith is believing things we cannot know. Faith and knowledge, then, are at opposite ends of the spectrum. The more facts we have, the less room there is for faith. God is most pleased when we cling faithfully to our convictions in spite of overwhelming evidence against them.

If this is your view of faith, following this route will lead you into a spiritual ditch. First, apologetics—giving evidence in defense of the truth—would be misguided. Yet Peter says we should always be ready to make an *apologia*, a defense, for our hope (1 Peter 3:15). Plus, Jesus and the apostles routinely offered arguments and gave evidence for their claims.

Second, if knowledge and faith are inversely proportional (as knowledge increases, faith decreases), then the more evidence we find against Christianity, the better. Our knowledge would shrink to nothing, providing ample opportunity for an abundance of blind faith. Affirming something you knew to be false would be the greatest virtue, if you took this view. God would be most pleased with those who had every reason to think the resurrection never happened, yet still believed.

The apostle Paul, however, called such a person pitiful. "If Christ has not been raised . . . your faith also is vain. . . . You are still in your sins. Then those also who have fallen asleep in Christ have perished. If we have hoped in Christ in this life only, we are of all men most to be pitied" (1 Cor. 15:14, 17–19).

According to Paul, if we believe contrary to fact, we believe in vain. We are not heroes to be praised but fools to be pitied.

What has gone wrong here? The problem is with the premise, "Faith is believing things we cannot know." This is not a biblical understanding of faith. Faith and knowledge are not opposites in

Scripture. They are companions. The opposite of faith is not fact but unbelief. The opposite of knowledge is not faith but ignorance. Neither unbelief nor ignorance is a virtue in Christianity.

EARTH DAY FOR EVOLUTIONISTS?

Has anyone else noticed a contradiction implicit in the annual Earth Day celebrations? The vast majority of devotees at such fetes are Darwinists who believe humans have an obligation to protect the environment. Starting with a naturalistic worldview, though, why should anyone care?

For millions of years, Mother Nature has spewed noxious fumes and poisonous gases into earth's atmosphere and littered the landscape with ash and lava. The most natural condition in the universe is death. As far as we know, the earth is unique. Death reigns everywhere else.

Species have passed into extinction at a steady rate from the beginning of time, the strong supplanting the weak. Why shouldn't they? Each is in a struggle for survival, a dance of destruction fueling the evolutionary process. May the best beast win. That's the logic of naturalism. Yet the sense of obligation to steward the earth is strong. Why?

The moral motivation for Earth Day simply does not follow from Darwinism. It makes perfect sense, though, if God entrusted human beings with stewardship over the planet. Taking the Roof Off—following an idea to its logical conclusion—shows that Earth Day makes sense for theists but not for Darwinists.

Here's a variation of the same idea. If there is no God and we evolved by chance, there is no fundamental difference between animals and humans. However, we permit a farmer to divide the weak from the strong in his pack of cows, yet we're appalled when Hitler does the same with people. Why is the first right but the second wrong, given a Darwinian starting point?

"MODIFIED PRO-CHOICE"

The modified pro-choice position is a politician's favorite abortion double-talk: "I'm personally against abortion, but I don't believe in forcing my pro-life view on others."

I once had a discussion with a man who offered this nonsense to me at a conference. I asked him the question I always pose when I encounter such a notion: "Why are you personally against abortion?"[12]

He responded with the answer I almost always get. "I believe abortion kills a baby," he said, "but that's just my personal view."

I then repeated his view back to him for clarity. "Let me see if I understand you," I said. "You are genuinely convinced that abortion kills an innocent child, yet you think the law should allow women to do that to their own babies. Did I get that right?"

He objected to my wording, but when I asked him what part of his view I had mischaracterized, he was silent. I hadn't misunderstood it. That *was* his view.

> The logic of the modified pro-choice position reduces to, "I think it's wrong to kill my own children, but I don't think we should stop other people from killing theirs."

JUST YOUR INTERPRETATION

The "that's just your interpretation" parry when you make a biblical point is usually vulnerable to Taking the Roof Off. Use the first Columbo question ("What do you mean by that?") to find out if the person thinks all interpretations are equally valid and yours is just another in an infinite line of alternatives.

If you suspect that this is his view, take the roof off. Treat his words as infinitely malleable. Tell him, for example, that you are sorry to hear that he believes all disabled infants should be executed. When his jaw drops, tell him that's your interpretation of what he said. Does he have a problem with that?

Don't leave him hanging, though. Clarify your point: some interpretations are better than others. If the person you are talking with thinks you have distorted the Scripture, then invite him to show you the error, not dismiss you with this weak response.

WHAT WE LEARNED IN THIS CHAPTER

Taking the Roof Off is a technique designed to show that some views prove too much. If taken seriously, they lead to counterintuitive or even absurd results. Another name for this tactic is *reductio ad absurdum*.

This tactic has three steps. First, we reduce the point of view to its basic argument, assertion, principle, or premise. Second, we give the idea a test drive to see if any absurd consequences result when we consistently apply the logic of the view. Third, we invite the person to consider the unusual implications of her view and the truth that follows from the *reductio*.

Taking the Roof Off works because humans are made in the image of God and must live in the world God created. Any person who denies this fact lives in tension between the way he says the world is and the way the world actually is. To protect themselves from this contradiction, people erect a self-deception—a roof—to shield them from the logical implications of their beliefs. With our tactic, we try to remove that roof to deprive them of their false sense of security, and then we show them the truth.

Chapter 14

STEAMROLLER

F ew people readily admit that their beliefs are wrong. Some put up a real fight, even when your points are reasonable and your manner is gracious. Did you ever wonder why people do that? Why do people ignore good arguments?

I think there are four reasons for resistance, and I would like to explain what those are. Then I will give you a step-by-step plan to deal with that overconfident, overbearing, and often overwhelming interrupter I call a steamroller.

WHEN ARGUMENTS DON'T WORK

In chapter 2, I talked about the importance of arguments—not angry squabbles or silly quarrels but points of view buttressed by reasons. Jesus used them. Paul used them. Peter used them. We should use them too.

When arguments are done well, they honor God. But arguments have limits; they don't always work. When that happens, some people are tempted to think that arguments themselves are useless.

This is a mistake. If you're searching for that perfect line of logic capable of subduing any objection, you're wasting your time. There is no magic, no silver bullet, no clever turn of thought or phrase that's guaranteed to compel belief.

Yes, rational objections can be a barrier to belief. The Christian message simply doesn't make sense to everyone, or it raises questions or counterexamples that make it difficult for some to even consider Christianity until those issues are addressed.

But rational appeals often fail to persuade for other reasons. At least three additional issues may compel the person you're talking with to ignore your point. They have nothing to do with clear thinking, even when objections based on reason are the first to surface. If your thoughtful response fails to have an impact, is not acknowledged, or—worse—doesn't even seem to have been noticed, maybe one of the following reasons is lurking in the shadows.

First, people have *emotional reasons* to resist. Many have had annoying experiences with Christians, or painful encounters with abusive churches. Others realize that to embrace Christianity would be to admit that cherished loved ones now dead entered eternity without forgiveness and with one fate awaiting them: darkness, despair, and suffering forever. Emotionally, this is something the person simply cannot bear.

Others know they would face the rejection of family and friends or perhaps suffer financial loss, physical harm, or even death if they considered Christ. These powerful deterrents can make the most cogent argument seem inadequate and unconvincing.

Second, some balk because of *prejudice*. Their minds are already made up. They have prejudged your view before ever really listening to your reasons. They are interested only in defending their entrenched position, not in considering other options.

Cultural influences are powerful here. Resistance based on prejudice can be especially strong for those with religious beliefs or with nonreligious beliefs (like naturalism) held with religious intensity. Often Christians defend their denominational distinctives in a prejudiced way. They plow ahead with blinders on, spouting the party line with no thought given to the merits of an alternate view.

Finally, some people are just plain pigheaded. Their real reason for resistance is no more elegant or sophisticated than simple *rebellion*.

Jesus said that people love the darkness rather than the light because their deeds are evil (John 3:19). So they persist in their mutiny, waging to the bitter end their unwinnable battle against God.

As you can see, you and I have limited control over how other people respond to us. That is largely in God's hands. We can remove some of the negatives or dispel some of the fog, and we ought to try to do both. But at the end of the day, a person's deep-seated rebellion against God is a problem only a supernatural solution can fix.

When someone forcefully disagrees with you, do not expect him to surrender quickly. Changing beliefs is not easy to do, especially when a lot is at stake. Usually, it is a slow process for someone to admit they are mistaken about something important.

Sometimes a person's impulse to resist is so strong, he will get verbally abusive. You need a plan to help keep you in the driver's seat of conversations with those people who have controlling personalities and bad manners. The tactic I suggest is a defensive maneuver called Steamroller.

STEAMROLLER

Once in a while, you will encounter people who try to overpower you. They don't overwhelm you with facts or arguments. Rather they roll over you with the force of their personalities. Their challenges come quickly, one after another, keeping you from collecting your wits and giving a thoughtful answer.[1]

If this sounds familiar, then you have been steamrolled. Men are frequently guilty of steamrolling, especially when talking with women, but women can be offenders too.

Steamrollers have a defining characteristic. They constantly interrupt. As soon as you begin to answer, they hear something they don't like in your explanation, interrupt, then pile on another objection or challenge. If you try to go down the new rabbit trail, they interrupt again, changing the subject, firing new challenges, yet never really listening to anything you say. You find yourself constantly off balance and on the defensive.

Some steamrollers are more distracted than discourteous. They're unable to stick to a line of thinking for more than a few moments, so they bounce around in a disorderly way, launching out with new challenges without absorbing the point you've been making. They're not disingenuous, but they're not really listening either, so you're not making progress, regardless of how good your answers are.

Though there are benevolent steamrollers—overly excitable but not hostile—most are insincere with their questions. Steamrollers are not usually interested in answers. They are interested in winning through intimidation. It is easier for them to ask the hard question than to listen to an answer that is more than a shallow, ten-second sound bite.

Because steamrollers are so aggressive, you must manage them aggressively, though you don't need to be rude. For some Christians, it will take courage and intestinal fortitude to face up to such a powerhouse at first. However, once you learn the following three steps to stop a steamroller, you will discover that getting back into the driver's seat is easier than you thought.

Step 1: Stop Him

The first step in dealing with a steamroller is a mild one. Even though you may feel pushed to your limits by the annoyance, don't fire back in kind, guaranteeing a head-on collision. Don't buckle at the knees either. "Once your opponent has intimidated you and knows it, you've lost," says William Dembski, a veteran of many encounters with hostile challengers of intelligent design.[2]

Instead your first move should be a genial request for courtesy. Stop the intrusion by momentarily putting the discussion on pause. Then briefly request permission to continue your point without being interrupted. Use a little body language if you need to, raising your hand a bit for emphasis.

It takes longer to describe it than to do it. Simply hold up your hand

and gently say, "Sorry, I'm not quite finished yet," and then continue. Often this is all you need to do to restore order to the conversation.

If the steamroller is especially aggressive, be calm and wait for an opening. Do not try to talk over him if he isn't cooperating at first. When you get a pause, don't be afraid to ask for adequate time. Quickly negotiate an informal agreement. You ask him to give you something—patience and courtesy—so that you can give him something in return—an answer. Here are some variations.

- "Is it okay with you if I take a few moments to answer your question before you ask another? I'll give you a chance to respond when I get done. Will that work?"
- "That's not a simple issue. I need a moment to explain myself. Is that okay?"
- "Let me respond to your first challenge. When I'm done, you can jump in again with another. Is that all right?"
- "That's a good question, and it deserves a decent answer, but that will take a few minutes. Are you okay with that?"

Notice the negotiation here. You make a petition, and he grants it. With more aggressive steamrollers, it is especially important for them to verbally consent to your request. (Of course, if a person answers no to any of these questions, you might ask him why he brought the challenge up in the first place.)

Be careful not to let annoyance or hostility creep into your voice. That would be a mistake, especially with this kind of person.

> Don't let a steamroller get under your skin. Being defensive and belligerent always looks weak. Instead stay focused on the issues, not on the attitude. Talk calmly and try to look confident.

Be sure to respond adequately to one question before you are forced to tackle another, but don't take unfair advantage of the time you buy with this little negotiation. Make your point, then ask, "Does that make sense to you?" This invites him back into the conversation. Give him the courtesy of offering you a reply without interruption. You do not want to be a steamroller yourself.

This first step is especially effective with a benevolent steamroller hopping from topic to topic in a disconnected way. Stay friendly while gently restraining their enthusiastic disorder. Keep them on track with one point before you let them pull you off to another.

Step 2: Shame Him

If the steamroller breaks trust with your agreement—or if you can't succeed in stopping him in the first place to negotiate an orderly conversation—proceed to phase 2 of the Steamroller tactic. This step is more aggressive. It also takes a bit more courage because you will now be directly confronting the rudeness of an impolite person. You might consider using his name at this point. It will soften the exchange.

> What's in a name? Plenty. A person's name is sweet to him. Keep this in mind when conversations begin to take a hostile turn. At the first sign of tension, pause and ask their name if you don't know it already. Then use it in a friendly manner as you continue. It helps take the edge off the encounter.

You tried to stop the steamroller. That didn't work. Now you want to shame him for his bad manners, but you want to do it with integrity. Start by taking the same basic approach you did in step 1. This time, though, make an explicit request for courtesy.

First, ignore any new challenges he has introduced. Do not follow his rabbit trails. Second, address the steamroller problem directly. If you are not able to get the floor right away, let him talk. When he finally pauses, look him in the eye and calmly say something like this:

- "Can I ask you a favor? I'd love to respond to your concern, but you keep breaking in. Could I have a few moments without being cut off to develop my point? Then you can tell me what you think. Is that okay with you?"

- "Can I ask you a quick question? Do you really want a response from me? At first, I thought you did, but when you continue to interrupt, I get the impression all you want is an audience. If so, just let me know and I'll listen. But if you want an answer, you'll have to give me time to respond. So do you want me to respond or just listen? I need to know before I can continue."

- "Here's what I have in mind. You make your point, and I'll be polite and listen. When you're done, it will be your turn to be polite to me and not interrupt while I respond. Then I'll let you have your say without breaking in. I need to know if that's okay with you. If not, this conversation is over. What would you like to do?"

Notice that each example I have offered is progressively more direct. You have to judge which one is appropriate for the circumstances you face. The last one is very aggressive. If you started this way, you would be out of line. With some people, though, a direct approach like this is the only thing that will save the conversation. Use it only after the other person has used up a lot of grace.

Remember, steamrollers are strong customers who sometimes need to be addressed with equal strength, yet coupled with civility. This can be harder if you're an easygoing sort with a gentle spirit, but unless you toughen up at this stage, you'll get nowhere.

Step 2 should work. The steamroller might even be ashamed and apologize. If he does, accept the gesture graciously, then return to the original issue and deal with it. Say, "Let's go back to the beginning. Your challenge, as I understand it, is this: [repeat the question]. Now, here is how I'd like to respond."

This second step is effective at taming even the most belligerent steamroller. Don't be snippy or smug. Stay focused, stay pleasant, stay gracious, but stay in the driver's seat.

If this doesn't work, go immediately to step 3.

Step 3: Leave Him

First you stop him, then you shame him. If that doesn't work, you leave him. When all else fails, let it go. Walk away. If the steamroller won't let you answer, listen politely until he's finished, then drop it. Let him have the satisfaction of having the last word, then shake the dust off your feet and move on. Wisdom dictates not wasting time with this kind of person.

> When I face an aggressive challenger, I often give him the last word. Not only is this gracious, it's also powerful, conveying a deep sense of confidence in one's own view. Instead of fighting for the final say-so, give it away. Make your concluding point clearly and succinctly, then say, "I'll let you have the last word." But don't break this promise. Grant him his parting shot, and then let it rest.

This last step is dictated by a simple bit of insight: not everyone deserves an answer. This may sound odd at first. Characteristically, an ambassador is always ready, alert for any chance to represent Christ, not backing away from a challenge or an opportunity. Sometimes, though, the wisest course of action may be to bow out graciously.

Jesus warned, "Do not give what is holy to dogs, and do not throw your pearls before swine" (Matt. 7:6). He followed his own advice too. Jesus was amazingly tight-lipped before Pilate; he "gave him no answer" (John 19:9). At times, he was also evasive with religious leaders intent on tricking him: "Neither will I tell you by what authority I do these things" (Matt. 21:27).

Knowing when to step back requires the ability to separate the dogs and the hogs from the lost sheep looking for a shepherd.

But how do you know when someone has crossed the line? When do we have an obligation to speak, and when should we save our pearls for another time?

Part of the answer can be found in Jesus' next words in Matthew 7:6: "or they will trample [the pearls] under their feet, and turn and tear you to pieces." Be generous with the truth, except with someone who shows utter contempt for the precious gift being offered. He will simply trample it in the mud and then viciously turn on you.

If you sense someone pawing the turf and readying for a charge, it may be time to leave. Don't waste your efforts on people like this. Save your energy for more productive encounters. Say something like:

- "It seems to me this conversation is not going in a productive direction. I'm going to let you have the last word, and then I'm moving on."
- "I'm having a hard time getting my point across, so I'm going to just let this go for now. Thanks for your thoughts."

Of course, there are times when you will find yourself in a Jeremiah situation—being faithful to speak the truth even though it falls on deaf ears. But those occasions are not the rule. Usually, wisdom dictates we ration our efforts.

There is an exception to this principle, however. I have learned from my radio show that sometimes my real audience is not the person I'm talking to but the people who are listening in, eavesdropping on the conversation.

This happens more often than you may think, even if you are not a radio host. Sometimes a word spoken to a hardened heart bounces off and hits a soft one. You may not even know that anyone else is listening. Years later, you discover that the Holy Spirit had a different audience in mind for your efforts. This has happened to me a number of times. Lee Strobel calls this "ricochet evangelism."

Dealing with a steamroller is rarely a smooth and tidy enterprise.

When you encounter abuse, don't take it personally. It's not about you. It's about Christ. When you falter, don't get discouraged with the process. I get caught flat-footed too sometimes. Take it as a learning experience for the next time around.

The principle? Make the best of the opportunities you have, then trust the Holy Spirit to be the witnessing partner who makes the difference. You do your part, then let God do his.

WHAT WE LEARNED IN THIS CHAPTER

In this chapter, we discovered that there is more than one reason why a person might reject our thoughtful arguments. There is nothing magical about a sound line of logic. For some people, reason doesn't matter. Some other barrier stands in the way.

Sometimes people have emotional reasons for resisting. Bad experiences with Christians or with churches, or pressures from family or culture, are enough to blind a person to our appeals. Others balk because of prejudice. They never really consider our message, because their minds are already made up. Finally, for many people the best explanation for their resistance is simple rebellion. The fundamental problem with most people is that they do not want to bend the knee to their Sovereign.

Finally, we learned how to recognize and restrain a steamroller. Steamrollers overpower you with strong personalities and interrupt constantly. I suggested three steps to manage a steamroller and regain control of the conversation. Step 1, stop the interruption graciously but firmly, then briefly negotiate an agreement. Step 2, shame him by making a direct request for courtesy. Step 3, leave. Never match a steamroller's incivility with rudeness. Instead let him have the last word, then calmly let it go.

Chapter 15

RHODES SCHOLAR

If you read magazines like *Time* or *Newsweek*, you might have noticed a trend. Just before Easter and Christmas, these publications often feature cover stories about the history behind these two central events on the Christian calendar. The articles have provocative titles like "What *Really* Happened to the Body of Jesus" or "The Untold Truth about the First Christmas."

Generally, the authors take a "what scholars say that your pastor does not want you to know" approach. They cite academics who use a "scientific" approach to history to expose the false notions held by the foolish faithful.

INFORMED OR EDUCATED?

Cover stories like these sell lots of magazines. They also discourage lots of Christians. Some wonder why these academic "facts" have been kept from them. Others don't know what to believe. They don't want to abandon their convictions, but they cannot in good conscience dismiss what appears to be the consensus of academic opinion simply because they don't like what they hear.

In situations like these, a tactic I call Rhodes Scholar is invaluable. It provides a way of assessing whether an appeal to an authority is legitimate or not. The tactic hinges on the difference between informing and educating. When an article tells you *what* a scholar believes, you have been informed. When an article tells you *why* he holds his view, you have been educated.

Here is why this distinction is so important. If you recall from chapter 5, an argument is like a house whose roof (what a person believes) is supported by walls (the reasons why he believes). You cannot know if the reasons are adequate to the conclusions—if the walls are strong enough to hold the roof—unless you know what those reasons are. If you know the reasons, you can assess their strength. Without them, you have no way of knowing if the conclusions are sound.

Popular articles always inform, but they do not always educate. As a result, you can't evaluate a scholar's conclusion. You simply have to take his word for it. But scholars can be wrong and often are. Their reasoning can be weak, their "facts" can be mistaken, and their biases can distort their judgment.

ASSESSING THE ACADEMICS

How do you find out if an authority has been compromised? Here's how. Regardless of a scholar's credentials, don't settle for opinions. Instead always ask for reasons. This is the key to Rhodes Scholar.

This tactic protects you from being victimized by a common error called the fallacy of expert witness. There is nothing wrong with appealing to authority, but it must be done in the right way. You must ask, "Why should I believe this person's opinion?" There are two ways to answer this question.

First, the scholar may be in a special position to know the facts. However, if an authority is in possession of special information that guides his counsel, then he should be able to point to that evidence to convince us he's on the mark.

Sometimes "authorities" give opinions that are outside of their area of expertise, though. When California passed its controversial embryonic stem cell research initiative, twenty Nobel laureates backed the measure. Only four were listed by name and discipline. I looked carefully at their comments.

One, a professor of biology and physiology, assured voters that the measure was ethical. Another, a specialist in cancer research, said the legislation would boost California's economy and have a salutary impact on health care costs. An Alzheimer's research director promised new jobs and increased revenues for state coffers.

As I scanned the comments and credentials, it occurred to me that a Nobel Prize in biology, chemistry, or medicine does not qualify a person to render sound counsel on economics or ethics. The appeal by these scholars, then, missed the mark because the principal objections to embryonic stem cell research are moral, not scientific or economic.

> Having twenty Nobel Prize winners on one's side may awe voters, but that fact alone does not legitimize the cause. You and I need more information before we can trust their endorsements.

Even when scholars speak within their field of expertise, they still owe us an accounting based on sound reasons. In a court of law, the expert witness is always cross-examined. Credentials alone are not enough to certify his testimony; he must convince a jury that his reasons are adequate. "All appeals to authority ultimately rest on the evidence that the authority has," Norm Geisler says. "The letters after his name don't mean a thing without the evidence to back up his position."[1]

There's a second way the Rhodes Scholar query, "Why should I believe this person's opinion?" can be answered. Sometimes a scholar is in a unique position to render a judgment. More than mere facts are in play here. Interpretation and professional assessment are factors.

In this circumstance, you face another pitfall. A scholar's judgment may be distorted by underlying philosophical considerations that are not always on the table. Note this critique of pluralist[2] John Hick's selective use of scholarship: "Hick seems intent on deciding questions of great spiritual significance by counting scholarly noses . . . without reminding readers that many of these scholars presuppose a picture of the world that excludes the possibility of divine intervention in the world."[3]

The point philosopher Douglas Geivett makes here is that sometimes one's destination is predetermined by where one starts. If a scholar begins an investigation convinced that miracles cannot happen, it will be difficult for him to conclude that something supernatural has taken place, even when there is overwhelming evidence in favor of it.

This problem is especially evident in science, where subjects like the origin of the universe (cosmology) or the origin and development of life (Darwinism) have worldview implications. The temptation is great to simply "count scholarly noses" without taking into consideration the powerful philosophical paradigm that dictates what kinds of conclusions are acceptable.

TWO FACES OF SCIENCE

Whenever you hear the complaint, "Intelligent design is not science," a subtle philosophical sleight of hand is in play. The charge capitalizes on an ambiguity between two different definitions of science.

The first definition is the most well-known. Science is a methodology—employing various tools like observation, experimentation, testing, and the like—that allows researchers to discover facts about the physical world. Thus any view that is not based on the right methodology is not a scientific view.

The second definition of science involves a philosophy—specifically, the philosophy of naturalistic materialism. All phenomena must be explained in terms of matter and energy governed by natural law. Any view that does not conform to this second definition is also not science.

There are two requirements, then, for an investigation of the natural world to qualify as scientific, according to current standards. First, one must use the right method—the scientific method.[4] Second, one must come up with the right kinds of answers—those consistent with a naturalistic, physicalistic, materialistic view of the world. Usually, these two requirements are not in conflict. Good methods produce answers in accord with matter in motion governed by natural law.

Sometimes, though, the evidence points in a different direction. The origin of life, for example, and the incredible biological diversity of the living world[5] consistently defy any naturalistic explanation. Instead powerful and persuasive empirical evidence points to design. This creates a problem for naturalists that is "solved" by trading on the ambiguity between these two definitions.

The "intelligent design is not science" charge appears at first to be directed at the methodology. Presumably, the reason evolution does qualify as a scientific enterprise and intelligent design doesn't is that Darwinists use the right methods and ID researchers do not (the facts of science inveigh against the faith of intelligent design). Thus (the assumption is) ID is no more science than astrology is.

This claim is a colossal distortion of the actual situation, though. First, a mountain of factual data has emerged in the last twenty years casting serious doubt on the entire Darwinian project, in spite of the clear suppression of such information by the larger academic community.[6] Second, ID researchers follow the exact same broad methodology as Darwinists, so their work is no less scientific in that sense than any other scientific pursuit. The real problem for naturalists is that ID researchers infer different conclusions from the same scientific evidence.

Enter the sleight of hand: When there is a conflict between the findings of the scientific method and the requirements of materialistic philosophy, the philosophy always trumps the findings. Modern science does not conclude from the evidence that design is not tenable. It assumes this prior to the evidence.[7] Any scientific methodology (first definition of science) that points to intelligent design is summarily disqualified by scientific philosophy (second definition of science) as "religion disguised as science."

> At first blush, it seems as if Darwinism is about scientific facts. But when facts suggest intelligent design, the second definition of science is immediately invoked to label design as unscientific.

Douglas Futuyma, author of a classic college evolutionary biology textbook, says, "Where science *insists on material, mechanistic causes* that can be understood by physics and chemistry, the literal believer in Genesis invokes *unknowable supernatural forces.*"[8]

Those who believe in intelligent design, however, claim that these forces are knowable, at least in principle. Consider this analogy. When a dead body is discovered, an impartial investigation might indicate foul play and not an accident. If the body is bullet-ridden, chances are the death was not a result of natural causes. In the same way, scientific evidence could, in principle, indicate an agent in creation rather than chance. This is not faith versus evidence but evidence versus consensus.

Clearly, the materialist paradigm is paramount, and everything must be done to save it. Harvard genetics professor Richard Lewontin was amazingly candid about this fact. In the *New York Review of Books*, he made this stunning admission.

> Our willingness to accept scientific claims that are against common sense is the key to an understanding of the real struggle between science and the supernatural. We take the side of science *in spite of* the patent absurdity of some of its constructs . . . *in spite of* the tolerance of the scientific community for unsubstantiated just-so stories,[9] because we have a prior commitment, a commitment to materialism. It is not that the methods and institutions of science somehow compel us to accept a material explanation of the phenomenal world, but, on the contrary, that we are forced by our a priori adherence to material causes to create

an apparatus of investigation and a set of concepts that produce material explanations, no matter how counterintuitive, no matter how mystifying to the uninitiated. Moreover, that materialism is absolute, for we cannot allow a Divine Foot in the door.[10]

Here Lewontin admits that the apparatus of science is geared not to find the truth, whatever it may be, but rather to produce philosophically acceptable answers. He openly admits that the game has been rigged.

Most who hold this prejudice are not so candid. The majority—confident their convictions rest on scientific fact, not materialist philosophy—are not even aware of any problem. They show their hand, however, with telltale responses like, "Intelligent design is not science," or, "ID is religion disguised as science."

These comments should always trigger questions: "What specifically disqualifies ID as science?" or, "Why dismiss the idea of design before you look at the evidence?" Invariably, your Rhodes Scholar probing will reveal the real reason behind the rejection: bias, not fact. Intelligent design of any sort is not the right kind of answer.

THE "HISTORICAL" JESUS

Science is not the only field where the game has been rigged. In the beginning of this chapter, I mentioned that this approach has also been applied to the Gospels. Whenever someone uses the word scientific to describe the way they look at history, they are signaling that materialistic philosophy governs the process.

Scholars from this school try to distinguish the "Jesus of history" from the miracle-working "Jesus of faith." They assume, of course, that there is a difference between the two. Why make this distinction?

In academics, everyone has a starting point. The place where many scholars begin is not always clear to the public, but it's critical to understanding and evaluating their conclusions. Magazine stories about Easter are quick to point out that most scholars reject the resurrection. But why do they reject it? A closer examination reveals their starting point. In a materialistic view of the universe, resurrections do not happen. Therefore any report of a corpse walking out of a tomb after three days must be a myth added to the records years later, regardless of any evidence to the contrary.

The late Robert Funk, formerly with a group of liberal biblical scholars known as the Jesus Seminar, made this clear: "The Gospels are now *assumed* to be narratives in which the memory of Jesus is *embellished* by mythic elements that express the church's faith in him, and by *plausible fictions* that enhance the telling of the gospel story for first-century listeners."[11]

The reasoning often goes something like this: The Gospels contain fabrications because they record events that are inconsistent with a scientific (materialistic) view of the world. Resurrection accounts, then, must be myth. Furthermore, if Jesus predicts an event that comes to pass decades after his death (the destruction of the Jewish temple in AD 70, for example), this must have been added after the event occurred, since prophecy (a kind of miraculous knowledge) is impossible. Since myths like this take time to develop, the Gospels must have been written late and could not be eyewitness accounts.

Notice the significance of the starting point. When an academic begins with naturalism, a series of "facts" fall into place before any genuine historical analysis begins: the resurrection is an invention; the miracles are myths; there is no prophecy in the Bible; the Gospels were written long after the events took place and not by eyewitnesses. Starting with one's conclusions, though, is cheating. Nothing has been proved; everything has only been assumed.

Using the Rhodes Scholar tactic—asking for the scholar's reasons, not just his credentials—helps us flush out both the facts and the philosophy that may be corrupting the interpretation of the facts. This allows us to assess the scholar's opinion for ourselves rather than simply having to take his view on faith.

Remember, reasons are more important than votes. If the reasoning is bad—if the "facts" are false or the judgments are tainted by philosophical bias—it doesn't matter if multitudes share the same opinion; the view is still compromised.

NOT ALL BIAS IS EQUAL

Can the charge of bias be leveled at Christians? Certainly, and sometimes the charge is justified. Whenever someone has already taken sides on an issue, it is possible he has not been evenhanded in his analysis.

It is not fair, though, to assume someone has distorted the facts simply because he has a stake in the matter. People who are not neutral can still be fair and impartial. If you think there has been distorting bias, you have to demonstrate it by looking carefully at the evidence itself.

A mom may think her high school daughter is brilliant. You might dismiss the claim as overly partial since her mom has a bias. But if the student maxed out her SATs, her mom also has a point. Clearly, not all forms of bias distort.

When a Christian deals with issues like science and history, it's fair to say he's biased in the sense that he brings certain assumptions to the process, just like everyone else. A Christian's bias, though, does not inform his conclusions the same way that biases inform the conclusions of scientists or historians restricted by a commitment to materialism.

The current bias of science is a bias that distorts, in many cases, because it illicitly eliminates certain answers before the game gets started. Many scientists and historians must come up with conclusions that leave a supernatural agent out of the picture—even when evidence points in that direction—because their philosophy demands it.

A theist is not so encumbered. She believes in the laws of nature but also is open to the possibility of supernatural intervention. Both are consistent with her worldview. She can judge the evidence on its own merits, unhindered by a philosophy that automatically eliminates divine intervention before giving the evidence an even-handed hearing.

Ironically, the Christian's bias broadens her categories, making her more open-minded, not less. She has a greater chance of discovering truth, because she can follow the evidence wherever it leads. That's a critical distinction. Can bias make a person open-minded? Under the right set of circumstances, absolutely.[12]

Ultimately, the issue isn't bias but distortion. It's unsound to say that because the gospel writers were Christians, their testimony cannot be trusted. Conversely, a nonbeliever's conclusions should not be dismissed because he is not among the faithful. In both cases, we have to look at the reasons themselves. This is the heart of Rhodes Scholar.

WHAT WE LEARNED IN THIS CHAPTER

The Rhodes Scholar tactic gives us a tool to use when someone invokes scholarly opinion against our view. It protects us from a common error called the fallacy of expert witness.

On one hand, appealing to scholarly opinion is a legitimate way to make a point. Sometimes an expert is in a unique position to know the facts or to render a judgment. On the other hand, experts are not always right. Be on the lookout for appeals to scholarship that are misapplied.

Sometimes authorities weigh in outside of their area of expertise. Other times, they get their facts wrong. Often philosophical bias distorts their judgment. The key to Rhodes Scholar is getting past the opinion of a scholar and probing the reasons for his opinion. This is the difference between being informed and being educated.

Whether an alleged expert is offering facts or judgments, always ask for an accounting. How did he come to his conclusions? What are the facts, specifically? Are there any biases that seem to be distorting the assessment? With the reasons on the table, you are in a better position to judge whether a scholar's conclusions are sound.

Don't be shaken by academic appeals. What an expert believes is not as important as why he believes it. Fancy credentials are not enough. What matters most are the reasons, not merely the opinions.

Chapter 16

JUST THE FACTS, MA'AM

There is an old TV police drama called *Dragnet* that you may have heard of but probably have never seen unless you watch reruns—really old reruns. Two lines from *Dragnet* are still remembered to this day. The first is, "The names have been changed to protect the innocent." The second is, "Just the facts, ma'am," Detective Joe Friday's trademark request of whomever he questioned as a witness.

Just the Facts, Ma'am is an easy tactic to use. It requires no cleverness or deft maneuvering. Only two things are necessary.

The first is an awareness that many challenges to Christianity are based on bad information. These objections can be overcome by a simple appeal to the facts. Syndicated talk show host Dennis Prager tells his callers, "First tell the truth, then give your opinion." His point: an opinion is only as good as the information it's based on. Bad information results in bad opinions.

The second requirement is that you need to know the facts. If you do, you can beat the objection. This is not an absolute requirement for this tactic, because sometimes you can spot a wrong answer even though you don't know the right one. But knowing the right answer is central to using Just the Facts, Ma'am, and often that information is just a few keystrokes away.

RELIGION KILLS?

Let me give you an example of a popular challenge to Christianity that is not based on fact, though many think it is. The protest goes something like this: "Religion is the greatest source of evil in the world. More wars have been fought and more blood has been shed in the name of God than for any other cause."

This myth is likely the most widely believed urban legend about religion. Atheist Christopher Hitchens's popular attack on theism is titled *God Is Not Great: How Religion Poisons Everything*.[1] Fellow atheist Sam Harris trades on the same fiction in *The End of Faith: Religion, Terror, and the Future of Reason*. Religious faith, he writes, is "the most prolific source of violence in our history."[2]

Now, one might point out that even if this were the case, it is not entirely clear what conclusions about religion would be justified from that data. One couldn't properly conclude that God does not exist or that Jesus is not the Savior or that the Bible is not reliable, simply by citing acts of violence done in the name of God or Christ.

> Since oppression and mayhem are neither religious duties for Christians nor logical applications of the teachings of Jesus, violence done in the name of Christ cannot be laid at his door. This conduct might tell you something about people. It tells you nothing about God or the gospel.

So there are logical problems with this complaint—it doesn't nullify any particular claim of any particular religion, especially Christianity—but the bigger problem is that this charge is simply not true. Though it is easy to characterize religion as a bloodthirsty enterprise replete with witch hunts, crusades, and jihads, the facts paint a different picture. Religion has not caused more wars and bloodshed than anything else in history.

In their massive, three-volume *Encyclopedia of Wars*, researchers Charles Phillips and Alan Axelrod show that of the 1,763 wars they chronicle over the last five millennia, only 123—less than 7 percent—were motivated by religion.[3] And religion played no part in the two greatest military conflagrations in history—World War I, with 16.5 million dead, and World War II, with 60 to 80 million perishing.

The historical facts show that significantly greater evil has resulted from denial of God than from pursuit of God. In the twentieth century alone, Dennis Prager notes, "more innocent people have been murdered, tortured, and enslaved by secular ideologies—Nazism and communism—than by all religions in history."[4]

Grab an older copy of the *Guinness Book of World Records* and turn to the category "Judicial," subheading "Crimes: Mass Killings." You'll find that carnage of unimaginable proportions resulted not from religion but from institutionalized atheism: more than 66 million Soviets wiped out under the communist leadership of Lenin, Stalin, and Khrushchev; between 32 million and 61 million Chinese killed under communist regimes since 1949; one-third of the 8 million Khmers—2.7 million people—killed between 1975 and 1979 under the communist Khmer Rouge.[5]

> The greatest evil has not come from people zealous for God. It has come from people who are convinced there is no God they must answer to.

The correlation between high body count and atheistic totalitarianism is not an accident. I presume Mr. Harris locks his doors at night, but it's not because he's concerned about deeply religious people in his neighborhood. People who care what God thinks characteristically control their behavior because they are convinced God is watching. Atheists have no such concern, so atheists with significant power have no such constraint.

I certainly am not suggesting that all atheists promote the kind of genocide I've described. Most oppose it. I am saying, though, that there is a natural kinship between particular worldviews and behaviors that logically follow from them. No, atheism doesn't dictate genocide. The worldview allows it, though. No moral principle inherent to atheism prohibits it, simply because there are no moral principles inherent to atheism to begin with.

Ironically, in his warning about the risks of religious belief, Sam Harris makes both of my points simultaneously—one, there is a kinship between dangerous ideas and dangerous conduct, and two, the dangerous idea of atheism easily gives way to deadly oppression. Listen: "The link between belief and behavior raises the stakes considerably [point 1]. Some propositions are so dangerous that it may be ethical to kill people for believing them [point 2].... There is, in fact, no talking to some people. If they cannot be captured, and they often cannot, otherwise tolerant people may be justified in killing them in self-defense."[6]

Kill people as an act of self-defense simply for their religious beliefs? You see what I'm getting at.[7] Though Christopher Hitchens titled his chapter on religious violence "Religion Kills," the simple fact is that nonreligion kills too—more often, more efficiently, and in greater numbers.

PRECISION IS PERSUASIVE

I want you to notice something about the facts I cited in the examples about conflict caused by secular ideologies. They were as precise as I could make them without being cumbersome. I gave specific details with exact numbers and clear-cut dates. Precision is an important element of Just the Facts, Ma'am because of a basic principle of persuasion: when citing facts in your defense, precise claims are always more persuasive than general ones.

Though your memory may not always be up to the task (mine certainly isn't), try to use specific information rather than general references whenever you can. When you communicate with factual precision, you convince your listeners that you know what you're talking about. Saying, "Thousands died in the terrorist attacks of 9/11," is not as compelling as saying that "2,977 human beings were buried beneath the rubble of the World Trade Center and the Pentagon, and entombed in the field in Pennsylvania, on September 11, 2001." Each bit of precision—the number 2,977; the date September 11, 2001; the locations of the attacks—adds force to your facts. It may take longer to say it, but with proper delivery it is much more compelling.

This kind of exactness can be a powerful persuader. I was once involved in a head-to-head encounter of sorts with Pulitzer Prize–winning historian Garry Wills before San Francisco's liberal Commonwealth Club, an encounter that was taped for national broadcast on NPR. In his opening salvo on the topic "Christianity in America," Professor Wills disputed the idea that the Founding Fathers of our republic were Christians. They were not Christians, he claimed, but deists.

The microphone was then passed to me. Fortunately, I had specific details at hand to make my point. "The phrase 'Founding Fathers' is a proper noun," I explained. "It refers to a specific group: the delegates to the Constitutional Convention. There were other important players not in attendance, but these fifty-five made up the core." I then cited from memory, as best I could, the following facts, which are a matter of public record: Among the delegates were twenty-eight Episcopalians, eight Presbyterians, seven Congregationalists, two Lutherans, two Dutch Reformed, two Methodists, two Roman Catholics, one unknown, and only three deists—Williamson, Wilson, and Franklin. The convention took place at a time when church membership usually entailed "sworn adherence to strict doctrinal creeds."[8]

This tally proves that fifty-one of the fifty-five members of the Constitutional Convention—virtually 93 percent of the most influential group of men shaping the political underpinnings of our nation—were Christians,[9] not deists.[10]

> Virtually every person involved in the founding enterprise of the United States was a Protestant whose denominational affiliation would be characterized in today's terms as evangelical or even fundamentalist.

When I was finished, I set my microphone down and waited, bracing for the rebuttal from my learned opponent. But he said nothing. After a few moments of awkward silence, the moderator moved on to a new topic. Dr. Wills had his facts wrong. Mine were not only correct but also precise, adding tremendous persuasive power to my rebuttal.

FOLLOWING A PLAN

Challenges to Christianity that fail because of faulty facts may seem difficult to spot at first, especially if you are not well versed in the issue in question. But the task becomes much easier if you have a plan, a series of steps to guide your effort. For Just the Facts, Ma'am, I use the same two-step plan whether I am having a conversation or doing a detailed analysis of a book or article.

First ask, "What is the claim?" This may seem like an obvious initial step, but you'll be surprised at how often we charge ahead without having a clear fix on a target. Take a moment to isolate the precise point being made (your first Columbo question helps here). Write it down in unambiguous terms if you need to. Sometimes the claim is clear, but not always. Assertions are often implicit or hidden under a layer of rhetoric and linguistic maneuvering. Pay careful attention to get an accurate sense of what the person is asserting.

A piece written by a student in a university newspaper claimed that pro-lifers have no right to oppose abortion unless they are willing to care for the children born to mothers in crisis pregnancies. Notice that the author was making two assertions here.

The first was the obvious moral point, which was easily dispatched. In my written response to the paper, I pointed out that it simply does not follow that because a person objects to killing innocent children, he is obliged to care for those who survive. Imagine how bizarre it would sound to argue, "You have no right to stop me from beating my wife unless you're willing to marry her." Clearly, the offender is not off the hook simply because others won't step in to take his place.

Implicit in the challenge, though, was a second assertion: the claim that pro-lifers are not doing anything for pregnant women who carry their babies to term. Thus the student felt justified in criticizing the pro-life movement.

This brings us to the second step of our plan. Once the assertion is clear, ask, "Is the claim factually accurate?" Sometimes answering this question takes a little investigation.

A short trip to the internet revealed that at that time there were roughly four thousand national and international pro-life service providers dedicated to the well-being of mothers in crisis pregnancies who choose life for their children. They provide medical aid, housing, baby clothing, cribs, food, help with adoption, even post-abortion counseling services—all at no cost. Amazingly, there were more crisis pregnancy centers in the country than abortion clinics. A quick check of the local phone directory showed there were ten such centers right in the same city as the university. In my response, I pointed out each of these details to show that besides being flawed in its reasoning, the student's objection had no factual basis.

CRACKING THE CODE

I followed my two-step plan when evaluating the historical claims of the blockbuster novel *The Da Vinci Code*, whose broadside on Christianity and the Bible created a public sensation and tremendous turmoil for Christians a number of years ago.

First, I isolated the claims. The author, Dan Brown, made it simple in most cases by stating his contentions clearly.[11] Here are some of them.

- In the first three centuries, the warring between Christians and pagans threatened to rend Rome in two.
- The doctrine that Jesus is the Son of God was fabricated for political reasons at the Council of Nicaea in AD 325 and affirmed by a close vote.

- Constantine arranged for all Gospels depicting Jesus as a mere mortal to be gathered up and destroyed.
- The Dead Sea Scrolls found in a cave near Qumran in the 1950s confirm the fabrication.
- Thousands of Christ's followers wrote accounts of Jesus' life. These evolved through countless translations, additions, and revisions. History has never had a definitive version.[12]

Because I now had specific items to assess, my job was much easier. The first challenge was simple. Even a cursory analysis of this period of history reveals there were no wars between pagans and Christians, and for a very good reason. Jesus' followers had neither armies nor the will to resist. Instead they considered it a privilege to be martyred for Christ. They wouldn't even fight tormentors like Diocletian, who executed Christians by the thousands just twenty years before Constantine.

The Council of Nicaea was not an obscure event in history. We have extensive records of the proceedings, written by those who were actually there: Eusebius of Caesarea and Athanasius, deacon of Alexandria. Two things stand out in those accounts that pertain to Brown's claims. First, no one at Nicaea considered Jesus to be a mere mortal, not even Arius, whose errant views made the council necessary. Everyone in the discussion believed Jesus was the Son of God. They disagreed on what that title meant. Consequently, the question of Christ's deity was the reason for the council, not merely the result of it.

After a pitched debate, the final vote wasn't close at all; it was a landslide. Of 318 bishops, only 2—the Egyptians Theonas and Secundus—refused to concur.[13] The council affirmed what had been taught since the beginning. Jesus was not a mere man; he was God the Son.

Regarding the famous Dead Sea Scrolls, Brown might be forgiven for not getting the date right (the first scrolls were discovered in the 1940s, not the 1950s). There is no excuse, however, for another misstep: the Dead Sea Scrolls say nothing of Jesus. There were no Gospels in Qumran. Not one shred or shard mentions his name. Brown's assertion is a complete fabrication.

As for the rest of the claims, I want to let you in on a little secret. Answering the second question—"Is the claim factually accurate?"— does not always require investigation. I mentioned earlier that sometimes it is possible to spot a wrong answer even when you do not know the right one. Here's how.

Before beginning any research, first ask, "Does anything about the assertion seem suspicious or unlikely on its face?" For example, early in *The Da Vinci Code*, Brown claims that over a period of three hundred years, the Catholic Church burned five million witches at the stake in Europe around the fifteenth century.[14] I was immediately suspicious of this "fact," so I took out my calculator and did the math. Rome would have to burn forty-five women a day, every single day, nonstop for three hundred years. That's a lot of firewood.

Furthermore, a quick internet search revealed that the population of Europe at the time was about 50 million. If half were female (25 million) and half of those were adults (12.5 million), then something like 40 percent of the entire adult female population perished at the hand of the Vatican. That's more carnage than the Black Plague of 1347, which killed only one-third. Let's just say this seems highly unlikely.

Many of Dan Brown's other claims can be quickly dispatched using the same technique.

- If the deity of Christ was an idea invented by Constantine and foreign to Christ's followers, who viewed him as a mere mortal, what explains the "close vote" at Nicaea?
- If the early records of Jesus' life are so corrupted and compromised with "countless translations, additions, and revisions," and if "history has never had a definitive version," from where does Brown derive his reliable, authentic, unimpeachable biographical information about Jesus?

- How does Brown know that thousands of Jesus' followers wrote accounts of his life, if the great bulk of these records was destroyed? This is the classic problem for conspiracy theorists. If all the evidence was eradicated, how do they know it was there in the first place?
- How was it physically possible for Constantine to gather up all of the handwritten copies from every nook and cranny of the Roman Empire in the fourth century and destroy the vast majority of them?

Each of these difficulties becomes obvious when you take a moment to ask if anything about the claim seems suspicious or implausible on its face. Granted, sometimes unlikely things turn out to be true. When that's the case, though, the evidence has to be clear and convincing. Usually, this question can save you some sleuthing.

Whatever the latest bestseller criticizing Christianity happens to be at the moment, use our two steps to do your own evaluation of its assertions.

ABORTION AND HOMICIDE

Here's another challenge that can be overcome by a simple appeal to facts. Some denounce the use of the word murder to describe abortion. Yet this language is consistent with the laws in nearly two-thirds of the states in the Union, at least in one regard. In the California statutes, under the category "Crimes against the Person," §187, murder is defined this way: "Murder is the unlawful killing of a human being, *or a fetus*, with malice aforethought" (emphasis added). After the definition, we find among the exceptions: "This section shall not apply to any person who commits an act which results in the death of a fetus if . . . the act was solicited, aided, abetted, or consented to by the mother of the fetus."

This exception in the California statute is troubling. The moral principle underlying all homicide statutes is that human beings have innate worth. Value is not derived from something outside of the individual; it is intrinsic to who they are. That's why destroying a human being is the most serious of crimes.

If the intrinsic value of unborn human beings qualifies them for protection under homicide statutes, why is something extrinsic—like the mother's choice—relevant? How does the mere consent of the mother change the innate value of the little human being inside her?

> Fetal homicide statutes like California's are odd because the only difference between legal abortion and punishable homicide is the consent of the mother.

However one answers this question, two facts remain. One, abortion is legal in states like California. Two, apart from the stipulated exceptions, killing the unborn is homicide. Those who do so have been prosecuted for murder.

On the use of the word murder to describe abortion, then, pro-lifers are not extreme. Labeling abortion that way may not always be rhetorically wise, but it is not inaccurate. It agrees with the rationale of the statutes of the majority of states in this country: unborn children are valuable human beings due the same protection as the rest of us. The problem is not with pro-life "rhetoric" but with inconsistent laws.

JUST THE CONTEXT, MA'AM

Resolving a challenge by appealing to the facts works with scriptural issues too. Here's an example. I have been asked why God prohibits killing in the Ten Commandments but then commands killing when the Jews take Canaan. That sounds like a contradiction.

The "contradiction" is dispatched by pointing out a simple fact. The sixth commandment does not read, "You shall not kill," but rather, "You shall not murder" (Ex. 20:13). There are different words for each in Hebrew just as in English, for a good reason. There is a moral distinction between justified killing (killing in self-defense, for example) and unjustified killing (murder). God prohibits the second, not the first. The scriptural facts show there is no contradiction.

In my debate with New Age author Deepak Chopra, he made an unusual statement about the text of the New Testament. He claimed that the King James Version was the eighteenth or nineteenth iteration of the Bible since the year 313. This comment reflected, I think, the idea many people have that the New Testament has gone through a series of translations and retranslations—"iterations"—before finally settling into the English versions we have today.

A simple appeal to the facts was all I needed to dispatch Dr. Chopra's challenge. All current English translations of the Bible start with manuscripts written in the original language—Greek, in the case of the New Testament—which are then translated directly into English. Instead of multiple iterations, there is only one step in language from the original Greek to our English versions.[15]

Here's another example of applying Just the Facts, Ma'am to a Bible passage that is almost universally misunderstood: "Do not judge so that you will not be judged" (Matt. 7:1). This is a verse everybody knows and quotes when convenient, even though they do not care about less convenient things the Bible has to say on other issues. Jesus qualified this command, though, in a way that most do not: "Why do you look at the speck that is in your brother's eye, but do not notice the log that is in your own eye? . . . You hypocrite, first take the log out of your own eye, and then you will see clearly to take the speck out of your brother's eye" (Matt. 7:3, 5).

A closer look at the facts of the context shows that Jesus did not condemn all judgments, only hypocritical ones—arrogant condemnations characterized by disdain and condescension. Not all judgments are of this sort, though, so not all judgments are condemned. In this passage, Jesus encourages a different sort of judgment once the hypocrisy has been dealt with: "*First* take the log out of your own eye, and *then* you will see clearly to take the speck out of your brother's eye" (emphasis added).

There are two other kinds of judging that are commanded in Scripture.

Judgments that are judicial in nature are proper when done by the proper authorities. Judges judge. They pass sentence. That's their job. Church discipline is of this sort.[16] Paul specifically commands us to judge believers. God will judge the world in his time (1 Cor. 5:12–13). Jesus himself did not come initially for this kind of judgment—he offered mercy, not justice—but he will certainly return with this kind of judgment, since he was appointed by the Father for that task.[17]

Judgments that are assessments—appraisals of right or wrong, wise or foolish, accurate or inaccurate, rational or irrational—are also commanded. Jesus' instructions in that same passage, "Do not give what is holy to dogs" (Matt. 7:6), require this kind of evaluation (What is holy? Who are the dogs?). Peter reminds us to "be of sound judgment," since "the end of all things is near" (1 Peter 4:7).

Some assessments are moral. Paul commands this kind of judgment in some circumstances: "Do not participate in the unfruitful deeds of darkness, but instead even expose them" (Eph. 5:11). Jesus said to make such assessments not "according to appearance" but by "righteous" standards (John 7:24). He chastised the Jews for their failures here: "Why do you not even on your own initiative judge what is right?" (Luke 12:57).

A judicial action, a factual assessment, a hypocritical condemnation—all are judgments. Only the third is disqualified by Jesus. The first two are virtues in their proper settings and are therefore commanded by Scripture. Those are the scriptural facts.

WHAT WE LEARNED IN THIS CHAPTER

As you can see, many who challenge Christianity base their case on misinformation or error. They simply have their facts wrong. Just the Facts, Ma'am is a maneuver you can use to help determine when this is happening. In this chapter, we learned how to apply the two-step approach of this tactic.

Whenever a challenge to your view is based on an alleged factual claim ("More blood has been shed in the name of religion than for anything else," or, "America's Founding Fathers were deists"), first ask, "What is the precise claim?" These two examples are clear, but sometimes assertions are hidden. Separate the precise point or points from the rest of the rhetoric. Ask questions to make sure you know what the person is alleging. This step is the same as the first step of Columbo.

Next, ask yourself if the claims are accurate. There are two ways to find mistakes. The internet is the most convenient place to do quick research.[18] Once you have isolated specific claims, verification is often a few keystrokes away. You may also have reference books or informed friends you can turn to for help.

You might save some time, though, by asking a different question before you start your sleuthing: "Does anything about the claim seem unlikely or implausible on its face?" If a dentist claims he has filled half a million cavities in his twenty-year career, you know he's confused. Just do the math.

Now, armed with the facts, you will be ready to address your friend's concerns. Keep in mind that when citing facts in your defense, precision is always more persuasive than generalities.

Listen and read critically, reflect on the claims, and check the background information. First tell the truth, then give your opinion. Like Detective Joe Friday, always say, "Just the facts, ma'am."

Chapter 17

INSIDE OUT

Years back, I lectured to a capacity crowd at the University of California at Berkeley. I made the case against moral relativism simply by pointing out how every day of our lives, we each encounter and ultimately violate genuine, deep morality.

This discovery, I noted to the audience, had explanatory power since it accounts for something else we all know—the personal feelings of guilt each of us experiences. Then I asked the question I pose frequently to groups like that: "Why do we all feel guilty?" I added, "Maybe guilt is just a cultural construction. But here's another possibility. Maybe we *feel* guilty because we *are* guilty. Is that option in the running?"

You may think this a bold stroke, but there was no risk for me at all. I have asked this question many times of audiences, and no one has ever stopped me afterward and said I was wrong. No one ever told me they never experienced guilt. They knew better. More to the point for this tactic, I knew better.

Even though I had never met a single one of them before that night, there was something I knew to be true for each of them on the inside that they couldn't keep from revealing on the outside, and they knew it too.

The Inside Out tactic is not so much a specific maneuver as a frame of mind, an insight to help you maneuver confidently, even creatively sometimes, in conversations. In a sense, you have inside information on others that they will eventually acknowledge, sometimes unwittingly, if you just pay attention.

A perfect example came from one of atheism's most colorful apologists, Richard Dawkins. According to his naturalistic worldview, morality is just a relativistic trick of evolution to get our selfish genes into the next generation. Nothing more, "no design, no purpose, no evil, no good, nothing but blind, pitiless indifference."[1] Yet in another work he railed against the God of the Old Testament as a vindictive, bloodthirsty, homophobic, racist, genocidal, sadomasochistic, malevolent bully.[2]

Do you see the problem? This is not Dawkins's naturalism speaking. Instead it's his commonsense moral realism doing the talking. His protest makes no sense in his minimalist molecules-in-motion world but is perfectly consistent with the world that actually exists—God's world.[3]

Notice here that there is something true on the inside for Dawkins—something he knows—that he cannot help but display on the outside in unguarded moments. When he's defending his philosophical turf, he tells the lie. When his guard is down, his humanity betrays him and he tells the truth in spite of himself.

Why does this happen?

MANNISHNESS

The Inside Out tactic is based on an insight I learned from the late Francis Schaeffer that has helped me navigate more confidently in conversations with others about Christ.[4] He called it the "mannishness of man." Strange phrase, agreed, but a provocative notion nonetheless.

Schaeffer's insight is tied to this question: "What does it mean to be human?" Here is one answer, the response of naturalism—the worldview currently governing science. According to pop "Science Guy" Bill Nye, we are just "a speck, on a speck, orbiting a speck, among other specks."[5] "We emerged from microbes and muck," Carl Sagan declared. "We find ourselves in bottomless free fall . . . lost in a great darkness, and there's no one to send out a search party."[6]

And they are right, of course, in a world without God. Humans are nothing but cogs in the celestial machine, cosmic junk, the ultimate unplanned pregnancy, left to build our lonely lives on the "unyielding foundation of universal despair," as atheist philosopher Bertrand Russell put it. Nihilism—bleak nothing-ism.

Yet no one really believes this, not deep inside. Solomon said God has set eternity in our hearts (Eccl. 3:11). There is a better answer—a more accurate answer—to the question, "What does it mean to be human?" And we all know it.

> In Schaeffer's words, "Man is different from non-man."[7] Human beings are special, unique, unlike anything else in the created realm, "crowned . . . with glory and honor," as David put it (Ps. 8:5 NIV). That is the mannishness of man.

At the core of our beings lies a mark, an imprint of God himself—not *on* us, as if foreign and attached, but *in* us, as a natural feature built into our natures. This mark is part of what makes us what we are, who we are. We would not be humans without it, but only creatures. Because of this mark, we are not kin to apes. We are kin to the God who made us for himself.

I do not want you to miss the significance of this simple statement: "God created man in His own image" (Gen. 1:27), the very first thing said about humans at the outset of God's story. It means that anyone reading these words—every person who has ever lived or died or hoped or dreamed anywhere on this planet at any time in history—bears something beautiful at their core, a beauty that can never be lost and cannot be taken from them.

No, we are not gods, but we are like God in an important way. God's image in us is what makes abortion a homicide and sexual slavery a travesty. It is the reason we are not free to treat each other like animals. It is why certain "inalienable" rights belong uniquely to us. It is also the basis for our friendship with God. We are like him so we can be near him in an extraordinary, intimate way.

In a very real sense, then, you have never met an ordinary person.[8] Because of the mark of God within our souls, we are each extraordinary in a way that no disfigurement—physical or moral—can ever change, no circumstance can ever alter, no thief can ever steal. It is God's forever gift to humanity, his image on our being.

Thus we are precious to him as nothing else is. Jesus said, "Are not two sparrows sold for a cent? And yet not one of them will fall to the ground apart from your Father. But the very hairs of your head are all numbered. So do not fear; you are more valuable than many sparrows" (Matt. 10:29–31).

Because we all live in God's world and are all made in God's image, there are things all people know that are embedded deep within their hearts—profound things about our world and about ourselves—even though we deny them or our worldviews disqualify them.

"That which is known about God," Paul wrote, "is evident *within* them; for God made it evident *to* them" (Rom. 1:19, emphasis added). That which is already on the inside, put there by God himself, eventually shows itself on the outside—in actions, in language, and in convictions. Our mannishness cannot be suppressed.

This knowledge can make a big difference in our conversations. Here is my tactical application of the mannishness of man: The profound truths we all know on the inside always eventually reveal themselves on the outside. All you need to do is listen.

Sometimes the Inside Out factor reveals itself in unusual ways.

TWO DEATHS

In the waning days of summer 1997, two well-known and well-loved women died within days of each other, but the public reaction to each death was radically different. Mother Teresa passed away peacefully at eighty-seven, her death a quiet conclusion to a noble life well lived. Princess Diana died in her prime at thirty-six, her death a tragic and "untimely" intrusion into a life still filled with promise.

Why did so many react so differently to the same kind of event—a life ending, a human being dying? From one point of view—an atheistic, materialistic one—no one dies before their time. Death is death and arrives when it arrives. There is no timeliness for anything, since there is no timetable—no schedule, no plan of how things are supposed to be. Everything just is.

> In a godless universe, where all meaning is of our own making, what could it possibly mean to say someone died an untimely death? It means that people know better. It means they know that life has ultimate purpose and deep significance that transcends private projects. In spite of their pontifications to the contrary, their mannishness gives them away.

And there are lots of things like this, if you look for them. People endorse moral relativism for convenience but then are mortified at the genuine evil that assails the world and struggle with guilty consciences for their participation in it. They deny conscious design in the universe but reflexively invoke the wonders of Mother Nature when overwhelmed by the magnificence of God's world. They deny Father, so they praise Mother.

Understanding this Inside Out pattern provides a powerful technique to get someone thinking. "The truth that we let in first is not a dogmatic statement of the truth of the Scriptures," Schaeffer wrote, "but the truth of the external world and the truth of what man himself is. This is what shows him his need. The Scriptures then show him the real nature of his lostness and the answer to it."[9]

Here's how Schaeffer's insight can be useful for us. Listen to the way people talk. Watch for when—from their own mouths—their acknowledgment of reality intrudes on their philosophies. Then exploit that tension by asking a question. In a world without purpose, why is Princess Di's death a tragedy? If there is no ultimate, universal morality, how can anything be really evil? Why try to talk someone out of a suicide? If there is no meaning to life, what's the point?

Mother Teresa finished her course, and Princess Diana did not. That is the victory and the tragedy of those events in the waning days of summer 1997. But only because there is a divinely intended purpose—a noble end humans have been designed for that sin, sadly, cuts short.

Here is another example of the inside truth finding its way to the outside.

MY FATHER'S WORLD

Something has always confused me about Earth Day celebrations. They seem to be based on a contradiction. Earth Day is a fete enjoyed by naturalists, on the main, who celebrate nature as ultimate and man's unique moral responsibility to protect it.

There, did you see it? Did you catch the contradiction?

To see the misstep, you must see something else first. Worldviews come in packages. They are like puzzles with particular pieces fitting together into a coherent whole. Foundational concerns either fit crisply with other details or foreclose on them.

In a naturalistic worldview, nature is all there is—physical things in motion strictly governed by the deterministic laws of physics and chemistry. In this package, then, there is no place for moral obligations of any kind because morality is based on free choices, not on physical determinism.

Further, Darwinism is a strictly materialistic process that produces strictly material goods. No pattern of genetic mutation and natural selection can cause an immaterial moral obligation to pop into existence.[10] Thus no living thing can have an obligation to protect any other. The locusts take what they can and leave nothing for the hapless boll weevil. Nor should they. May the best bug (the fittest critter) win. That's the program.

Nature's "balance" is maintained by the corporate tug-of-war for survival that all living things engage in (on this view), not by one species acting responsibly toward another. There are no moral hierarchies in nature, since nature has no resources to build them. Thus the notion that a specific animal, even a human one, has responsibility of stewardship over any other—not to mention Mother Nature's entire project—is foreign to naturalism and thus to Darwinism. There is nothing in an atheistic, naturalistic world that makes sense of man's obligation toward nature. That's the contradiction.

As I said, it confuses me, and it ought to trouble naturalists too, but it doesn't appear to. There is a reason for this, I think. To them, it just seems obvious—regardless of their underlying worldview—that humans are different in a qualitative way, making us responsible as stewards over the world entrusted to us. That's not the exact language they use, of course, but it's what the intuition driving Earth Day amounts to.

And they are right about this intuition, but certainly not in virtue of naturalism. Naturalists can talk all they want of human obligations, human meaning and purpose, human value, human significance—even human rights—but it's all chaff in the wind given their foundational understanding of reality.

Here is what the Earth Day crowd gets right: Man *is* different. Humans *are* special. People *are* responsible because they are not the same as anything else in nature. And we all know this, which is why the fact continues to stubbornly assert itself even with people whose worldview package cannot justify it. That's because this world is not Mother's world. It is Father's world.

Again, these are things we all know, it turns out. They reflect our deepest intuitions about ourselves and the world we live in. But why do humans have an obligation to the planet, given naturalism? This is a question we must ask, and waving the wand of evolution is not an answer, as we've seen.

> Carl Sagan says we are cousins of apes.[11] That is Mother's assessment, of course. Father says different: "God created man in His own image, in the image of God He created him" (Gen. 1:27).

Note one thing more. God said to mankind, "Be fruitful and multiply, and fill the earth, and subdue it; and rule over the fish of the sea and over the birds of the sky and over every living thing that moves on the earth" (Gen. 1:28). This is the accurate insight of Earth Day. We are both masters and stewards—regents on earth yet servants of the most high God.

BROKEN

I want to tell you another thing everyone knows. Something has gone terribly wrong. We call it the problem of evil, and it prompts us to ask, "Why is there so much badness in the world?" There is a wrinkle to this concern, though, another detail each of us also knows.

The world is broken, true enough. But we are broken too, and our brokenness is a huge part of what is wrong with the world. The world is broken because we are broken. Though man has inherent dignity, he is also cruel. The evil is "out there," as it were, but it is also "in here"—in us.

Things did not start out that way, of course. At the very end of the very beginning, once God had set everything in its proper place, we find this summary of all he had done: "God saw all that He had made, and behold, it was very good" (Gen. 1:31).

All was as it was supposed to be, just as God intended, everything working according to its purpose, man and woman one with each other and with the world, resting in their friendship with God.

When our first parents chose to follow the deceiver rather than their Sovereign, though, they broke fellowship with the Father, they broke communion with each other, and they broke harmony with the earth they'd been entrusted with. When Adam and Eve sinned, they broke the whole world. Human badness made the world go bad.

Because our parents became broken, each of us is now broken like them, since they reproduced children just like themselves, and their children have done likewise, one broken generation cascading down into the next. Each of us is still beautiful, to be sure. God's image cannot be erased. However, it can be defaced and disfigured, sullied and spoiled. And that is what has happened.

To say we are broken is accurate, but it is also easily misunderstood, since it does not go far enough. We are not machines that are malfunctioning. We are not bodies that are ailing. We are subjects who revolted, rebels who are now morally corrupted. We are guilty, and for this we must answer.

Again, each of us knows this deep down inside. It is the Inside Out point I traded on in my Berkeley lecture. We are the "others" doing those evil deeds we object to. Deep inside us is a gnawing awareness of our own badness, producing a feeling we universally recognize: guilt. At some point or another, if we are honest with ourselves, we feel the painful reality of our brokenness:

> There is none righteous, not even one;
> There is none who understands,
> There is none who seeks for God;
> All have turned aside, together they have become useless;
> There is none who does good,
> There is not even one.
>
> —*Romans 3:10–12*

Humans are beautiful, yes. But humans are also broken. And in our moral wretchedness, we are also profoundly guilty. We owe. We are in debt, not to a standard, not to a rule, not to a law, but to a Person—to the One we have offended with our disobedience. And this is not good news, since our guilt has severe consequences.

JUSTICE OR MERCY

Each of us longs for justice. We speak of it often, especially when we have suffered injustice. That is the inside revealing itself on the outside again. Justice is not ultimately satisfied in this life, though. It is satisfied in the next.

At the end of the Bible, we find a dark passage (Revelation 20). It tells of the final event of history as we know it, a great trial on a great plain where a great multitude of the accused—the guilty ones—stand before a Judge. The books of death are opened, each of our moral lives laid bare for all mankind to see—the record in the books the basis for a final reckoning, a last judgment.

Before the Judge stand all the beautiful, broken, guilty ones, each shut up under sin (Gal. 3:22). Every mouth is also shut, each voice silenced, unable to utter any defensive appeal or excuse (Rom. 3:19). The record in the books speaks for itself.

> Here is Sagan's "bottomless free fall"—mankind "lost in a great darkness." He is right about that, since we are all guilty, and no judge owes a pardon. Atonement must be made. The debt must be paid. Justice must be perfect.

There is something else, though. I did not leave the students at Berkeley in despair, abandoned under the weight of their own guilt—culpability we all shoulder, blame we all share.

"The answer to guilt is not denial," I told them. "That's relativism. The answer to guilt is forgiveness. And this is where Jesus comes in."

I have made that point many times to audiences, and every time I say those words, something moves inside me. Forgiveness. Mercy. Repair. Restoration. Rebirth. New life. Hope. This is what each of our souls longs for.

Sagan is right when he says we are lost, but he is wrong when he says there is no one to send out a search party. Clearly, humans need rescuing, and we cannot rescue ourselves. Help must come from the outside. From outside of us. From outside of Sagan's closed cosmos. From outside of this world.

And the search party has arrived. The Rescuer has come.

When [Jesus] comes into the world, He says,

> "Sacrifice and offering You have not desired,
> But a body You have prepared for Me;
> In whole burnt offerings and sacrifices for sin You have
>   taken no pleasure.
> "Then I said, 'Behold, I have come . . .
> To do Your will, O God.'"

> —*Hebrews 10:5–7*

Because our souls bear God's image, we are wonderful. Because we have rebelled against the God who gave us our beauty, we are broken, guilty, and ultimately lost. "The wages of sin is death," the Word tells us (Rom. 6:23). In the darkness, though, there is hope, because it then adds, "But the free gift of God is eternal life in Christ Jesus our Lord."

He is the one who calls to us, "Come to Me, all who are weary and heavy-laden, and I will give you rest. . . . For I am gentle and humble in heart, and you will find rest for your souls" (Matt. 11:28–29).

OUR RESTLESS SOULS

Augustine of Hippo most famously described the restlessness of the human soul and suggested its only proper place of repose. "You have made us for yourself, O Lord," he wrote in his *Confessions*, "and our hearts are restless until they can find rest in You."

I think it is safe to say that this restlessness, this sense of longing, this ineffable yearning to be filled—or maybe yearning to be fixed—is a universal human affliction, a malady that has nothing to do with our natural appetites, since satisfying them never sates the hunger of our hearts. This ache of the soul can be muted by other distractions, but it can never be entirely silenced.

Two facts of the human condition lie at the heart of our inescapable sense of longing. One is that we are broken. We have already spoken of that. The second is, it hasn't always been this way. There remains a remnant of former beauty the brokenness cannot efface.

As to being broken, we all know this on the inside. We face our own failures every day. Further, we know there is a place from which we have fallen. "What else does this craving, and this helplessness proclaim," wrote Blaise Pascal, the French mathematician and religious philosopher, "but that there was once in man a true happiness, of which all that now remains is the empty print and trace?"[12]

> We know it is not enough for us simply to *be*. Something has gone missing that must be replaced. We feel a "sweet pain . . . a primal memory deep in our souls reminding us of the way the world started— good, wonderful, whole, complete."[13]

We were made for something better, and we scrap and scrape to climb back up, to return to the heights. That struggle is central to just about every film we have ever seen and every story we have ever read. The "triumph of the human spirit," they say—God's image forcing its way to the surface, to the outside. The exceptions, of course, are the dark, nihilistic yarns, the dystopian tales that tell the lie that we are nothing.

Note the conflicting visions—the vision buried deep in our humanity, and the contrary vision flowing from the atheistic, nothingism view.

Atheism, of course, denies the guilt. It must. Without Good, there is no Bad. It also denies the beauty. Again, it must. If no God, no guided design, only biological accidents, physical parts stuck together without reason or purpose—cosmic junk. Man is nothing and his life means nothing. Atheism leaves us, once again, with naught.

No, our true longing is a hunger that atheism simply cannot satisfy, a thirst it cannot quench. Holly Ordway was an atheist who watched her soul suffer injury, corrupted by a belief that did not fit reality: "My atheism was eating into my heart like acid. . . . I could not have explained the source of my own rationality, nor of my conviction that there were such things as truth, beauty, and goodness. My worldview remained satisfying to me only insofar as I refrained from asking the really tough questions."[14]

Ordway was not drawn to God initially because of DNA, irreducible complexity, or the finely tuned constants of the universe. Rather she first saw God in John Keats, John Donne, and Gerard Manley Hopkins. She was alerted to God by beauty.

As an atheist, she had been feasting on despair for years, and she was starving. "However satisfied I declared myself intellectually . . . atheism . . . was a terrible place to live," she realized. "It was the winter of my soul."[15]

The thaw began when, as a newly minted college professor, Ordway reread the canonical poets of English literature and for the first time realized that the soul-satisfying beauty of their verse flowed naturally and natively from their Christian view of the world—God's world. "I sensed something deeper in the poems I was reading. I could feel power thrumming in the lines of the poems, an electricity of meaning, drawing from some source beyond my reach."[16]

The world of Hopkins, Keats, and Donne was a world where transcendent beauty made sense, where longing and hunger could be satisfied, where rising up from the fall was possible—a world where there was hope. Inside her, something moved—"My heart in hiding / Stirred . . . ," ". . . hope, wish day come . . ." (Hopkins).

A realistic hope, though, or empty wish? C. S. Lewis answers: "If I find in myself a desire which no experience in this world can satisfy, the most probable explanation is that I was made for another world."[17]

This other world was the one Ordway hungered for. This was the understanding that made sense of the actual world she lived in. But there was also a dark side to her discovery.

The understanding of reality that made sense of beauty and meaning and hope also made sense of this world's brokenness—both unintelligible in Holly Ordway's atheism. The disturbing part for her was this: the brokenness that was real was also moral and personal. "I considered myself a 'good person,'" she wrote, "but in my heart I was afraid to be judged on the real self behind my outward image."[18] She was guilty, and she knew it.

French philosopher Guillaume Bignon found his naturalistic atheism being challenged as he encountered Christ in the New Testament.[19] Nevertheless, the cross confused him. "Why did Jesus have to die?" he asked over and over again as he worked through the historical accounts of Jesus' life. It made no sense to him.

Then something unexpected happened. "God reactivated my conscience," he told me. "That was not a pleasant experience. I was physically crippled by guilt, not knowing what to do about it."

Suddenly it dawned on him. "*That's* why Jesus had to die. Because of *me*. Because of *my* guilt." He immediately surrendered all his brokenness to the only one who could repair it, giving all his guilt to the only one who could forgive. When he did, "the feelings of guilt just evaporated."

Atheism cannot do this. It cannot explain the beauty and wonder of being human. And it has no answer to human brokenness. It cannot provide the consolation of true forgiveness. Only God in Christ can solve the crisis in our hearts. That is the road home. Pascal again: "This [craving is what man] tries in vain to fill with everything around him . . . though none can help, since this infinite abyss can be filled only with an infinite and immutable object—in other words, by God himself."[20]

Because our souls bear God's image, we are beautiful. Because we have rebelled against the God who gave us our beauty, we are fallen, guilty, lost. We cry out.

Here is our remedy, stated simply in a Christmas card I received from a friend: "The birth of Christ . . . invites us to believe that the cries of a broken world have actually been heard—a Savior was born."[21]

There are times when clever arguments evade you. That's when a simple declaration of the truth may be all that's needed. "Come to Me . . ." is an offer of meat to hunger and drink to thirst. Touch the existential nerve, the deep, profound desire that throbs in every fallen human being made in the image of God.

Listen carefully in your conversations. Listen for when a person's mannishness speaks. When they tell the truth—and they must eventually—point it out. My question to the audience at Berkeley was a direct application of the Inside Out tactic. I addressed those students confidently, since I knew that even though a person can run from God, he cannot run from himself.

WHAT WE LEARNED IN THIS CHAPTER

The Inside Out tactic is not so much a specific maneuver as it is an insight into what it means to be human that helps us navigate in conversations. "Man," Francis Schaeffer wrote, "is different from non-man." We are not insignificant specks lost in a universe of specks but are unique and marvelous creatures bearing God's imprint.

This fact is a truth every human knows on the inside that informs other truths that eventually reveal themselves on the outside in words, actions, or attitudes.

Those truths include the deep awareness that humans have profound value and worth, that human beings were designed for a valuable purpose, that we are beautiful yet broken and guilty, and that our restless souls hunger for rescue.

Our job is to listen for when a person's mannishness speaks, to pay attention to when his language or reactions tell the truth even though his worldview tells the lie. Then—gently, charitably, graciously—ask him about it.

Chapter 18

MINI-TACTICS

Over the years, I have developed a handful of modest maneuvers that may help you like they've helped me in my conversations with others. I call them Mini-Tactics because the concepts are relatively uncomplicated and can be put into play easily when needed.

Most are simple strategies for dealing with difficulties. One is a defensive technique. Another is a general practice that will help all of your communication with others. Each of them should have a place in your tactical toolbox.

WHAT A FRIEND WE HAVE IN JESUS

Have you noticed how often people who are not otherwise committed to Christ or the Bible make theological points based on what Jesus either said or, presumably, did not say? In both instances, I have the same question: "So what? Why should it matter what Jesus said or didn't say?"

Of course, in one sense the answer is obvious: Jesus has credibility even with those who are not his followers. The person making the appeal is trying to bolster her view's legitimacy by conveniently enlisting Jesus as her ally.[1]

It's a smart move, and we can make use of it too. If Jesus' opinion on any one issue matters, maybe we should take his counsel on other things for the same reason. Here's the general principle guiding this tactic: pit the challenger against Jesus whenever you can.

That was my approach when I faced off with New Age guru Deepak Chopra for a national TV debate on Lee Strobel's *Faith under Fire*. Deepak is one of the few people in the world who can be immediately recognized by his first name. I knew it would be a mistake to position my credibility against Chopra's fame. I was the local boy from LA. In a "Chopra versus Koukl" matchup, I was outgunned.

There was someone else on my side, though, who had a lot more firepower than either of us: Jesus of Nazareth. If I could position the debate as Chopra versus Jesus ("Dr. Chopra says this, but Jesus says that"), I knew I would fare much better in the eyes of the viewing public.

> Put this basic principle into play: pit the challenger against Jesus, not you. Step aside whenever you can and let Jesus shoulder the responsibility for his own claims. It really helps balance the scales.

This move is especially important when dealing with the most offensive detail of our message—which is also *the* central claim of the gospel—that Jesus is the Savior for the world, the only one capable of rescuing us from judgment and restoring us to a relationship with the Father. That's why it's vital we let Jesus carry the load here when we can, since Jesus' view was crystal clear for anyone willing to take notice.[2]

When someone presses you on the "narrowness of Christianity," shrug your shoulders and say, "Well, I understand how you feel, but this was Jesus' view, not mine, and he repeated it often. So did everyone else he personally trained to carry his message after him. Do you think Jesus was mistaken?"

I suggested the What a Friend We Have in Jesus tactic to a dad whose daughter was competing in a statewide beauty pageant and was sure to face a question about same-sex marriage—an obvious attempt to marginalize anyone who didn't toe the politically correct line on homosexuality. He wanted my opinion on the safest way to answer the question, "What do you think about same-sex marriage?" and still be faithful to Christ.

Since Jesus said we should be innocent but shrewd, I worked out this response I think satisfies both requirements: "Since I am a follower of Christ, my view on marriage is the same as Jesus' view, one he made clear in Matthew 19. I'll sum it up this way. Jesus' view was *one man, with one woman, becoming one flesh, for one lifetime.* So on the definition of marriage, I stand with Jesus."[3]

You get the point. Disagree with the Christian on this, and you disagree with Christ. That's why this approach should be your first line of response when answering this kind of query. Since Jesus still has credibility with most people, it sets the opposition against him, not you.

Jesus' comments in Matthew 19 may also help you with a similar appeal to Jesus' authority: Jesus never said anything about homosexuality. Notice, this is an attempt to use the What a Friend We Have in Jesus tactic against the Christian. If Jesus didn't specifically condemn homosexuality—or same-sex marriage or gender dysphoria[4]—how can Christians condemn it? That's the thinking.

So here's my question in light of that challenge. What can we properly conclude from the record's apparent silence about Jesus' view on homosexuality? The answer is simple. Nothing. Nothing at all.

Here's the problem. Actually, there are three of them.

First, there is a difference between the record being silent about Jesus' opinion on something and Jesus being silent about it. Remember, the vast majority of what Jesus said and did was left out of the Gospels. Not enough room, as John himself admits (John 21:25).

Second, is the apparent silence significant? Think about it. The record is also silent on Jesus' view of slavery, capital punishment, spousal abuse, sex trafficking, racism, child abuse, and gay bashing, to name a few. Do we infer from this silence that he approved of these things?[5] Hardly.

You see the problem. It's difficult to conclude anything about what Jesus did not condemn, based on a limited written record of what he did condemn. It's simply a mistake to assume Christ must favor whatever he didn't explicitly object to.

Notice I said difficult, not impossible. Sometimes we can infer Jesus' view on something we have no record of by listening carefully to his view on a related thing he did weigh in on. This point brings us back to Matthew 19 and the final flaw of this approach.

As it turns out, Jesus had strong convictions about sexual subjects. According to him, the only kind of sexuality ("one flesh") that's proper is sex between a man and a woman in a lifelong, committed, marital relationship with each other (Matt. 19:4–6). Conversely, all forms of sex expressly prohibited in the Bible—adultery, fornication, homosexuality, and bestiality—are each automatically disqualified by Jesus' reasoning. His one, simple principle rules them all out. Pretty straightforward.

So it appears Jesus had a lot to say, indirectly, about the issues of homosexuality and same-sex marriage and gender dysphoria.

Take advantage of any opportunity you have to get Jesus on your side. Let him do the arguing for you. You may have to set this up in advance by asking, "What's your opinion on Jesus?" Most of the time, people will give a positive response. Let *them* establish Jesus as an authority—a great teacher, an important prophet, an avatar, a guru, a "Christ" of some sort—then leverage that in your favor.

STICKS AND STONES

My mom used to say, "Sticks and stones may break your bones, but names will never hurt you." Your mom probably told you the same thing. It's a clever aphorism encouraging us to brush off foolish people, ignore their empty insults, and move on. That's usually good advice.

It's not entirely accurate, though. First, names can hurt emotionally, even when we try to dismiss the slight. Second, when it comes to thinking carefully about weighty matters, name calling can be a distractive nuisance. If we want to stay on target in an important discussion, we need to take action.

This is where the Sticks and Stones tactic comes in. Like Steamroller, this is a defensive tactic. It's a maneuver to protect you from a certain type of ad hominem attack: name calling.[6] Here's how it works.

Whenever anyone tries to deflect your point by labeling you with a nasty name—bigot, homophobe, Islamophobe, racist, whatever—always ask for a definition. It's the same thing I encouraged you to do with the passive-aggressive tolerance trick mentioned in chapter 7.

The rhetorical force of these words is often so powerful, you'll have a hard time overcoming them unless you flush out their meanings into the open. Pejorative labels succeed at marginalizing you because of their ambiguity. Plus, the person using them has deftly changed the subject—from the issue at hand to a question of your character, which is irrelevant to the discussion. Don't fall for it.

There are two advantages of asking for a definition. First, it stops the momentum of the illicit attack and puts you back in the driver's seat. Second, it forces the other person to think about what he just did.

Once he spells out what he means, ask him why his definition applies to you. Then ask why he thinks it's helpful to impugn your character instead of showing where your idea went wrong. Ridicule is not an argument, after all. Your questions could help take some of the edge off the attack. Name calling is an explicit act of hostility, though, so be sure to be gracious and calm when you ask for a definition and offer your follow-up questions.

Most people don't realize they've made a false move when they revert to personal smears. They've been so thoroughly socialized to use this approach, they don't realize that it's both intellectually unsound and bad manners.

MOVING TOWARD THE OBJECTION

The next Mini-Tactic was the result of a little epiphany—a moment of revelation—I had while prepping for my national radio debate with atheist and *Skeptic* magazine founder Michael Shermer. Here's the "inspired" insight: sometimes it's better to move toward an objection rather than away from it, to embrace a charge rather than run from it.

I was introduced to this maneuver in a movie. In the opening scenes of *Clear and Present Danger*, a man with connections to the president is found dead in what appears to be a drug deal gone bad. To contain the PR damage, the president's advisors suggest he immediately downplay the relationship and distance himself from the problem.

Analyst Jack Ryan (played by Harrison Ford) suggests just the opposite. "If they ask if you were friends," he counsels, "say, 'No, he was a *good* friend.' If they ask if he was a good friend, say, 'We were *lifelong* friends.' It would give them no place to go. Nothing to report. No story."

> Don't run away from the problem; run toward it and defuse it. Don't evade; invade. Embrace it, undermine its relevance, and take the wind out of its sails. In certain situations we face, that's good advice.

I fully expected Shermer to fire off the atheist's standard response to evidence for intelligent design: "If you argue for ID, then you're going to have to deal with the problem of imperfect design." If God designed living organisms, their design would be perfect. Clearly, there are design flaws, it seems. Therefore there was no divine designer.

If that point came up, I planned to follow Ryan's recommendation. I'd say, "Michael, you're absolutely right. If I'm going to argue for an intelligent designer, then I *am* going to have to deal with that problem. But you're not going to get off that easily. One apparent anomaly[7] doesn't nullify the overwhelming evidence for design. That would be like denying that a wristwatch was designed because it runs three minutes slow. You're straining at a gnat but swallowing a camel."

This particular challenge to ID isn't really an argument against the evidence for design. It's a distraction from that evidence.[8] By moving toward the challenge, I'd blunt the objection by telegraphing to the radio audience that I was aware of the difficulty and wasn't shaken by it. Shermer would have "no place to go. Nothing to report. No story."

As it turned out, that issue didn't come up in our debate, but something like it did. Shermer pointed out that if the Bible is a guide to morality, then I'd have to pick and choose which biblical commands to embrace. My response: "You're absolutely right, Michael."

Yes, I explained, I would have to do the hard work of sorting the rules out. But that's true of every ethical system, even his. I faced no bigger challenge than he did with his "objective" evolutionary morality.[9] I agreed with the problem, then demonstrated its insignificance.

I know of Christians who are stumped when atheists charge, "There are lots of gods you don't believe in too: Zeus, Jupiter, Thor. We atheists just believe in one less God than you." It turns out, the atheist is exactly right on this point, but it does him no good.

Believing in one less God than a monotheist is what distinguishes atheists from Christians, after all. Nothing meaningful follows from this observation. The flummoxed Christian could have simply said, "Yes, you're right. You do believe in one less God than I do. That's what makes you an atheist and me a Christian. We all already know that. So what's your point?" and then watched the challenge fizzle.

The next time someone raises an issue or a problem, instead of backpedaling, think for a moment whether there might be a way to move toward the objection and embrace it and thus defuse it. Here are some more examples.

Challenge: The church is filled with hypocrites.

MTO: Actually, the church is filled with worse people than hypocrites—liars, swindlers, fornicators, adulterers, drunks, self-centered egotists, sinners of all sorts. That's why they need Jesus.

Challenge: There are 130,000 words in the New Testament, but there are more than 400,000 variant readings—mistakes, differences, and errors.

MTO: Of course there are lots of variants. That's what you'd expect when you have thousands of ancient manuscript copies. But the existence of thousands of copies of the Greek New Testament is the very thing that makes it possible for us to accurately reconstruct the original, in spite of the variants.[10]

Challenge: There's so much evil and suffering in the world. How can there be a God?

MTO: Of course there's so much evil in the world. That's what you'd expect if the Christian account is true. The Bible doesn't just explain it. It predicts it. We live in a world humans broke, and a broken world produces broken people and broken situations.

Challenge: Jesus is a crutch; God is a crutch.

MTO: You're right. Handicapped people need crutches, though. We need God to help us, to hold us up, and to forgive us.

Challenge: Your God committed genocide when he destroyed the Canaanites.

MTO: Of course God destroyed them. If you had witnessed the things they did—including burning thousands of children and even infants alive in sacrifice to Molech—you would have asked, "How could there be a God who allows these people to do such evil?" It wasn't genocide. It was judgment.[11]

Challenge: I'm not religious; I'm spiritual.

MTO: Of course you're spiritual. God made you that way so you could know him.

Challenge: Every culture has a flood story like you have in the Bible. It's just a myth.

MTO: Of course every culture has a flood story of some sort. That's what you'd expect if there really was a great flood that wiped out most of the human population. Do you think every culture independently invented a fiction like that?

Challenge: That's just your interpretation.

MTO: You're right. That is my interpretation. How about this? Let me read the whole passage to you, and then you let me know from the context what you think I got wrong and why.

A naysayer's objection is often meant to push us off balance and put us on the ropes. In some cases, though, rather than go on the defensive, it's best to cast the negative as a positive. Tell them they're right, then show them it doesn't work in their favor the way they think it does. Help them see that their complaint is not ultimately relevant, decisive, or damaging when seen in its proper perspective.

Moving toward the objection instead of backing away from it can change the dynamic and cause a complaint to go dead in the water.

WATCH YOUR LANGUAGE

Here is a simple communication tip that will make you much more effective as an ambassador for Christ: watch your language. I don't mean avoid vulgar or obscene vocabulary (I presume you're already doing that). I mean something else.

Consider this. When you settle into your seat on an airplane and the flight attendant addresses the passengers on the intercom, do you pay attention to the "flight attendant noise"? I don't, and neither do most seasoned travelers. We've heard it before and tune out.

In the same way, much of our Christian lingo sounds like religious noise to outsiders. Terms like "faith," "belief," "the Bible," "receive Jesus," even "sin"—as important as it is to talk about it—fall on deaf ears. They've heard it before and tune out what to them is religious "blah, blah, blah."

Worse, Christian jargon can be misleading. This is especially true of the word "faith," which suggests a kind of useful fantasy, a leap of religious wishful thinking in complete disregard for reason or evidence. Nothing like this is in view, of course, with the original biblical word, *pistis*. Still, it's the way many people (including Christians) mistakenly perceive it.

To solve the lingo problem, I've made a habit of finding (and using) substitute words—synonyms for religious terminology—to brighten my conversation and improve my communication.

Instead of quoting "the Bible" or "the Word of God" (both easily dismissed), why not cite "Jesus of Nazareth," if he's the one you're quoting, or "the people Jesus personally trained to follow after him" (the apostles) or "the ancient Hebrew prophets"? These substitute phrases mean the same thing, of course, but have a completely different feel to them. And that's the point. It's much easier to dismiss a religious book than the words of respected religious figures.

When referring to the Gospels, try citing "the ancient biographical evidence" or "the primary source historical documents" for the life of Jesus of Nazareth. That's the way historians see them, after all. And notice I've been using the phrase "Jesus of Nazareth" instead of "Jesus Christ" or even the more religious-sounding "Christ." My phrase communicates a feet-on-the-ground, real person of history. Plus, those words are fresher to contemporary ears.

I also advise that you banish the word "faith" from your vocabulary. I have. It works against us every time we use it, even when talking with Christians.[12] Substitute "trust" for the *exercise* of faith ("I have placed my trust in Jesus"), which is the precise meaning of the original biblical term anyway, and "convictions" for the *content* of faith ("These are my Christian convictions"—that is, "This is what I've become convinced of").

For the same reason, don't talk about your "beliefs." It's too easy to misunderstand this word as a reference to *mere* beliefs, subjective true-for-me preferences. Rather say, "This is what I think is true," or, "These are my spiritual [not 'religious'] convictions."

"Non-Christians" and "unbelievers" are still useful terms, but be careful when you use them. Sometimes they subtly communicate an us-versus-them mentality. Instead substitute the phrase "those who don't share our views" or "people who differ with us" or "those who don't know the Lord."

I've even been avoiding the word "sin" lately, not out of timidity about the topic but because the English word doesn't seem to deliver anymore. Instead I talk about our "moral crimes" against God, our "acts of rebellion," or our "sedition against our Sovereign." By contrast, abandon terms like "blown it" and "messed up" as synonyms for sin. They simply do not capture the gravity of our offenses and end up trivializing our wickedness before God.

> The word "forgiveness" still seems to have emotional power, but sometimes substitutes like "pardon," "clemency," and "mercy" can put a fresh face on it.

Rest assured, there's nothing wrong with using substitute words. Biblical translation is always a matter of choosing appropriate synonyms for original Greek or Hebrew terms. The goal here isn't to soften the original meaning but rather to replace stale, religious language with words that are more vivid, powerful, and precise—adding more punch to our point.

Help yourself to my substitute words, or make your own list of synonyms. Try to find down-to-earth ways of communicating your convictions to others (notice I didn't say "sharing your faith") so they don't tune you out.

I'll warn you in advance, though: it's really hard for Christians—particularly seasoned ones and especially those in ministry—to break the religious lingo habit. You'll need to make a deliberate effort, but the commitment will pay off by removing a massive barrier to meaningful communication. Get rid of those worn-out words and phrases, and those you speak to will take you more seriously.

Watch your language. That's my rule every time I write, speak, or broadcast. I want the clearest, most compelling words I can find to resolve a difficulty or communicate the truth.

THE POWER OF "SO?"

Many challenges offered by skeptics amount to little more than intellectual trash talk. These are clever-sounding complaints that have rhetorical impact and effectively intimidate the opposition but have nothing to do with any reasonable case against God or Christianity. Here is where a bit of reflective thinking coupled with a simple Mini-Tactic can be golden.

I want to teach you the tactical power of a humble two-letter word. This modest word is a little giant, putting the ball back into a skeptic's court and putting you in the driver's seat. When used properly, it can stop a challenger in his tracks, turn the tables, and get him thinking.

That little word, used as a question, is "So?"

Use this tactic when it's clear to you (that's the reflective thinking part) that the charge fired at your convictions doesn't hit any meaningful target. Put another way, even if we agree with the claim, nothing useful follows from it. Your response is to sympathize with the challenge and then simply say, "So?"

It's not uncommon to hear a dismissive "Christians are stupid" from a critic.[13] My response: "You're right. Some of them are. So?"

There are plenty of dull, simpleminded, gullible religious people. So what? Lots of nonreligious people are mentally dense too. Can Christianity be true if some Christians are dumb? Sure. Can atheism be false even if an atheist is brilliant? Of course. The observation, even if true, takes us nowhere. It's just trash talk.

Here's another: "Christians are hypocrites." My response: "Yep, some are. I admit it. So?" Churchgoers have all sorts of vices, but this tells you nothing about Christ. Sure, some religious people don't live up to their convictions. Others are simply fakers, pretenders, and frauds (that's what the word hypocrite means). Therefore, what? Christianity is false? That doesn't follow.

Here's a final example, one I've heard frequently: "You're a Christian because you were raised in America. If you were raised in Iraq, you'd be a Muslim." My answer: "Probably. So?"

Even if true, what does that tell us about the merits of Christianity versus Islam? Nothing. What does that tell us about the merits of theism versus atheism? Nothing. This may be an interesting observation about culture or anthropology. But it tells you nothing at all about the truth or error of any specific religious claim.

> Whenever someone faults an idea by attacking something about the person who holds it and not by addressing the idea itself, you know they're being irrational. You know it's trash talk.

Faulting someone's psychology is not evidence against her beliefs. Finding problems with religious people tells you nothing about God. Here's why: you cannot refute a view by attacking something else.

The question for the atheist is simple: "Does God exist?" He will never get anywhere close to an answer to that question by focusing on human anthropology, human psychology, or human behavior. Each of those is irrelevant to the question. Any appeal that does not speak directly to that question is an immaterial, irrational distraction.

These attempts are nothing more than genetic fallacies or psychogenic fallacies[14] or ad hominems—all irrational missteps, not thoughtful responses. Anyone advancing such an appeal is being unreasonable.

So listen carefully to a challenge, then ask yourself what follows even if the claim is accurate. If there's nothing that you're aware of, point it out using this tactic. Then see what happens.

Rhetorical tricks like any of these may be daunting to the untutored who can't see through them, but they don't work. Weed out the trash talk using the Power of "So?" Mini-Tactic and you'll have much less nonsense to deal with.

WHAT WE LEARNED IN THIS CHAPTER

Mini-Tactics are modest, uncomplicated maneuvers you can easily put into play when needed to help you in conversations with others.

The What a Friend We Have in Jesus tactic trades on the high regard people have for Jesus as an authority, even when they are not his followers. The general principle for this tactic is to pit the challenger against Jesus whenever you can. Get Jesus on your side and let him do the arguing for you. When someone disagrees with you, then, they'll be disagreeing with Christ.

Sticks and Stones is a Mini-Tactic meant to blunt the rhetorical force of distractive name calling. Whenever anyone tries to deflect your point by calling you a name, always ask for a definition. Your question stops the forward momentum of the attack and forces the other person to face the fact that ridicule is not an argument.

Moving toward the Objection is a tactic that's useful when it's to your advantage to agree with a charge rather than oppose it. Sometimes it's possible to cast a negative as a positive. By embracing the complaint when you can, you defuse it by casting it in a different light, undermining its relevance and taking the wind out of the critic's sails.

Watch Your Language is a general guideline reminding you to banish Christian lingo from your vocabulary. It means nothing to non-Christians and little to most Christians, plus it can sound annoying. Religious jargon can also be misleading. To fix the problem, use appropriate synonyms for stale religious terms. Try to find down-to-earth ways of communicating your convictions to others so they don't tune you out.

The Power of "So?" employs a simple question that disputes the relevance of challenges that sound compelling at first glance but turn out to be irrelevant to any case against God or Christianity. Whenever someone faults an idea by attacking something about the person who holds it and not by addressing the idea itself, agree with the point for the sake of argument, then ask, "So? What follows from that point that's relevant to God's existence or the truthfulness of Christianity?"

Chapter 19

MORE SWEAT, LESS BLOOD

At the beginning of this book, I made a promise. I said I would guide you, step by step, through a game plan that would help you maneuver comfortably and graciously in conversations about your Christian convictions.

I wanted to give you the tools you needed to help make your engagements with others look more like diplomacy than D-Day. I suggested an approach I call the Ambassador Model. It trades on friendly curiosity rather than confrontation. Then I introduced you to a handful of effective tactics to help you navigate in conversations.

I have done my best to keep my promise. Reading this book, though, does not guarantee that anything will be different in your conversations. How you proceed from here will be up to you. I want to talk now about your next steps.

When I was younger, I was an army reservist during the Vietnam era. If I were joining the military now, though, I think I would choose the marines. Two things about the marines impress me.

The first is the motto of the U.S. Marine Corps: *Semper Fi*. This is short for *semper fidelis*, a Latin phrase that means "Always faithful." The second is a training maxim I learned from a former marine who picked it up during the rigors of officer candidate school. This adage is in the back of my mind every time I prepare for a public encounter with an opponent who is dedicated to defeating my convictions: "The more you sweat in training, the less you bleed in battle."

I want to end this book with some suggestions that will help you sweat more and bleed less, and thus stay always faithful to the task ahead of you.

First, I would like to offer eight insights I gained from a conversation I overheard while flying home from vacation one summer. Next, I want to explain the best way I know to build a small fellowship of like-minded ambassadors for Christ who value the life of the mind. Finally, I want to share with you some lessons about the importance of hostile opposition and what I learned about courage under fire from a pair of timid, door-to-door evangelists.

EIGHT QUICK TIPS

On a flight back from the Midwest, I listened while a Christian brother in the row directly behind me vigorously shared his faith with passengers on either side. I was glad for his effort (my wife and I were both praying for him), and he made some fine points. But some of his tactics were questionable. Here are some things I learned from that experience that might make your efforts more effective.

First, be ready. The Christian brother behind me was clearly on the alert for chances to represent Christ. Seated between two other passengers, he had a captive audience on either side for almost four hours, and he was determined to make the most of the opportunity.

Though you do not need to squeeze each encounter dry (as he seemed to be doing), you should at least be willing to test the waters to see if there is any interest. Good ambassadors are vigilant, always watchful for what might turn out to be a divine appointment.

Second, keep it simple. On the way to sharing about the cross, our Christian passenger ranged from young earth creationism to Armageddon. That is a lot to have to chew on to get to Jesus. The basic gospel is challenging enough. Generally, you will have to deal with a few obstacles that come up. But if the listener is interested, why complicate things with controversial issues unrelated to salvation? Remember, you want to put a stone in his shoe, not a rock pile. If other issues don't come up, don't bring them up.

Third, avoid religious language and spiritual pretense. Our dear brother was obviously a Christian. His dialogue was littered with spiritual lingo and religious posturing. Everything about his manner screamed fundamentalist. Even when this is genuine, it sounds weird to outsiders. Words and phrases like "saved," "blessed," "the Word of God," "receive Christ," and "believing in Jesus as Savior and Lord" may have meaning to you, but they are tired religious clichés to everyone else.

As I encouraged you to do in the last chapter, experiment with fresh new ways to characterize the ancient message of truth. Consider using "trust" instead of "faith," or "follower of Jesus" instead of "Christian." I try to avoid quoting "the Bible." Instead I quote the words of "the ancient Jewish prophets" (the Old Testament), of "Jesus of Nazareth" (the Gospels), or of "those Jesus trained to take his message after him" (the rest of the New Testament).[1]

Avoid spiritual schmaltz like the plague. Even though a person is attracted to Christ, he may still be reluctant to join an enterprise that makes him look odd. Don't let your style get in the way of your message.

Next, focus on the truth of Christianity, not merely its personal benefits. I appreciated our evangelist's focus on truth rather than experience. When one of his fellow passengers said he liked reincarnation, the Christian noted that liking reincarnation could not make it true. The facts matter. By focusing on the truth claims of Jesus instead of making a more subjective appeal, he gave his message a solid foundation.

Give reasons. This brother understood that making assertions without giving good reasons would be an empty effort. He was ready to give the support needed to show that his claims were not trivial. Jesus, Paul, Peter, John, and all the prophets did the same. Even in a relativistic age, people still care about reasons.

Stay calm. Don't get mad. Don't show frustration. Don't look annoyed. Keep your cool. Our friend stayed composed the entire time. The more collected he was, the more confident he seemed. The more confident he seemed, the more persuasive he sounded.

If they want to go, let them leave. When you sense that the one you are talking with is looking for an exit, back off a bit. Signs of waning interest—wandering eyes, a caged look, darting glances toward the doorway—are clues that she's probably not listening anymore. Don't force the conversation. Instead let the exchange end naturally. Remember, you don't need to close the sale in every encounter. God is in charge. He will bring the next ambassador along to pick up where you left off. When the conversation becomes a monologue (yours), it's time to let it go.

Don't let them leave empty-handed. If possible, give the person a tangible way to follow up on what you challenged him to consider. Our friend had an arsenal of tracts, booklets, and Christian paper-backs to leave behind to keep the thinking process going. You might offer your business card, a Christian website (for example, *www.str.org*), or something to read. A copy of the gospel of John is a good choice. It's small, inexpensive, and focuses on Christ. Offer it as a gift, suggesting, "It might be best for me to let Jesus speak for himself."

These eight ideas remove obstacles that get in your way as an ambassador. They will make it easier for others to focus on your message without being distracted by your methods. The irony is that when our method is skillful, it fades into the background. But when our method is clumsy or offensive, then *it* becomes the focus instead of the truth we want to communicate.

DRY TINDER

Another key to making you a better ambassador is the company you keep. You may have found that this book has opened up a whole new spiritual landscape you're anxious to explore. This can be exhilarating, but it can also be frustrating if your Christian friends have not experienced the same epiphany. There is a solution, though.

Awhile back, I spent most of one day with seven seemingly ordinary women who captured my attention, respect, and admiration. They were not philosophers, theologians, authors, or captains of industry. They were mostly mothers and housewives juggling car pools, laundry, and tired husbands.

Every couple of weeks they gathered together with their Bibles and study materials in a small group simply known as Women of Berea. Their main purpose was not prayer or fellowship, though both of those things happened. Rather their goal was study and discussion, engaging their minds in careful thinking on things that mattered.

When people ask me how to get their church interested in loving God with their minds as Christians, I have a simple bit of advice that these women understood: You can't start a fire with wet wood. You must begin with dry tinder.

> In nearly every church, there are brothers and sisters who share your hunger but have yet to share your discovery. They are dissatisfied, yearning for something more substantial, but do not know where to turn. These people are your dry tinder.

Do not make it your goal to change your church just yet. First, find people of kindred spirit. Gather up the dry tinder, plant your spark, and kindle a flame. Aim to start a modest fire with a cluster of believers who value using their minds in their pursuit of God. Once the fire gets ignited, don't be surprised if some of the wet wood around you begins to dry out and starts to blaze.

Commit to meet together on a regular basis: weekly, biweekly, monthly—whatever fits your schedules. Individual commitments to your group may be short-term for a particular study project or part of a long-term relationship similar to C. S. Lewis's friendships with J. R. R. Tolkien and others in a group they called the Inklings. It's up to you.

"Culture is most profoundly changed," Chuck Colson said, "not by the efforts of huge institutions, but by individual people."[2] Edmund Burke called them "little platoons," small groups of ordinary folks making a difference where their feet hit the sidewalk.

Meet together for a limited but definite period of time to study a particular topic. As a group, you might listen to recorded talks, discuss a book, or assess a video you discovered online. You might role-play differences of opinion, using the tactics you've learned from this book. Or you might work together to construct an intelligent, reasoned response to the points you heard on a talk show or saw in a letter to the editor. Encourage each other to step out of your comfort zone and apply what you're learning.

Your group could become a catalyst influencing others in your church, a vital resource that your Christian friends can turn to when they have questions. The Women of Berea soon began to have an impact beyond their own ranks, drying out the wet wood around them by being good ambassadors for Christ. The key to effectiveness outside your group is to stay visible, be committed to excellence, and keep a good attitude. This is not a time for high-mindedness but for usefulness.

Remember, look for the dry tinder—like-minded people of kindred spirit. There are more of them around than you may think. You just have to find them. You could be the match that kindles the tinder that starts a bonfire of excitement in your church. You just need to be willing to take the initiative to lead others in the pursuit of thoughtful, intelligent convictions.

HOSTILE WITNESSES

Part of that pursuit involves a certain kind of vulnerability. None of us wants our views proven wrong, especially our most cherished ideas, regardless of which side of the fence we're on. But if we want to cultivate a well-informed faith, we need to be aware of our own powerful instincts for ideological self-preservation.

This instinct is so strong that sometimes we are tempted to intellectually circle the wagons and guard against the slightest challenge to our beliefs. This strategy provides a false sense of security, however. The opposite approach offers much more safety. Instead of digging in behind fortifications to protect against attackers, we should encourage critique by hostile witnesses.

In academic circles, this is called peer review. Philosophers, scientists, and theologians present their ideas in professional forums and solicit critique. They test the merit of their thoughts by offering them to people who are inclined to disagree.

A number of years ago, I attended a three-day conference titled Design and Its Critics. The best minds in the intelligent design movement were assembled to make their case. But they were not alone. They had invited the top Darwinian thinkers in the country to listen to their ideas and take their best shots. It was one of the most invigorating and intellectually honest encounters I have ever witnessed.

> Peer review is based on a sound notion. If our ideas are easily destroyed by those acquainted with the facts, they ought to be discarded. But if our ideas are good, they will not be upended so easily. In the process, we will learn what the other side knows. We may even be surprised at how weak the substance of their resistance really is.

The lesson of hostile witnesses was driven home to me quite unexpectedly one day. While sitting in my library prepping for a radio show, I heard a knock on my front door. When I answered, two middle-aged women smiled at me pleasantly, bundles of apocalyptic literature in hand. They asked if I wanted to see their material.

There were two at the door, but only the one in front—the one who had knocked—spoke. The second stood quietly in the back, watching. Jehovah's Witnesses go out in pairs, usually one experienced Witness and one newer disciple. The neophyte makes the initial contact, while the mentor waits protectively in the background, ready for a flanking maneuver if the young cadet gets into trouble.

I knew the encounter would be brief. First, I had little time to make an impact because I had to leave for the radio studio. Second, door-to-door missionaries like these usually have little time for anyone who is biblically literate. I knew that once I showed my hand, they would disappear quickly and look for an easier mark. Still, I didn't want to send my visitors away empty-handed.

"I am a Christian," I began. I directed my comments to the younger convert, the one less influenced by the Watch Tower organization and hopefully more open to another viewpoint.

"It's clear we have some differences, including the vital issue of the identity of Jesus. I believe what John teaches in John 1:3, that Jesus is the uncreated Creator. This would make him God."[3]

Mention of the deity of Christ was all that was needed to bring the rear guard into action. The woman in the shadows spoke up for the first time. I honestly wasn't prepared for her response.

"You're entitled to your opinion, and we're entitled to ours," was all she said. No question, no challenge, no theological rebuttal. This was a dismissal, not a response. She turned on her heel and started for the next house, trainee in tow, in search of more vulnerable game.

I cast about for something to say that might slow their retreat. "You're also entitled to be wrong in your opinion," I blurted out, but the retort had no effect. I admit it was a poor response, but it was all I could think of at the moment. "Clearly, we both can't be right," I added, trying to mend the breach, "even though we're both entitled to our opinions."

I was hoping for some kind of reaction, some kind of engagement, but my challenge went unanswered. As they marched down the walkway, I fired my final salvo, vainly hoping for a response. "Obviously, you're not interested in hearing any other point of view than your own."

Then they were gone.

GUN-SHY

In the moments that followed, a host of questions flooded my mind. Did I use the right approach? (Apparently not.) Would a different tack have been more effective? (Probably.) Did anything I say leave a good impression? (Unlikely.) Did I plant even a seed of doubt or stimulate any reflection in their minds? (Hard to say.)

I will probably never know the full answer to those questions, but the meeting was still educational. Notice a couple of things about this short exchange.

What did these two missionaries do when they encountered someone who was biblically literate? What was their first response when I mentioned my background and then gave a thumbnail sketch of an argument striking at the heart of their most cherished doctrine? They backed off. They bailed out. They ran away. What's wrong with this picture?

If you were convinced that the medicine you held in your hand would save the life of a dying patient, would you turn away, letting him perish because he did not like the taste of the treatment? In the same way, isn't it strange that a door-to-door evangelist commissioned to save the world would take flight at the first sign of opposition? These Jehovah's Witness missionaries were in a battle for human souls, yet they fled at the first sound of gunfire.

This encounter taught me three things about these missionaries that were also lessons for me. First, they were not confident in their message. Why should I take a single moment to consider their alleged message from God if the messenger herself would not lift one finger to defend it? Why should I respect the cause of a soldier who retreats at the first sign of resistance?

Second, these missionaries could not have been interested in my salvation. If they were genuinely concerned about rescuing my lost soul, their first impulse would have been to find out what I thought and why (the first two steps of our own game plan), then attempt to correct what they considered to be my dangerous, errant theology.

Isn't that why they go door to door—to witness to the lost, to give them the truth about God as they understand it? Yet they didn't even listen to my point of view, much less try to correct my error. That tells me they didn't care much about my eternal destiny.

Third, they did not take the issue of truth seriously. Religious evangelism is a persuasive enterprise. The evangelist thinks her view is true and opposing views are false. She also thinks the difference matters, which is why she's trying to change other people's minds. Follow the truth, you win; follow a lie, you lose—big-time.

A commitment to truth—as opposed to a commitment to an organization—means an openness to refining one's own views. It means increasing the accuracy of one's understanding and being open to correction in thinking. A challenger might turn out to be a blessing in disguise, an ally instead of an enemy. An evangelist who is convinced of her view, then, should be willing to engage the best arguments against it.

One of two things would then happen. She might discover that some objections to her view are good ones. The rebuttal would help her make adjustments and corrections in her thinking, refining her knowledge of the truth. Or it might turn out she is on solid ground after all. Developing answers to the toughest arguments against her position would strengthen both her witness and her confidence in her convictions.

COURAGE UNDER FIRE

Here is the main takeaway for you: don't retreat simply because you face opposition. Too much is at stake. Be the kind of soldier who instills respect in others because of your courage under fire. Make your case in the presence of hostile witnesses. Throw your gauntlet into the arena and see what the other side has to say. It's one of the most effective ways to establish your case and to help you cultivate a bulletproof faith over time.

Do not lose heart if your audience seems to get the best of you sometimes. That happens to each of us sooner or later. There is an easy explanation for why we sometimes feel ill-treated or ignored, a simple reason why the scoreboard often reads, "Lions 10, Christians 0." Jesus warned us in advance, "A disciple is not above his teacher, nor a slave above his master. . . . If they have called the head of the house Beelzebul, how much more will they malign the members of his household!" (Matt. 10:24–25).

This is how our Savior was treated, and this is what he said our lot would be. We should never expect a fair shake or whine when it isn't given. We are not to play the victim. That is disloyalty to Christ. Os Guinness writes, "Followers of Christ flinch at times from the pain of wounds and the smart of slights, but that cost is in the contract of the way of the cross. . . . No child of a sovereign God whom we can call our Father is ever a victim or in a minority."[4]

This is why Jesus finished his comments with, "Do not fear them. For there is nothing covered that will not be revealed, and hidden that will not be known" (Matt. 10:26 NKJV). Listen carefully to those words: "Do not fear." He repeats them three times (vv. 26, 28, 31). Jesus is with us. And he promises a final day of reckoning. As I heard someone say once, "There is a justice, and one day they shall feel it."

But even this ultimate victory should not be our immediate concern. If you want to know how I fight off discouragement, consider these words of former US ambassador Alan Keyes that for many years were posted in my study: "It is not for us to calculate our victory or fear our defeat, but to do our duty and leave the rest in God's hands."

As ambassadors, we measure our legitimacy by faithfulness and obedience to Christ who alone will bring the increase. The most important gauge of our success will be not our numbers or even our impact but fidelity to our Savior.

That opportunity for faithfulness might be a salesman at the front door, a chance encounter at the bank, a casual conversation on an airplane, or a chat with a waitress in a restaurant. It could be anyplace, anytime. If you apply the right tactics, with God's help, a lost and confused person will see not only the problem—his own rebellion—but also the solution—Jesus Christ. The question you need to answer in advance is, "When God opens that door, will I be ready?"

Study these tactics and learn how they can help you in various situations. They will serve you well when you need them—if you put them into practice. Remember, if you don't do it, it doesn't work.

Know the truth. Know your Bible well enough to give an accurate answer. Tactics are not a substitute for knowledge. Cleverness without truth is manipulation.

Push yourself beyond your comfort zone. Begin to mix it up with others before you feel adequately prepared. You'll learn best by putting your tactics into play, even though you may falter a bit at first. That is part of the learning process. Along the way, you'll discover what the other side has to offer, which often is not very much.

Do not be discouraged by outward appearances. Don't get caught in the trap of trying to assess the effectiveness of your conversations by their immediate, visible results. Even though a person rejects what you say, you may have put a stone in his shoe. These things take time. Remember, the harvest is often a season away.

Finally, live out the virtues of a good ambassador. Represent Christ in a winsome and attractive way. You—God's representative—are the key to making a difference for the kingdom. Show the world that Christianity is worth thinking about.

With God's help, go out and give 'em heaven.

THE AMBASSADOR'S CREED

An ambassador is:

- *Ready.* An ambassador is alert for chances to represent Christ and will not back away from a challenge or an opportunity.
- *Patient.* An ambassador won't quarrel but will listen in order to understand, then with gentleness will seek to respectfully engage those who disagree.

- *Reasonable.* An ambassador has informed convictions (not just feelings), gives reasons, asks questions, aggressively seeks answers, and will not be stumped by the same challenge twice.
- *Tactical.* An ambassador adapts to each unique person and situation, maneuvering with wisdom to challenge bad thinking, presenting the truth in an understandable and compelling way.
- *Clear.* An ambassador is careful with language and will not rely on Christian lingo nor gain unfair advantage by resorting to empty rhetoric.
- *Fair.* An ambassador is sympathetic and understanding toward others and will acknowledge the merits of contrary views.
- *Honest.* An ambassador is careful with the facts and will not misrepresent another's view, overstate his own case, or understate the demands of the gospel.
- *Humble.* An ambassador is provisional in his claims, knowing that his understanding of truth is fallible. He will not press a point beyond what his justification allows.
- *Attractive.* An ambassador will act with grace, kindness, and good manners. He will not dishonor Christ in his conduct.
- *Dependent.* An ambassador knows that effectiveness requires joining his best efforts with God's power.

NOTES

Preface to the Second Edition

1. I will talk about this concept in more detail in chapter 2.

Chapter 1: Diplomacy or D-Day?

1. Note, for example, Paul's comments in Ephesians 6:10–20.
2. At Stand to Reason, we have excellent training material helping pro-lifers make the case that abortion takes the life of a valuable human being—baby killing, if you will, but we don't encourage using that phrase. We don't want to look like we're relying on rhetoric to make our point when we have such good arguments ethically, scientifically, and philosophically. In this case, though, the pro-choice person introduced (and legitimized) the phrase. See *Making Abortion Unthinkable: The Art of Pro-Life Persuasion* and *Precious Unborn Human Persons*, in addition to other pro-life materials, at *www.str.org*.
3. I develop the concept of gardening versus harvesting in the preface. Be sure to take a look at it if you haven't done so already.
4. Sometimes offensive and defensive apologetics are called positive and negative apologetics, respectively.
5. Hugh Hewitt, *In, But Not Of* (Nashville: Nelson, 2003), 166.
6. If you follow our podcast live on the web *(www.str.org)* or using the STR app, you'll notice I take pains not to abuse callers who disagree with me.
7. I owe this excellent insight to the wonderful apologist the late Bob Passantino.

Chapter 2: Reservations

1. Because 2 Timothy is a pastoral epistle, Paul's specific application of this exhortation in context is to Timothy as an elder over a group of Christians. His point has relevance for all in the body of Christ, though, since contending for truth is a broad biblical value, and the means of defending the truth is the same for all—the Scripture applied thoughtfully to accomplish its divine intent (see 2 Tim. 3:16–17).

2. For example, Acts 26:28; 28:23–24; 2 Corinthians 5:11.

3. My close friend and bestselling author (*Cold-Case Christianity* et al.) J. Warner Wallace is a noteworthy case in point. And he is just one of many.

4. This verse is almost universally misunderstood to be a reference by Jesus to the Christian's ability to hear God's voice, an interpretation that is completely foreign to Jesus' meaning. In John 10, those who hear Jesus' voice (a phrase explicitly characterized by John as a figure of speech) are unbelievers, not believers. Note the order in verses 27–28. The sheep hear and thus come to Christ ("they follow Me"), after which Jesus gives them eternal life.

5. I am thankful to Kathy Englert, who introduced me to this concept many years ago.

6. Jesus modeled this same approach. When he encountered hostility from a group of Samaritans, he simply ignored them and "went on to another village" (Luke 9:51–56).

7. Books on our side abound too—excellent, thoughtful, scholarly, and compelling refutations of virtually every challenge raised—but most people have not read them either, including most Christians.

Chapter 3: Getting in the Driver's Seat

1. Hugh Hewitt, *In, But Not Of* (Nashville: Nelson, 2003), 167.

2. Ibid., 172–73.

3. Ibid., 173, emphasis added.

4. See also Matthew 17:25; 18:12; 21:28–32; Mark 12:35–37; Luke 7:40–42; 14:1–6; 10:25–37; John 18:22–23. In total, the Gospels record nearly three hundred questions Jesus asked.

5. I'm grateful to Kevin Bywater for the improvements he helped make to the questions used in Columbo.

Chapter 4: Columbo Step 1

1. Sometimes I'm asked how to transition more directly into spiritual things. You might try asking the question, "Where are you in your own spiritual journey?" or, "What do you think happens to you when you die?" and then see what they say. Have patience. Draw them out. Listen. Let them tell their story.

2. Remember, "What do you mean by that?" is a *model* question. There are many variations you can use to adapt it to your situation.

3. This last statement is also an example of the Suicide tactic you'll learn later in the book.

4. This is the initial step of all critical thinking, by the way. To evaluate any idea, always clarify the claim first. You can't possibly begin to assess a point until you understand it, something many critics of Christianity often seem to miss.

5. The Stand to Reason booklet *Jesus, the Only Way* contains one hundred verses proving this point. They are taken from the teaching of Jesus and those he personally trained to carry on after him. For the sake of argument, Jesus and his followers might have been mistaken about his claim to exclusivity, but make no mistake about what claim they were making. The booklet is available at *www.str.org*.

6. This is also an example of the Suicide tactic.

7. I believe in such arguments and even offer them (for example, "Has God Spoken?" at *www.str.org*), but I don't think this is the most effective way to persuade someone on this issue. Encounter *with* the Word beats arguing *about* the Word.

Chapter 5: Columbo Step 2

1. I got this term from apologist Bob Passantino.

2. I first heard this quip from apologist Phil Fernandes.

3. Dan Brown does this famously in his popular work of fiction *The Da Vinci Code*.

4. This, by the way, is the second step of critical thinking: determining the reasons that support a claim.

5. When neighborhood evangelists knock on your door, you might also ask, "Why should I trust that your organization [the Mormon Church, the Watch Tower Bible and Tract Society] speaks for God?"

6. This question is also a fair one to ask of any Christian, by the way.

7. Richard Dawkins, *The Blind Watchmaker* (London: Norton, 1996), 89.

8. This kind of evidence is also needed for the evolution of flight in mammals, reptiles, fish, and insects—each supposedly evolving flight mechanisms along independent biological lines.

9. The same liability applies to the claim that miracles recorded in the Gospels were an invention of the Catholic Church to help consolidate its power over the people or that the early manuscripts were doctored to make Jesus look divine.

10. Philosopher Richard Swinburne calls this the "principle of credulity," a notion accepted by most philosophers and by all ordinary folk.

Chapter 6: Two Reliable Rescues

1. Getting out of the Hot Seat is a different kind of challenge than dealing with a steamroller—someone who overwhelms you with belligerence and constant interruption. When in the hot seat, you're outmatched by a person's information and skill at communicating, not by his aggression and rudeness. I'll show you how to handle a steamroller in chapter 14.

2. Remember, this is a model response. Feel free to adapt it to your circumstances.

3. An ad hominem (literally, "to the person") is a fallacious attempt to make points for one's side by attacking the opposing person instead of addressing his opposing arguments.

Chapter 7: Columbo Step 3

1. This phrase was suggested to me by my friend philosopher Frank Beckwith.

2. At this point, he might attempt to sidestep the implications of your question by saying, "I think my views are right *for me*. You're trying to force your views on others; I'm not." I call this the postmodern two-step because it's intellectually dishonest. The whole reason the other person is engaging you is to correct you. He thinks you should adopt his more "tolerant" view instead of the "arrogant" and "intolerant" view you hold. He wants to change your mind because he thinks his view is correct and yours is wrong, the very same thing that brings his charge of intolerance down on you.

3. This is another example of an ad hominem attack.

4. My approach here is also a subtle form of the Practical Suicide tactic you'll learn about in chapter 11. His attempt is self-defeating because he is doing the very thing he is accusing me of doing.

5. Jonathan Wells, *Icons of Evolution: Science or Myth?* (Washington, DC: Regnery, 2000), 79–80.

6. Materialism (also called naturalism and physicalism) is the view that nothing exists but material (physical) things in motion governed by natural law. Though there are exceptions, it is the standard worldview of atheists, humanists, secularists, Darwinists, and communists.

7. Notice, the professor is now making a controversial claim. This means he bears the burden of proof for it, prompting the next Columbo question.

8. The professor has made what is known as a category error. This mistake happens when asking a question or making an assertion that hinges on a quality or activity that does not properly belong to that category of things. If I were to ask, "How much do your thoughts weigh?" or, "What does the color yellow sound like?" I would be guilty of this mistake. Science cannot foreclose on anything in the nonmaterial realm using its empirical methods any more than a person can rule out the existence of an invisible man because he hasn't seen him.

9. The term *a priori* refers to that which is known before, or "prior to," a process of discovery—in particular, discovery by sense experience. It's often used to describe philosophical commitments that are brought to the table as defining elements of a discussion before other relevant evidence is considered. These commitments determine how the evidence will be viewed or whether it will be considered at all. *A priori* is contrasted to *a posteriori*, that which is known after looking at the evidence of sense experience. The conclusions of science can properly be based only on a posteriori evidence, not on a priori assumptions.

10. Please do not miss something else going on here that is critical. I was clear with him about the bad news first before going on to the good news. No one cares much about insulin until they get diabetes. The bad news is what makes the good news good. Do not neglect this point.

11. Notice that I used forensic terminology—legal language—to make my point clear ("pardon," "rap," "penalty," "crimes"). There are two reasons for this. First, since he was a lawyer, legal terms were familiar

to him. I was using language he could understand and identify with. It's always a good policy to contextualize your points in this way, using elements from the person's own environment or experience when possible. Second, forensic language is the same language Paul uses in the New Testament to describe the atonement, since it accurately characterizes elements of Christ's work on the cross.

12. This is called the moral argument for the existence of God.

13. This question distinguishes objective evil from some relativistic variety that's not adequate to ground the problem of evil we're talking about.

14. The phrase *non sequitur* literally means "it does not follow." It describes a step in thinking that has no relevance to the step preceding it, a conclusion that does not follow from any earlier statements or evidence. To claim that the Gospels are unreliable because they were written by Christians, for example, is a non sequitur. It does not follow that simply because the gospel writers were disciples of Christ, they distorted their descriptions of him. Just the opposite might be argued. Those who were closest to Jesus were in the best position to give an accurate record of the details of his life—a point that is not a non sequitur but a reasonable conclusion from the evidence.

15. C. S. Lewis opens with this argument in *Mere Christianity*, his fine introduction to the Christian faith. I develop this idea in more detail in chapter 12. You can also find my more nuanced discussion of it in chapter 14 of *The Story of Reality* (Grand Rapids: Zondervan, 2017).

16. I am fully aware that Darwinism, strictly speaking, is meant to explain only the development of life through natural selection and mutation (called the neo-Darwinian synthesis) and not the origin of life, since reproductive biological systems must first be in place before natural selection can work to move evolution forward. However, the larger evolutionary project is meant to explain the entire biological enterprise—from the origin of life to the development of the complete, complex taxonomy of all living things—by purely materialistic mechanisms. Thus abiogenesis—life from nonlife—is the necessary starting point for Darwinism proper, which is why so much ink has been spilled (fruitlessly) by Darwinists trying to explain how life arose spontaneously in the first place—for example, Darwin's pond, biochemical predestination, the Miller-Urey experiments in 1952, and so on.

17. Of course, I'm not suggesting we never take a strong stand, only that as a tactical consideration, we present our views in a way that keeps our options open. Since our own understanding of truth is fallible, it is wise not to press our point beyond what our evidence allows. This is appropriate epistemic humility.

Chapter 8: Perfecting Columbo

1. Gregory Koukl, *The Story of Reality* (Grand Rapids: Zondervan, 2017), 50.
2. Watching debates or interactions online is also a great low-stress way for you and your Christian friends to sharpen your skills. It gives you a chance to discuss together what you might have said or how you would have maneuvered in those situations.
3. My standard way of doing this is to use the built-in microphone feature in my smartphone to dictate an email to myself. That gives me text I can cut and paste into a document and review later. It's a practical application of one of my basic rules: never lose a good thought or a profitable idea.
4. I call this approach to abortion Only One Question because answering a single question about abortion is the key to cutting the Gordian knot on this controversial issue. Here is that question: "What is the unborn?" As I have argued elsewhere (for example, in the booklet *Precious Unborn Human Persons*, available at *www.str.org*), if the unborn is not a human being, no justification for abortion is necessary. However, if the unborn is a human being, no justification for elective abortion is adequate, because we do not take the lives of valuable human beings for the reasons people give to justify their abortions. My theoretical question to the actor's wife trades on that strategy.

Chapter 9: Turnabout

1. The "believe just like you" part would have been limited to the issue of Jesus and forgiveness.
2. Incidentally, I'm careful how I use Columbo in an on-air, crossfire environment because the clock is always ticking. The more time the other person is given, the less opportunity I have to make my points. I do not want to surrender valuable airtime to my opponent by asking questions he may take a long time answering. It's difficult to get the floor back once I've given it away. The exception to this rule is when I

am the host. In that case, I am the man with the microphone and can keep the conversation from becoming too one-sided.

3. The best single source I suggest for a short, concise tutorial on the biblical understanding of faith is chapter 21, "Trust," in my book *The Story of Reality* (Grand Rapids: Zondervan, 2017).

4. Causing people to doubt, not clarifying ideas, is one of the biggest differences between Boghossian's approach and my own teaching here in *Tactics*.

5. Just to be clear, Mormons are not Christians, though they are some of the nicest people you'll ever meet. Theirs is a religion that is distinct from historic Christianity—same vocabulary, different definitions. These distinctions don't matter to an atheist, but they should matter to you.

6. Peter Boghossian, *A Manual for Creating Atheists* (Durham, NC: Pitchstone Publishing, 2013), 126. STR's Amy Hall alerted me to this passage and helped me develop some of these ideas.

7. For more detail, see Gottfried Leibniz's version of the cosmological argument.

8. Boghossian, *A Manual for Creating Atheists*, 126.

9. Ibid.

10. For more on this issue, see my article "'Misquoting' Jesus? Answering Bart Ehrman," at *www.str.org*.

Chapter 10: Suicide

1. I heard this line from my friend philosopher David Horner.

2. To be more precise, A cannot be non-A at the same time, in the same way. In Aristotle's words, "One cannot say of something that it is and that it is not in the same respect and at the same time."

3. This quip came from my clever friend Frank Beckwith.

4. These last three are memorable malaprops from Yogi Berra.

5. The argument fails, though, as many have shown. There is no inherent contradiction between God's goodness, God's power, and the existence of evil. For more detail, see Gregory Koukl, *The Story of Reality* (Grand Rapids: Zondervan, 2017), 87–90.

6. This is not a meaningful limitation on the Divine, however. God's omnipotence ensures that he can do anything power is capable of doing. Yet no amount of power can make a square circle. It would be a problem, though, if God's rational nature were compromised by contradiction.

7. According to postmodern thinking, truth does not exist in the sense most of us use the word. There are no claims about the way the world really is that we can know to be accurate. Instead there are many socially constructed accounts of reality, and each one is "true" for those who believe it.

8. C. S. Lewis, *God in the Dock* (Grand Rapids: Eerdmans, 1970), 272.

9. For a more thorough discussion of this problem, see "Theistic Evolution: Drifting toward Darwin" at *www.str.org*.

10. Empiricism, the claim that knowledge is restricted to that which can be perceived by the senses, self-destructs in the same way. The truth of empiricism itself cannot be perceived with the senses.

11. Note, for example, Matthew 7:13–14 and John 14:6.

Chapter 11: Practical Suicide

1. See my discussion on the biblical teaching on judging in chapter 16.

2. Note the Columbo question.

3. Alvin Plantinga, "Pluralism," in *The Philosophical Challenge of Religious Diversity*, ed. Philip Quinn and Kevin Meeker (New York: Oxford Univ. Press, 2000), 177.

4. C. S. Lewis, *Mere Christianity* (New York: Macmillan, 1952), 5.

5. Gregory Koukl and Francis Beckwith, *Relativism—Feet Firmly Planted in Mid-Air* (Grand Rapids: Baker, 1998), 143.

6. Jeffery L. Sheler, "Unwelcome Prayers," *U.S. News and World Report* (September 20, 1999).

Chapter 12: Sibling Rivalry and Infanticide

1. Incidentally, in the Christian view the conflict is resolved because God's love is not sentimental but sacrificial. He can execute justice while also making provision for mercy and forgiveness.

2. C. S. Lewis, *Mere Christianity* (New York: Macmillan, 1952), 31.

3. G. K. Chesterton, *Orthodoxy* (Chicago: Moody, 2009), 66. Ironically, the chapter this citation appears in is called "The Suicide of Thought."

4. I don't think this is a sound way of reasoning, because it commits the is/ought fallacy. I am only adopting this claim for the sake of argument (see chapter 13, "Taking the Roof Off").

5. Lewis, *Mere Christianity*, 31.

6. Richard Taylor, *Ethics, Faith, and Reason* (Englewood Cliffs, NJ: Prentice-Hall, 1985), 83–84.

7. *The Quarrel*, directed by Eli Cohen, distributed by Honey and Apple Film Corporation, Canada, 1991.

8. If the atheist does not affirm the existence of objective evil but is merely pointing out what appears to be a contradiction in the theist's worldview, he escapes this particular dilemma, and we would use a different strategy to address the problem of evil. Usually, however, the atheist raising this objection believes in genuine evil.

9. Here is how one might address this problem as a Sibling Rivalry: (1) God does not exist as moral lawmaker. Therefore there are no moral laws to break. Therefore evil does not exist. (2) Evil exists. Therefore transcendent moral laws exist. Therefore a transcendent moral lawmaker exists. Therefore God exists. Either there is no God and no evil, or evil exists and so does God. The option that does not seem possible is that evil exists, but God does not. These notions are in conflict, victims of Sibling Rivalry.

10. J. P. Moreland, *Christianity and the Nature of Science* (Grand Rapids: Baker, 1989), 104.

Chapter 13: Taking the Roof Off

1. Francis Schaeffer, *The God Who Is There*, in *The Complete Works of Francis Schaeffer*, vol. 1 (Wheaton, IL: Crossway, 1982), 138.

2. Ibid., 140–41.

3. Ibid., 110.

4. Romans 13:3–4; 1 Peter 2:14.

5. The scientific research, by the way, tells a completely different story, according to a number of studies. The identical twins research provides convincing evidence that homosexuality is not innate. Using a registry of twenty-five thousand twins, Northwestern's Michael Bailey showed that homosexuality occurred in both twins only one in nine times (11 percent). For details, see Michael Bailey et al., "Genetic and Environmental Influences on Sexual Orientation and Its Correlates in an Australian Twin Sample," *Journal of Personality and Social Psychology* 78 (2000): 524–36. Neither is same-sex attraction immutable. One study of 385 men from the Netherlands found 51 percent of them who had same-sex attraction said their SSA disappeared at a later stage in life (Theo Sandfort, "Sampling Male Homosexuality," *Researching Sexual Behavior*, 1997). In another study of 20,747 high school students, 68 percent of the fifteen-year-olds

with SSA had opposite-sex attraction by age twenty-one ("Prevalence and Stability of Sexual Orientation Components During Adolescence and Young Adulthood," *Archives of Sexual Behavior*, 2007).

6. This also confuses what *is* with what *ought to be*, making it an example of the is/ought fallacy.

7. This tale is almost certainly an urban legend. I include it for two reasons. First, even if apocryphal, it still illustrates this tactic well. Second, this story has circulated so widely that you might encounter this "proof" of atheism and need a response.

8. I owe this insight to my friend and colleague Scott Klusendorf.

9. This was the very approach I took with the witch from Wisconsin in chapter 1. It's possible the person might counter that a fetus is not a human being in the same sense that a one-year-old is. My response is, "I suppose you could also say that a one-year-old is not a human being in the same sense that a fourteen-year-old is—as in growth and maturity—but she would be a full human being, even so."

10. A word of warning here. For some, this line of arguing is no longer effective. Princeton ethicist Peter Singer, for example, readily admits that "we have to face the fact that these arguments [for abortion] apply to the newborn baby as much as to the fetus. . . . If, for the reasons I have given, the fetus does not have the same claim to live as a person, it appears that the newborn baby does not either." And he is right, of course. He's not the least bit daunted by this *reductio*, though, since he advocates—quite consistently—that if abortion is morally permissible, then infanticide is permissible for the same reasons. Sadly, more and more people are following his lead. Most, however, are still properly repulsed at the thought of infanticide. See Peter Singer, *Practical Ethics* (Cambridge: Cambridge Univ. Press, 1997), 151.

    Another pair of philosophers boldly pressed the same point in the *Journal of Medical Ethics*: "After Birth Abortion: Why Should the Baby Live?" https://jme.bmj.com/content/early/2012/03/01/medethics-2011–100411.

11. Former KABC talk show host Al Rantel.

12. Note, this is a variation of the first Columbo question. I'm gathering more information about his view.

Chapter 14: Steamroller

1. You might be wondering how being in the hot seat (mentioned in chapter 6) is different from getting steamrolled. In the former, you are

merely overmatched. With steamrollers, you are overwhelmed. You may be up to the task of answering the objection, but you are never really given the opportunity.

2. William Dembski, ed., *Darwin's Nemesis* (Downers Grove, IL: InterVarsity Press, 2006), 102.

Chapter 15: Rhodes Scholar

1. Norman Geisler and Ronald Brooks, *Come, Let Us Reason* (Grand Rapids: Baker, 1990), 99.
2. A pluralist, in this sense, is a person who holds that all religions are equally legitimate paths to God.
3. Douglas Geivett, "A Particularist View," in *Four Views on Salvation in a Pluralistic World*, ed. Dennis Okholm and Timothy Phillips (Grand Rapids: Zondervan, 1996), 266–67.
4. Strictly speaking, there is no single "scientific method" as such—one specific set of research activities that all scientists follow. Instead science employs a variety of tools, with each area of research using the scientific procedures appropriate to its own field. See J. P. Moreland, *Christianity and the Nature of Science* (Grand Rapids: Baker, 1989), 101.
5. And the origin of the universe, I might add.
6. Note, for example, Stephen Meyers's *Signature in the Cell* (New York: HarperOne, 2009) and *Darwin's Doubt* (New York: HarperOne, 2013) or Douglas Axe's fine *Undeniable* (New York: HarperOne, 2016). Atheistic philosopher Thomas Nagel was remarkably candid about significant difficulties facing Darwinism in his *Mind and Cosmos: Why the Materialistic Neo-Darwinian Conception of Nature Is Almost Certainly False* (New York: Oxford Univ. Press, 2012).
7. A view like this is an example of an a priori view, meaning it is in place prior to any consideration of the empirical evidence. See note 9 in chapter 7 for a review of this concept.
8. Douglas Futuyma, *Science on Trial: The Case for Evolution* (Sunderland, MA: Sinauer, 1983), 12, emphasis added.
9. See page 82 for a description of what Lewontin means by the phrase "just-so stories."
10. Richard Lewontin, "Billions and Billions of Demons," *New York Review of Books* (January 4, 1997), emphasis in original.
11. Robert Funk, Roy Hoover, and the Jesus Seminar, *The Five Gospels: What Did Jesus Really Say?* (New York: Macmillan, 1993), 5, quoted in

J. P. Moreland and Michael Wilkins, *Jesus under Fire* (Grand Rapids: Zondervan, 1995), 4, emphasis added.

12. I owe this insight to J. P. Moreland.

Chapter 16: Just the Facts, Ma'am

1. Christopher Hitchens, *God Is Not Great: How Religion Poisons Everything* (New York: Twelve, 2007).

2. Sam Harris, *The End of Faith: Religion, Terror, and the Future of Reason* (New York: Norton, 2004), 27.

3. Charles Phillips and Alan Axelrod, *Encyclopedia of Wars* (New York: Facts on File, 2005), as referenced in Vox Day, *The Irrational Atheist* (Dallas: BenBella, 2008), 103–4.

4. Dennis Prager, *Ultimate Issues* (July–September 1989).

5. Donald McFarlan, ed., *Guinness Book of Records 1992* (New York: Facts on File, 1991), 92.

6. Harris, *The End of Faith*, 52–53.

7. To sharpen the point, note Harris's sentiment that religion is so bad that it should be eradicated, just like slavery was eradicated: "I would be the first to admit that the prospects for eradicating religion in our time do not seem good. Still, the same could have been said about efforts to abolish slavery at the end of the eighteenth century." Sam Harris, *Letter to a Christian Nation* (New York: Knopf, 2006), 87.

8. John Eidsmoe, *Christianity and the Constitution* (Grand Rapids: Baker, 1987), 43.

9. That is, Christians of some stripe. I'm making no claim regarding the doctrinal purity of any particular person, since individual convictions varied, just as they do now. I am simply pointing out the religious view that the vast majority of the Founders publicly identified with. It wasn't deism.

10. Though fifty-five attended, only thirty-nine signed the document.

11. Find a detailed response in "The Da Vinci Code Cracks" at *www.str.org*.

12. Dan Brown, *The Da Vinci Code* (New York: Doubleday, 2003), 231–34.

13. Philip Schaff, *History of the Christian Church*, vol. 3 (Grand Rapids: Eerdmans, 1994), 623, 629.

14. Brown, *The Da Vinci Code*, 125.

15. For a thorough treatment of the claim, "The Bible has been changed," see my article "'Misquoting' Jesus?" at *www.str.org*.

16. Matthew 18:15–20; Galatians 6:1.

17. John 3:17; 12:47; 5:22, 27; Acts 10:42; 17:31.

18. The website *www.str.org* is a good place to start.

Chapter 17: Inside Out

1. Richard Dawkins, *River out of Eden* (New York: Basic, 1996), 133.

2. Richard Dawkins, *The God Delusion* (Boston: Houghton Mifflin, 2006), 31.

3. I'm not suggesting that Dawkins's specific complaint is sound, but rather that objectivist moral assessments like this are completely at home in the actual world, not in his faux reality.

4. You'll notice the overlap between Schaeffer's insights described in chapter 13, "Taking the Roof Off," and those informing the Inside Out tactic.

5. Bill Nye's June 5, 2010, Humanist of the Year Award acceptance speech in San Jose, California.

6. Carl Sagan, *Pale Blue Dot: A Vision of the Human Future in Space* (New York: Random House, 1994), 6, 51.

7. Francis Schaeffer, *He Is There and He Is Not Silent*, in *The Complete Works of Francis Schaeffer*, vol. 1 (Wheaton, IL: Crossway, 1982), 278.

8. I owe this insight to C. S. Lewis.

9. Francis Schaeffer, *The God Who Is There*, in *The Complete Works of Francis Schaeffer*, vol. 1 (Wheaton, IL: Crossway, 1982), 140–41.

10. For a more thorough explanation of why Darwinism as a system is incapable of generating objective moral obligations, see "God, Evolution, and Morality," parts 1 and 2, at *www.str.org*.

11. Sagan, *Pale Blue Dot*, 6, 51.

12. Blaise Pascal, *Pensées* VII (425).

13. Gregory Koukl, *The Story of Reality* (Grand Rapids: Zondervan, 2017), 83.

14. Holly Ordway, *Not God's Type* (Chicago: Moody, 2010), 27.

15. Ibid., 27, 32.

16. Ibid., 31.

17. C. S. Lewis, *Mere Christianity* (New York: Simon and Schuster, 1952), 106.

18. Ordway, *Not God's Type*, 51.

19. Guillaume Bignon, "How a French Atheist Becomes a Theologian: Inside My Own Revolution," *Christianity Today* (November 17, 2014), *www.christianitytoday.com/ct/2014/november/how-french-atheist-becomes-theologian.html*.

20. Pascal, *Pensées* VII (425).

21. My thanks to Jonathan Noyes.

Chapter 18: Mini-Tactics

1. I say "conveniently" because this appeal is often made by people who seem completely unconcerned with Jesus' opinion until it appears he sides with them. This looks suspiciously like special pleading.

2. To help you make this point, I assembled a little booklet called *Jesus, the Only Way—100 Verses*. It documents precisely what Jesus and his disciples taught about religious pluralism. You'll find nine lines of reasoning clearly showing that none of them thought that all spiritual roads lead to God. Rather everyone needs Jesus. Find it at *www.str.org*.

3. Here is the full text: "Have you not read that He who created them from the beginning made them male and female, and said, 'For this reason a man shall leave his father and mother and be joined to his wife, and the two shall become one flesh' [Gen. 2:24]? So they are no longer two, but one flesh" (Matt. 19:4–6).

4. Gender dysphoria is the psychological feeling that one's gender is different from one's biological sex.

5. The Gospels are biographical sketches, not exhaustive records of Jesus' sentiments. The vast majority of his ethical opinions were irrelevant to the main message: the person and work of Christ.

6. I mentioned the ad hominem fallacy—attacking the person instead of the idea—in chapter 6.

7. Many of the so-called design flaws have turned out, on closer examination, to be important functional features of the organism.

8. It is also, ironically, a theological objection—a perfect God wouldn't be such a poor designer—by an atheist who is attempting to disqualify theological elements from scientific discussions.

9. Shermer persistently denied he was a relativist, then persisted in grounding his morality in relativistic ways—Darwinian evolution or social contract theory. Both sources of moral grounding are completely dependent on a subject, either evolved individuals or shifting social groups, and are thus subjectivist—relative, that is. It's characteristic of relativism that morality changes as the individual changes, either through evolution or through changing convictions reflected in the social contract.

10. The vast majority of the variants are spelling errors, by the way, and have no bearing on our ability to reconstruct the original with confidence. For more detail, see my article "'Misquoting' Jesus? Answering Bart Ehrman" at *www.str.org*.

11. For more on this concern, see my article "The Canaanites: Genocide or Judgment?" at *www.str.org*.
12. I discussed this problem a bit in chapter 9. Taking advantage of "faith" language is a foundational strategy that many atheists use to cripple the Christian by distorting that word.
13. I related a version of this move in chapter 2.
14. The genetic fallacy is the error of faulting an idea simply based on its origin (genesis) when the origin is irrelevant to the legitimacy of the claim. The psychogenic fallacy is the same error when the source faulted is a psychological one.

Chapter 19: More Sweat, Less Blood

1. Find more examples of helpful word substitutions in the article "Watch Your Language," available at *www.str.org*.
2. Chuck Colson, *Kingdoms in Conflict* (Grand Rapids: Zondervan, 1987), 255.
3. An irrefutable biblical argument for the deity of Christ, based on John 1:3, is featured in the article "Deity of Christ: Case Closed," found at *www.str.org*.
4. Os Guinness and John Seel, *No God but God* (Chicago: Moody Press, 1992), 91.

Tactics Study Guide with DVD

Gregory Koukl

In a world increasingly indifferent to Christian truth, followers of Christ need to be equipped to communicate with those who do not speak their language or accept their source of authority.

In the *Tactics Study Guide with DVD*, apologist and radio host Gregory Koukl demonstrates how to get in the driver's seat in discussions about faith, keeping any conversation moving with thoughtful, artful tact. Readers will learn how to maneuver comfortably and graciously through the minefields, stop challengers in their tracks, turn the tables, and—most importantly—get people thinking about Jesus with conversations that look more like diplomacy than D-Day.

Drawing on extensive experience defending Christianity in the public square, Koukl demonstrates how to:

- Initiate conversations effortlessly
- Present the truth clearly, cleverly, and persuasively
- Graciously and effectively expose faulty thinking
- Skillfully manage the details of dialogue
- Maintain an engaging, disarming style even under attack

The *Tactics Study Guide with DVD* provides a game plan for communicating the compelling truth about Christianity with confidence and grace.

Available in stores and online!

The Story of Reality

Gregory Koukl

Biblical Christianity is more than just another private religious view. It's more than just a personal relationship with God or a source of moral teaching.

Christianity is a picture of reality.

It explains why the world is the way it is. When the pieces of this puzzle are properly assembled, we see the big picture clearly. Christianity is a true story of how the world began, why the world is the way it is, what role humans play in the drama, and how all the plotlines of the story are resolved in the end.

In *The Story of Reality*, bestselling author and host of *Stand to Reason* Gregory Koukl explains the five words that form the narrative backbone of the Christian story. He identifies the most important things that happen in the story in the order in which they take place:

1. God
2. Man
3. Jesus
4. Cross
5. Resurrection

If you are already a Christian, do you know and understand the biblical story? And for those still seeking answers to the questions of life, this is an invitation to hear a story that explains the world in a way nothing else will. This story can change your life forever.

Available in stores and online!

The Story of Reality Study Guide and DVD

Gregory Koukl

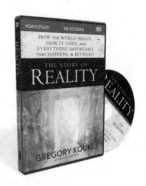

Biblical Christianity is more than just another private religious view. It's more than just a personal relationship with God or a source of moral teaching.

Christianity is a picture of reality. It explains why the world is the way it is. When the pieces of this puzzle are properly assembled, we see the big picture clearly. Christianity is a true story of how the world began, why the world is the way it is, what role humans play in the drama, and how all the plotlines of the story are resolved in the end.

In *The Story of Reality Video Study*, together with the accompanying *Story of Reality* and *Story of Reality Study Guide*, bestselling author and host of *Stand to Reason* Gregory Koukl explains the words that form the narrative backbone of the Christian story. Each session identifies the most important things that happen in the story in the order in which they take place, beginning with an examination of reality and God, and moving though man, Jesus, the cross, and the resurrection.

If you are already a Christian, do you know and understand the biblical story? For those still seeking answers to the questions of life, this is an invitation to join a story that explains the world in a way nothing else will. Be a part of the story that can change your life forever.